SOMEBODY'S
SOMEONE

SOMEBODY'S SOMEONE

A MEMOIR

REGINA LOUISE

WARNER BOOKS

An AOL Time Warner Company

Author's Note: This work is a memoir. It contains no fictional or composite characters. All incidents and stories are true; however all names have been changed.

Warner Books, Inc., 1271 Avenue of the Americas, New York, NY 10020

Visit our Web site at www.twbookmark.com

 An AOL Time Warner Company

Printed in the United States of America

First Printing: June 2003
10   9   8   7   6   5

Library of Congress Cataloging-in-Publication Data
Louise, Regina.
    Somebody's someone : a memoir / Regina Louise.
      p. cm.
    ISBN 0-446-52910-9
    1. Regina Louise.   2. Abandoned children—Texas—Biography.   3. Abused children—
Texas—Biography.   4. African American children—Texas—Biography.   I. Title.

HV883.T4 R44 2003
362.73'092—dc21
[B]
                                                                        2002038006

For the half-million-plus children,
caught in the social welfare system, who just
want to be Somebody's Someone

ACKNOWLEDGMENTS

Thanks first and foremost to the little girl who reminded me of the times I'd wished upon stars, and to my ancestors for their whisperings in my ear.

To Jane Anne Staw, my beloved writing coach, who gave me a resounding "YES" when everyone else said no. I love you, Janey! Donna Levine, thank you for the faith. Arielle Eckstut, my agent extraordinaire, what can I say? You convinced me that you were the one for me and here we are at the finish line; here's to us! Thank you so very much. Melissa, Jim, and everyone at Levine/Greenberg—thank you for the support. Caryn Karmatz Rudy, you beautiful soul, I am so grateful to have you as my editor. You've made so many things possible for me and I can't praise you enough. And more than that, you've given me my first home in more ways than one. Thanks for choosing me, while I was choosing you (and not poking fun at the fact that I travel via Amtrak). Molly Chehak, thank you for doing your best to get back with me, it's much appreciated. A BIG thanks to all the amazing sales, marketing, and publicity folks at Warner Books (you all know who you are) who took the time to meet with me and hear my story. I loved the lunch and conversation.

A special acknowledgment to all my clients. You've all been so willing and patient throughout the invention of my second career. Your commitment to continually supporting me is nothing short of miraculous; THANK YOU all!

For my sister, I only wish that this book brings the closure for you that it has for me.

Elizabeth Hartley and Phillip Thomsett of Vidal Sassoon, thank you for giving me a chance.

Lisa Faustino, I will be eternally grateful to you.

Yasna Stefanovic, Dee Mosbacher, and Nanette Gartrell, you gals rock! And I love my pen.

Nicole Garrett-Fitt, I adore you and thanks for reading the first few pages and eagerly looking forward to more. Clay Cahoon. OHMIGOD! You're awesome and I adore you.

Parris McKnight and Karen West (formerly of Barnes and Noble booksellers), a big kudos to you, ladies. Thanks so much.

Antonio, GIRL! You are my sister!

Brian and Shelly O'Neil, thanks for the use of your "cabin." And J.B. Cahoon, thank you for brothering my son; we are so fortunate to have you in Michael's life.

Scott Miller! You are my peoples! Debra, Stephanie, Erin, Caroline, thank you for being great people.

Rebecca Slovin, thank you for all the support and the word-of-mouth. You are a true "Maven" and I am so lucky to know you.

Susan Choi, thank you for being so generous. I am fortunate to know you.

Dean, you're the man. Your dedication and desire to support me has been consistent throughout this process. I have nothing less than profound respect for you. Thank you, gargantuan.

Ave Marie Montegue, you have been so instrumental in supporting me with my project. I am very grateful to you. I look forward to more Kwanzaa celebrations.

To Julia Youngblood of Serpent Source Foundation for Women Artists, thank you for being there for me from beginning to end. Your initial words of inspiration will never be forgotten. I only wish for all women to have the fortune of crossing paths with you. Your financial support helped me afford the time needed to mine this project inside out. I only hope to one day be able to return your generosity.

To Brett Hall-Jones and the Squaw Valley Community of Writers, thank you for giving me a place within your community. It is a great pleasure to feel as though I fit in among such a talented group of artists. And Diana Fuller, thank you for the chance to experience the Screenwriters Workshop. It was simply out of this world!

To Denise (DAHLLLL) and all the staff at Hedge Brook Retreat for Women, thank you for hosting me. I'd love to return someday.

Finally, I want to send a gargantuan thank-you to my family of friends; without you this couldn't have been possible: Jimmy, Lauren, and Marissa Gordon; Carol, Emmett, Beth, and Alex Zaworski; and last but not least, Miss "Queen" Anne Gordon-Quinn. I love you all so much. Thank you for accepting me unconditionally; may God bless you all.

Laine Demetria, when I first met you and asked the question "Can Humpty be put back together again?" you handed me a small stone and said it signified me finding my way back to myself. For you, I thank God every day. I love you so big.

Diana, my breath of fresh air, how could I have done it without you? Since you've entered my life, I am more whole than I have ever dreamed of being, and some of that I owe to you. Thank you so much, sweetie; not only for the time and dedication, but for accepting me for who I really am. You have my love.

Last, but most definitely not least, for my reason for living—my precious son, Michael—it is because of you that I do what I do. Thank you so very much for being my muse to do it differently.

SOMEBODY'S
SOMEONE

Them that's got shall get
Them that's not shall lose
So the Bible said and it still is news
Mama may have, Papa may have
But God bless the child that's got his own
That's got his own
                    —Billie Holiday
                      "God Bless the Child"

CHAPTER ONE

SINS OF THE MOTHER

IF SOMEBODY WAS TO ASK ME how I came to be here, I swear b'fore God that I wouldn't know what to say to 'em. My whole life, I always wanted to be able to hear stories 'bout how I came into the world a wanted and special child. But the folks I lived with told stories 'bout my mama that wasn't meant for children's ears. Truth be told, seemed like nobody could even dig up a idea of how I got inside my mama, let alone what happened afterwards. Since no one was gonna tell me what I wanted to hear, I let myself believe that God had gave me a mouth and mind of my own to do what I seen fit, and I set about imaginin' what my beginnings would've been like. That way, if folks was to ask me 'bout myself, I'd have an answer ready for 'em.

There she'd be, my mama, sittin' in her hospital room in a rocking chair, arms wide open to collect me—her head leaning to the side as she smiled and reached out. I'd be folded up in a soft pink blanket that smelled like flowers from God's backyard. After the nurse laid me in my mama's arms, she'd drag her breath in and know that everything was the way it was s'posed to be. Then for the fun of it, my mama would pull my li'l arm out to see whose hands I'd got. Maybe they'd be stubby and fat like Uncle So-and-so's? Or even lean and long like Great-gran'mama Whatchamacallit. And somehow, knowing that she was thinking 'bout me, I'd reach out and bind my little fingers round her one and know we belonged to each another. We'd feel just like the white families do on them TV shows I watched. 'Cause finally, there I'd be, the one my mama'd been waiting her whole life for—a li'l girl to call her own.

In no time a'tall, she'd name me. Not just any ole ugly name, like Lula Mae or Donna Janine. No, it'd be one that had been hanging round her mind, waiting for me to come so she could finally give it a rightful resting place. After that, she'd unwrap me like a present and count all my fingers and toes to make certain they was all there. Then the nurse would call my daddy and he'd come, and drive us all home. We'd live happily ever after. And that would be the end.

If anybody was to ask me, that's what I'd tell 'em.

Truth was, from as far back as folks could recollect, me and my sister Doretha lived off and on in a foster home with a woman named Johnnie Jean Thornhill. We called her Big Mama since using her first name was out the question if you was under a hundred. And the times when we wasn't with Johnnie Jean, we'd be trying to get back together with our mama, Ruby, whose only talent—accordin' to the grown folks—was running round town drunk and cussing up a storm while trying to take up with other women's husbands. This meant that those few visits we did have always got cut short and Big Mama'd have to come and pick me and Sister up from wherever my mama would've left us. Nobody would tell me this stuff to my face—I had to play like I was 'sleep most of the times to hear the whispers of the grown folks.

When I did ask somebody 'bout the exact reason my mama left, and how it came down, everybody got deaf and dumb all a sudden like that girl Helen Keller that I read 'bout so I had to play possum real good and just sit and listen. I finally got the answer and then some. I learned that Doretha had come some five years b'fore I was even thought of. They say that Ruby's not wantin' Sister started way b'fore Doretha was even born. It was all on account of Ruby being thirteen with nobody to claim what was laying in her belly, and since Big Mama could get extra money for taking in a pregnant girl, she convinced Ruby to stay on. And once Sister was born, Big Mama took to her like she was her very own. Apparently, five years later, nobody was stepping up to claim her second child either—that would've been me, Regina Louise—but I never got that far to hear how I came.

If you let Doretha tell it, she didn't even know I was her sister till she was almost nine and me four. But that was almost seven years ago, and I couldn't recall knowing her any different. And the part 'bout Ruby being her mama was something she never talked on. And if you did, it was sho' to put her in a bad way. I learned quick how to stay on Sister's good side. If the truth was to *really* be told, I never even knowed Ruby was gone till she called one day and said she was on her way to get me and my sister. But she never showed up.

The first time Ruby didn't come wasn't so bad. I just told myself that she hadn't been to the house in such a long time that she prob'ly forgot the address and was still driving round looking for it. But the many times after that, when she'd promise and still didn't come, there'd be a achin' in the middle of my bosom anytime I'd hear her name talked 'bout.

If anybody bothered to ask me, I'd tell 'em that the worst thing 'bout a mama leaving her children was that there ain't nobody to take up for 'em if trouble seemed to find 'em. And at Big Mama's, folks sho' needed taking up for.

Careful not to disturb the raggedy screen door that barely kept the man-eatin' mosquitas from tearin' our asses up, I leant my body into the frame and stared up at the sky. I could tell by the way the clouds moved that God was gonna start cryin' soon. I wondered who had pissed the angels off this time. The white lady from the Church of the Nazarene told me that whenever somebody committed a cruel act against one of God's children, their guardian angel would run and tell him, and he would cry for their pain—that's where raindrops come from. The white lady said that when the clouds changed quickly from fluffy white to smoky gray, well that's when the angelic messengers was runnin' 'cross the heavens. And when every breath you take holds the promise of his tears mixin' with the dirt, it was guaranteed to be a grand event. Thunder! Lightnin'! And sometimes if the crime was unforgivable, he might just throw golf balls made of ice at 'em. I know one thing: I felt sorry for whoever it was this time, but I sho' was glad it wasn't me.

That screen door was what sep'rated where we lived from the other folks who also lived on our land. See, there was two houses plus a silver Airstream trailer on our one property. Me and Sister lived with Big Mama and her husband Daddy Lent in one house. Since our house was so small, Sister and I shared a room. That made two rooms left: one for Big Mama and Daddy Lent, and the last one for none other than Lula Mae Bledsoe—the dangerous one.

The other house was for Big Mama's real daughter Aint Bobbie and her four children plus one. The plus one was a nobodies' child named Donna Janine—who Aint Bobbie took care of even though she wasn't hers. As for the trailer—it was used for the overflow of visitors that we would sometimes have.

I 'magined that living with Big Mama wouldn't have been so bad if it wasn't for ole Lula Mae—she was Big Mama's oldest ex- foster child, who'd moved out and back in. And on account of her Christian ways, Johnnie Jean couldn't turn nobody away who was in need. That means Lula Mae was part of the family again—right along with her two kids, Ella and Sherry, who didn't have no daddy to speak of. You should've seen how spiteful that ole Lula was to folks. Talking 'bout people behind they backs and in front of they faces for that matter. She acted like everybody in the whole world had jumped her from behind and left her for dead, and she'd be damned if they was gonna get away with it. Many times the things I overheard her saying 'bout me, my mama, and a lot of other folks wasn't fit for the ears of a junkyard dog on its last leg. I even heard the grown folks say Lula was more ornery than a tick full of turpentine. Big Mama said that Lula Mae was meaner than she could ever be, and that was a good thing. That way Lula could do all of Big Mama's dirty work and not get in the way with Big Mama making it into heaven.

If you didn't do what Lula Mae asked faster than she could get the words out her mouth, she'd be on you like flies to a pile of shit. All I could say was that, even though her kids might've had they mama living right with 'em, she was no real mama to them—that's why right now, I had her baby strewn 'cross my side. She'd been with me since I finished up my chores this morning. If anybody'd bothered to ask, I would've much rather been rolling down the river with Huckleberry Finn and Jim the slave. But instead I had to be the child's keeper. Secretly I didn't mind being with the baby that much—I just sometimes rather be round Huckleberry.

Ever since my teacher Miss Schenkel loaned me *The Adventures of Huckleberry Finn,* I would 'scape to his world every chance I got. I read that book so many times I lost count somewhere round ten. Over and over Miss Schenkel would ask me to return the book back to her, and each time I'd tell her I'd misplaced it. I got to telling her that so much, she just told me to keep it. And I did. The truth was I always kept the book hiding in the underside of my pillowcase. I put it there every night after reading it, just in case Huckleberry and Jim would think to come and get me so we could ride down the Mississippi on they raft.

My mind returned to me as I pushed Huckleberry to the side. The sweat had slid down the back of my legs and pooled its way to the bottom of my feet. We needed some shade. Holdin' baby Ella on my hipbone, I decided that we should go outside to the front yard and wait for the rain to break through. There was so much heat hanging in the air I thought I'd lose my mind. As I stepped outside onto the dirt in my flip-flops and tried to breathe in the muggy air, I felt like I was being smothered with a wet blanket. But I didn't let the stickiness bother me too much, on account that Big Mama'd said it's what makes the women of the South stay younger-lookin' longer.

Outside we sat down under a big oak tree, on a pallet somebody'd left out, so its branches could shade our skin from the heat of the too-hot sun. I placed the baby b'tween my legs and licked the dust from the pacifier that was pinned to her bib— then I put it in her mouth. Within no time Ella's dark Karo syrup–colored eyes was rollin' into the back of her head—till she fell off to sleep.

Since right after she was born, Ella was like my own child. She was with me almost all the time. Ofttimes, seemed like I was the only one who wanted to get next to the baby other than her mama. You see, Ella was born clubfooted, which mean that her feet was turned backwards from the ankle. She had to wear special shoes that was screwed on to a curved metal bar— they was meant to force her feet forward. As long as the brace was on, her little ankles looked fine, but when them shoes was off, you didn't know which direction her toes was heading. Since the braces made her twice as heavy, nobody wanted to tote her round when she wore 'em. Everybody else complained 'bout how they back hurt and how uncomfortable holding Ella was. Not me—no siree. I never whined. I'd pick that child up and sling her 'bout my side, and we'd be on our way.

Instead of being with her child, most of the time, Lula Mae could be found watching her soaps and yelling at me to take her baby and git.

I tried not to argue with Lula. Instead, every chance I got I aimed to get her to like me, but the harder I worked, it just seemed to make her more and more ill-tempered, which meant that she was either apt to cuss me out or find a reason to go upside my head with whatever she could get her hands on. Sometimes it was a rosebush switch with the stickers left on it, and other times it might be an extension cord pulled from a old iron or maybe even one of those orange Hot Wheel track pieces. But the worst of all of 'em was the Green Monster: the cut-off green water hose. And when the beatin's wasn't 'nough, she'd haul off and start cussing—saying things like, "Yo' mama ain't shit, and if you don't watch out you gonna be just like her. And all I know is I betta' not ketch you even looking at a boy with yo' fast-ass self."

I hated how Lula always had something to say 'bout me being "hot" or "fast." I never understood why I always had to hear that kind of mess, when I hardly had nothin' to do with boys, except for maybe Huck—and since he lived somewhere in Mississippi he didn't count. So other than him, I wasn't studying boys in no kinda way. Deep inside, I kinda figured out the reason I was called those names was 'cause of my mama and the reputation she'd made for herself by chasing after married men and leaving us for other folks to look after. I finally came to figure that where I come from, it wasn't a matter of whether or not you yourself was guilty of what you was being accused of, but that what your mama did could hang over your head like heavy, dark clouds on a sunshiny day. I guessed when she left us my mama didn't figure that Lula Mae was gonna be the one to look out for me and Sister, on account that Big Mama was getting old and was more concerned with having a spot in heaven than takin' care of young girls.

Seeing how low-down my mama maybe was, I tried real hard to make it easier for Lula by helping her with Ella. Most times, unless I was doing my schoolwork, or reading, Lula didn't even have to ask me, 'cause I kinda figured that the less Lula had to take care of kids, the less right she'd have to be hateful. I started out by going to the baby if she cried out at night. The walls of the house were so thin you could almost hear everything throughout the entire property. I'd even change her diaper and warm a bottle for her if she was hungry. Since combing hair was one of my favorite things to do, I had no qualms 'bout caring for Ella's. It was easy to comb her hair 'cause Ella and her sister Sherry had what black folks called "real good" hair, not like mine. Theirs was soft to the touch, and each curl would wrap itself round your finger like a Slinky round your wrist. I would just section her jet-black tiny curls into plaits rubbed with Alberto VO5, so she wouldn't get tangles. I wanted baby Ella to be hardly any trouble a'tall to her mama. I guess I was hoping that somehow I could make what my mama did go away from Lula's mind. But it made no difference to Lula if I was good or bad. She must've just looked at me and seen Ruby, and I figured it was reason 'nough to keep her plain old ornery and plumb full of hate. There was very few things that scared me, but Lula Mae's nasty temper'mint and God was at the top of the list. The only thing that could top them was being beat with that Green Monster hose, and told not to cry when the whoopin' was done.

'Cross the yard from where me and the baby was sitting, I seen Donna Janine, the nobodies' child, standing on the curb talking to some high-yellow-skinned boy. I don't know what she thought she was doing, 'cause she knowed that talking to boys was off-limits on account we already had 'nough mouths to feed. From far away, the boy looked like he could've been kin to her, but I knowed better: she had no peoples in these parts. According to the whispers, Donna Janine was a product of a inna'racial thing, and her white mama couldn't take her home for fear that her own peoples would kill her for sleeping with a Negro and then bringing some half-breed baby round 'em. So, Donna Janine was left with the rest of us. For years, folks in Austin who didn't want they kids could drop 'em off at Johnnie Jean Thornhill's. And for a small price, she would take anybody in. I heard she even had insurance policies on ever'body she took care of just in case they was to drop dead. Again, it was 'cause of her Christian background that she couldn't let folks go hungry or without. I know this to be true firsthand since she'd taken in my mama Ruby b'fore me. That's right, I was living in the same foster home my mama'd lived in, which maybe shoulda made it feel more like home to me, but since my mama wasn't with me, it didn't feel much like a home a'tall.

Big Mama's motto was, "If you play, you should pay," and that was that. A lot of folks must've agreed with her, 'cause over the years there sho' was a lot of kids that came and went.

Accordin' to the grown folks, there was only one thing that Donna Janine's mama forgot to tell Big Mama when she dropped her child off: the fact that she was crazier than a bedbug. Donna Janine had that look in her eyes like them folks who you ain't s'posed to point and stare at 'cause they different than you—the kind that came to school early on them yellow buses. The only difference was, she could talk and walk like most other folks round her, and she didn't have stringy spit runnin' from her mouth. I'd heard that the way she became mentally off was 'cause she got jumped in the girls' locker room at her school by a gang of heathen girls on account of her talkin' trash. I heard tell that they cracked her skull open with a combination lock and watched some of her brain slip out. My sister told me that some folks had found Donna Janine in the back of a Laundromat, curled up in one of them baskets and returned her to her mama, then they told her 'bout Big Mama. However she got that way, Donna Janine turned out to be somebody not to mess with. There was something way off in her.

Every now and again when she got overly upset or caught off guard, she would fall out wide on the floor and go wet on herself, while her eyes would turn so all you could see was the whites of 'em. A coupla times Big Mama'd yell at me to try and hold her tongue still with a Popsicle stick, to keep her from biting her ole tongue off. All you had to do is see that mess one time, and you knowed better than to bother Donna Janine.

But that girl hurt more'n herself. Not only could she tell bald-faced lies longer than Lake Travis, but she could steal you blind faster than you could smell a roadrunner's fart. All us kids learned quick not to say anything round her, 'cause if we did, she'd take what you'd say and turn it into the most outlandish concoction anybody'd ever heard. And since the grown folks was 'fraid she'd snap into one of them fits where somebody was gonna have to clean up her piss, they just believed whatever she told 'em.

I'd found out the hard way 'bout Donna Janine's thieving ways. One day, after spending the better part of my morning digging round the neighborhood for empty soda-water bottles, I decided to go and turn my findin's in at the 7-Eleven corner store. I wanted some Little Debbie nickel cakes more than anything, and it was for certain that I'd make 'nough money for two cakes, being that they only cost a nickel. I wanted one oatmeal cake with white icing and the other would be vanilla with pink filling. I could already see myself nibbling round the thin smooth edges of the cookie first, then making my way to the thick center. I'd also figured there may be change left for a coupla pieces of banana taffy candy. After getting my bottles all bagged up in two old pillowcases, I headed for the dirt trail that led from our house directly to the front of the store. I don't think I got four good steps down the driveway b'fore Donna Janine shows up out of nowhere and invited herself along. I guessed I didn't mind, seeing how she was willing to help me carry the Coke and Pepsi bottles, as long as she didn't think she was getting some of my money.

Once we was in the store, I got my thirty cents and bought the nickel cakes and the other candy I wanted and still had change left over. I was 'bout to go outside and wait for Donna Janine until her whistle made me look up and see her. She was motioning with her hand for me to come on over to where she was standing—the too-expensive candy aisle.

"Come here, Gina. Let me show you how to get any kind of candy you want wit'out having to spend your hard-found money," Donna Janine whispered to me, while at the same time shoving a big ole candy bar down the front of my panties.

"Ain't what we doing s'posed to be against the Bible?" I asked.

"Looka here girl, that's why God created thieves. He made it so that all the li'l folks who was meant to have they share could get it. God wouldn't want for some to have and others to not, so take this and walk out the door. I'll meet cha on the other side."

"Wait a minute now." I asked, real confused, "Won't God punish me for stealing?"

"Hell nah! My mama told me that as long as I was under twelve years old, then God didn't bother keeping track of all the things I did. But, she said that after twelve that was a different story, 'cause then you was a grown-up. And since you is still eleven, and I'm sixteen, you have some time left to do good by those who don't have."

Well by the way she put it, it did seem like I had heard something 'bout that "being twelve" thing b'fore. And since her mama had told her it was okay, I let her talk me into taking that Milky Way candy bar.

I pushed the king-size thing deeper b'tween my legs and headed straight for the front door. As my feet turned in and almost tripped me up every step I took, you could hear the paper crackle. But I kept going. I could feel the candy seesaw against my thighs as it poked out, making me look like a boy with wet swim trunks on. When the store clerk looked up at me, I knowed I was caught, and I got scared, and as I waited for him to move round to my side of the counter, I peed all over the candy bar. He made me pay for it by turning in my other goodies and my spare change.

"Don't ever let me see you face round here no more," he said. "If I do, I'll tell you peoples."

I promised he'd never see me again; then I ran out that store for home like a hunted-down jackrabbit. Along the way I seen a Almond Joy wrapper that wasn't there b'fore. I knowed that to be Donna Janine's favorite candy, but Donna Janine was nowhere to be found. By the time I reached our house, Big Mama was waiting on me with a rosebush switch in her hand. No questions was asked—she whooped me like there was no tomorrow, and told me that every time she thought about my stealing, she'd beat me again. I learned that day to leave that crazy Donna Janine alone.

Baby Ella must've been teething, 'cause she was rubbing her gums with the grass she kept pulling up. Seemed like the more

I tried to take it from her, the more she fought to get it back. "Stop girl!" I whispered to her, hoping she could understand me. "Stop! 'Fore your mama think I feed you blades of grass. Heaven only knows what kinda trouble that would lead to." After a small tug of war, the baby gave in and started sucking on her pacifier again.

Sittin' under the tree, all I could think on was what fun me and Big Mama was gonna have that night at the town carnival, which was in the grocery store parking lot. The carnival came every year, and since I was a tiny girl, I loved nothing more than hoping it was my turn to go. Big Mama only took one child to the carnival every year. This time it was my turn. Last year she took my older sister, and Donna Janine had had her turn the year b'fore that.

Hallelujah! I had waited a long while for it to be my turn to go. I was gonna pretend that it was the county fair, like the one that Huckleberry and Tom would go to. Maybe the Widow Douglas would be there with all her pies and cakes and fixin's. And maybe they would have a corn-on-the-cob eating contest or bobbin' for apples. Maybe if I was lucky, I could enter and win a watermelon seed–spitting contest. Lord knowed I could already taste the shiny, red, hard, candy apple crunchin' b'tween my teeth. While my mind was wanting to take me to the carnival, I sensed that Donna Janine wasn't so glad about me going. She had come up to me after Big Mama'd told us that I'd be goin' and called me a "titty sucker" and said that she hoped I'd choke b'fore I had a chance to go. I tried my best not to worry 'bout what that fool girl said.

So I was sitting on the pallet, trying to put everything right in my thinking, when Donna Janine called to me.

"Hey, Regina, bring the baby over so my friend can see her."

One thing 'bout Ella, besides her feet problem, is she was the prettiest black baby this side of the Rio Grande. The grown folks said that if the Gerber baby food folks ever needed a new face, Ella was the one for the job, with her good curly hair and dimpled cheeks. Folks always wanted to grind they first finger into the dimpled part of her cheek and pinch her fat face. I cain't say that she liked that too much, but other'n that, she was a pretty smiley chile.

Seeing nothing wrong with a simple look, I strolled over to where Donna Janine and the fella was standing. B'fore I could say a word, the high-yellow-skinned boy took Ella outta my hands and started throwing her up in the air, back and forth like she was some kinda rag doll or something. I could see that she liked that 'bout as much as having her cheeks pinched. So, after she started hollering bloody murder, I took her away from the boy and pulled her close to me like I'd seen Buffy do with Miss Beasley on *Family Affair*.

"Sssh, it's all right, hush up now," I whispered in Ella's ear as I rocked her from side to side.

Just as I was 'bout to give Mr. Stupid a piece of my mind, the rain came pouring down. Oh how I loved it; I'd been waiting all day for God's tears to come and cool us off! I could hear that ole Lula yelling through the open window, asking what the matter was with Ella. Not wanting to miss God's tears, I just called out that she was fine. I was having such a good time, swaying the baby in my arms and playfully quieting her down, I never seen Donna Janine leave. Instead I was holding my mouth open, trying to get all the water in it I could. Within no time our hot bodies was cooler, and the baby was holding on to me real tight and she was finally quiet. We wasn't having fun five minutes b'fore Donna Janine showed up out of nowhere, saying, "Lula

Mae wants you right now. You's gonna get it and get it good!"
Then she snatched Ella outta my hands, hard and serious-like,
scaring the daylights out the baby and making her cry again. I
had no idea what that fool girl was talking 'bout, but I sure was
going to find out.

As I turned and headed for the house I could see that the
screen door to Big Mama's house was partly open, and that Lula
was standing in the middle of it with her hands on her hips. My
heartbeat got louder the closer I came to the porch. I didn't
know what the trouble could be. I hadn't done nothing. But
there was Lula, seeming like she was just waiting for me to get
closer so she could pounce on me, like a rattlesnake waits on a
rat. Making each step more important than the last, I minded
the cracks—I wanted to be careful to protect my mama's back.
Somehow I figured if I tried to help her, she might be able to
rescue me too someday.

By the time I got to the porch I was moving at a snail's pace.
I tried to distract myself by snapping my fingers to the beat of
my heart, but the wetness on my hands made 'em slide off each
other, creating a dull thumping sound. When I looked up from
my hands, there was Lula Mae, standing right in front of me,
holding the door open with her big ugly foot. Her face was so
twisted in knots she looked like one of them old dried-apple
dolls. And her mouth was pinched up like the hind part of a
polecat. Her hair was plaited so tight from the roots that it
curled and flipped at the ends, making her look like a black
Pippi Longstocking.

"Where my baby at?" her lips asked me, 'cause her teeth
never moved.

"Ova there." I pointed a palsied finger, aiming towards the
curb of the street, where Donna Janine stood holdin' Ella.

"Come a l'il closer; I cain't hear ya, heifah," Lula told me.

With all the strength I had, I lifted my foot to the next step. The sound of my heart was drowning out all else, even my eyesight somehow.

"Donna Janine said you was playing in the street wit' my baby."

"Nah! That's a lie," I screamed. "She's lying again. I cain't stand her." I shoulda knowed better than to keep tryin' to talk Lula Mae down. It only meant that she'd pitch a bigger fit and I'd be hit harder. But I couldn't stop screaming, "She's lying again!" I could feel it in my belly that I was in for a whoopin'. But this time it was gonna be different.

The last time Lula beat on me I made a pact with God. I told him that the next time she hit me for no reason it meant that she was wanting to kill me, and that I would take it as his way of letting me know I should run away. I promised him, and unlike my mama, I'd planned on keeping my word.

"Didn't you hear me the first time I told you to come closer, heifah? Don't make me have to tell you twice and snatch your smart-mouth self up them steps."

I was scared. She was gonna get me. I could tell by the way her eyes moved tightly together, pullin' her forehead towards her nose. And when her nostrils grew wide 'nough to see her brains, I knowed I was in for it.

But this time, I wasn't gonna pay no mind to her. Something came over my mind, and I turned to run. I put all I had into that first pump, but b'fore my other foot hit the ground, Lula was on me like white on rice. Her fingers was buried deep in the rubber bands that held my ponytails together. As she drug me into the house, I swear b'fore God that I heard and felt my hair pull away from the scalp—it reminded me of what weeds being pulled out the ground sounded like. B'fore I could try and say or do anything else, she had yanked me into the bathroom and locked the door. I slammed my face against the commode as I tried to break loose. I was tossing and turning, trying hard to get free of her grip.

"Let me go!" I screamed. "I didn't do nothing; Donna Janine is lying!" I was only making the situation worse, but I didn't care anymore. Lula's hold on me tightened.

"Shut yo' stupid ass up," she yelled at me. Out of nowhere, the Green Monster appeared, ready to do Lula's business.

Lula raised that rubber monster above her head, holding on to the little gold nozzle to make sure she had her grip. Just as I reached for the door, I could hear the water hose gaining speed as it whistled through the air and slammed onto my skin, like a snake whip. *Whoosh, whoosh, thwack.* "*You little bitch, you ain't shit!*" *Thwack-whoosh-thwack.*

"*How you gonna stand in the middle of the street wit' my baby?*" *WhooshWhoosh Thwack.* "*You just like you whorish-ass mama.*" *Thwack thwack thwack.*

"*You ain't good for shit!*"

"Please stop. . . . I didn't do nothing to you, why you hittin' on me?" *Snap!* "Please! Don't hit me no more." *Whoosh-thwack.*

"*I'm tired of fuckin' looking at you.*" *Thwack . . .*

"*Even if yo mama don't want yo' ass, that don't mean I don't want my baby.*"

I tried to grab hold of the water hose. . . . I felt Lula was gonna kill me, but I couldn't get away. I was grabbing for the hose to try to stop her.

"*Oh, you bad now, you gonna grab it from me.*" *SlamSlam!* She kept on hitting me. I knew for sure that was a sign from God. . . . I knew it was time for me to go. "*All's you good for is to ask too many goddamned questions and get yo' ass whooped." Slam!* "I wish Big Mama had left you where she found you, right in that ho' bag motel where yo' triflin' mama left you!"

She was lyin' 'bout my mama now. Her words hurt pretty bad, but not as bad as the Green Monster.

"Lula! Pleeeasse don't hit me no more!"

"Who you talking to? You talkin' to me?"

The look in her eyes told me she had no plans to stop hittin' on me. That garden hose kept flying through the air to bite my flesh. *Thwack!* I could see the hate running through her veins. Somewhere in the distance, I heard Big Mama coming. She was yelling at Lula to stop!

"Lula Mae Bledsoe, you let that chile go, you hear. That's 'nough. . . . She cain't take no mo'."

There was a loud knocking on the door. "Leave her be!" More banging, then Lula got another lick offa me.

"You ain't shit now, and you ain't never gonna be shit either! And just like yo' mama, you gonna have kids by the time you thirteen! All you ever gonna know is how to lay up with some man and have babies you don't want!" Whack!

Lula got her last lick, sealing in her wicked spell of evil sayin's and hateful doin's. The door flew open as Big Mama pushed it in. She fell on top of Lula. I took the first chance I got, gathered myself up, jumped over their bodies, and ran. I ran like hell! Past Big Mama, through the screen door, and over them juniper bushes lining the front porch! All the while asking the question, "Now that I gotta live up to my word, God, where do I go?" I didn't care. I kept on runnin'.

I kept on running 'cause my life depended on it. My body was so numb I couldn't feel the gashes in my arms and legs where the Green Monster had left its bite, or the stinging in my body from the skin being gone—pieces of me was left stuck to the hose, but I didn't feel nothing. Lula wouldn't have to worry 'bout ever seeing me again. 'Cause as God was my witness I wasn't never going back there!

Over my back, I could hear Big Mama's voice. She was screaming at me, "Gina, Gina, where's you going—is you coming back in time for the carnival tonight?"

I didn't know where I was going. I hated the carnival and never wanted to go again. I couldn't stop to answer her. All I knowed was I had to keep moving. I looked over my shoulder and waved her on.

"When you coming on back?" I heard her asking me again. "When you coming back, Gina?"

There wasn't no words to answer her with. I kept telling myself to run. Just keep on running. It was all I could do.

CHAPTER TWO

MY DADDY'S MAMA

I RAN FROM MY HOUSE like the wind was a special friend looking out for just me. It pushed me as if I had wings. And I soared all the way to the closest house I could think of—the Perezes'. Theresa Perez was my buddy, and sometimes we'd walk to school together. She'd tell me all 'bout why she was Cath'lic and I wasn't, and how she and her folks had some kinda special tie to God. I never let her nonsense bother me too much on account I was able to make pacts with God, and I bet myself Theresa didn't know nothing 'bout that. Usually I'd go to her house early in the mornings and eat whatever her mama'd cook b'fore making our way to school—so her folks knowed me pretty good. Plus, they'd seen this sort of thing b'fore with me. Not too long ago, Lula had tore me up good, but not as badly as now. That time, I'd gone to the Perezes' to be with Theresa, and Mrs. Perez had cleaned me up pretty good, shaking her head and cryin' all the while. Today I looked way worse—the traces of Lula Mae's hate was clearer than witch hazel; and if she hadn't stopped when Big Mama'd said, I'd maybe been beat to death. I didn't wanna make Mrs. Perez cry again, but I didn't see that I had anywhere else to go.

By the time I reached the Perezes' front yard, I could barely breathe. I had run the whole way without stopping once. I sat down on a tree stump at the edge of they yard and tried to catch some air. My chest was so tight I used the butt of my hand to rub back and forth 'cross the place that hurt. I was real thirsty and wanted a drink, but more than that, I wanted to have Ruby, my mama, come and see what that mean hussy of a woman had done to me. I knowed Ruby would take up for me if she'd seen how I looked right then. Plus she would be madder than hell if she'd heard all them mean and nasty things Lula'd said 'bout her. Whoever heard of a mama leaving her child in a motel by themselves. Anybody could see that those hateful sayings she was telling me 'bout my mama was all nothing but works of evil. And what 'bout her calling me a whore; Lula was just mad that she wasn't high-spirited with pretty eyes with a man to dote on her.

All lies, that's what they was. All lies. I couldn't wait to the day that I'd see Ruby to tell her 'bout all that wickedness ole Lula said. Anyway, it wasn't my fault, what my mama did. I sho' felt sorry for Lula Mae and her kids, but Lula had no call to take out on me what was done b'tween grown folks. I had nothing to do with they problems. I'd get back at that Lula Mae some day, when I got grown.

As my breathin' calmed, I got to studyin' my body. Lula had whooped me like she was beating down the gates of hell. My arms and legs had dried blood all over 'em; it must've dripped when I was running. In some places I saw the pink and white of my inside flesh, and in others there was swollen welts. It reminded me of the time my stupid sister Doretha went and teased a German shepherd dog, and it damn near bit her thigh off. That dog's teeth dug so deep in her skin that she had to go and have 'em sew her leg meat back together. And since nobody knowed if the stray animal had the rabies or not, she had to take a hundred shots in her belly so that she wouldn't foam at the mouth. I kinda wondered if Lula Mae had rabies and if so, would I need to get them rabies shots too.

"Oh no, not again. *¿Niña, niña, qué pasa?*"

Mrs. Perez must've seen me sittin' on the tree stump through her kitchen window. She came hurrying towards me yelling, *¿Niña, niña, qué pasa?*" I only knowed a li'l Mes'can, but I understood what she was asking me. She wanted to know what the matter was. I tried to tell her, but I choked on the tears as I spoke.

¿Niña, qui ente hizo esto? Who make this happen?" Mrs. Perez asked me again.

"Donna Janine lied and told Lula that I was trying to kill her baby, so Lula beat me with a water hose." As I 'tempted to let her know my side I couldn't help but think how crazy it all was. Lord knows I loved that baby like she was my own kin. I took care of her best I could, and I'd never try and hurt her. The place behind my eyes started to puff up with water again, and I didn't try and stop 'em from coming in no way; I just let the tears fall as they pleased and listened while my heart moaned in quiet.

After shaking her head, and swearing words of *"puta"* and *"cabrona,"* Mrs. Perez led me into her kitchen, where she handed me a wet paper towel and kept one for herself. Most of the welts was real swollen and too painful to the touch, so Mrs. Perez tried to be as gentle as she could. Goodness gracious, the more I looked at me, the more my mind couldn't make sense of the whole thing. All I could see was that one minute I was home and now I wasn't. I didn't even know what I'd done wrong. The tears kept sliding.

"Shh, *mija*. It's okay. Shh," Mrs. Perez whispered to me. She took my head and leaned it on her chest and petted me like a baby. It made me cry harder and want for a mama I didn't have. I felt the wind take my breath and draw it in real deep as Ruby's name echoed in my mind. It sounded like somebody inside me was screaming from a far-off place. I don't know why, but something inside me always called her name whenever I cried.

It seemed like Mrs. Perez was home alone, 'cause Theresa was nowhere in sight. Secretly, I was happy. I didn't need my friend to see me all torn up like this. I figured it would sho' 'nough scare her half to death.

"Whatchu gonna do, *mija?*" Mrs. Perez asked me, the skin above her eyes raised high. "Ju cain't go back dare."

Again, the water hose welts started to sting and remind me of where I had just come from. I wanted real bad to stay with the Perezes, but I didn't know how to ask if I could. Anyway I didn't wanna stay too long just in case Lula decided to come looking for me so she could finish me off. I just knowed that nothing in the world could make me wanna go back home. I realized for the first time that when I left Big Mama's I never thought past getting to the Perezes'. And now that I was here, I had to worry 'bout what to do next. As I let Mrs. Perez's question sink into my mind, I quickly started to go through all the folks I knowed that might be interested in me. There was only one other grown folk who I could think of that didn't live out in south Austin, but I was scareder than the dickens to call her up.

As I thought 'bout it, ever so slowly, I began recollectin' the face of the nice ole lady who'd come out to the Thornhills' to tell me she was my real peoples and she wanted to get to know me. The first time I met her I was playing "Ole Mary Mack" with one of my play cousins, and she rode up our driveway in a big brown car. I'd never seen a car that big b'fore. I tried not to pay much mind to her 'cause I didn't wanna mess up my game, but I couldn't help but take notice that she had the largest, shiniest forehead I'd seen in all my life. The way she wore her hair, all pushed back off her face, brought to my mind the man who sits on the front of a dollar bill—except she was black. Even while she got out her car, I never stopped playing "Ole Mary Mack," I just kept a lazy eye on her. My game was gettin' good.

"Hey, Gina, I was eavesdropping and heard Big Mama talking to the lady who came in that nice car. The lady say she yo' gran'mama." Carl, Big Mama's youngest gran'son, came running towards me with a mouth full of other people's business.

"You a damned lie," I hollered at him—mad for making me mess up my game.

"No I ain't, neither. I did hear 'em say that. You just wait," he insisted, then licked his tongue out at me and ran off. I'd later learned that Carl was tellin' the truth.

"Odetta Fontaine." I surprised myself by speakin' aloud.

Not waiting for me to answer her question, Mrs. Perez had picked up a ball of cornmeal from a bowl. She looked over at me as she started smashing pieces of the dough between her hands.

"My so-called daddy's mama," I explained, hoping Mrs. Perez could understand me. I say so-called 'cause if you ask me, anybody that did what my daddy did wasn't fit to be knowed. I had a hard time believing that I had a real daddy, so when Miss Odetta called on me I thought it was even odder he'd sent her instead of coming hisself. I never did understand that. I'd thought on Odetta every now and again since the first time I met her. On account we didn't see one another on a regular basis, she slipped past my everyday knowing, just like my unpracticed multiplication tables. But now she might be the only one I could call.

Mrs. Perez was pulling stuff out of cabinets and was making what I s'posed was dinner—after all, it was getting dark outside. The truth be told, the last thing I wanted to think 'bout was food. That Odetta woman was sitting on the edge of my mind.

Even though I'd swore to the heavens I'd never go all the way back to them mem'ries of the one time me and Doretha visited with Ruby the summer I s'posedly met my daddy, Glenn, I couldn't stop the thoughts from having they way. I didn't try and fight it. I just laid the wet paper towel Mrs. Perez gave me 'cross my stinging welts on my arms and closed my eyes.

I could still hear the spitefulness in Sister's voice as she's yelling and telling us how she didn't wanna go and see Ruby. Me and Big Mama just stood by and watched as Daddy Lent dragged her to the car and tried to fold her into it. "I hate her. She ain't no kin to me." I couldn't believe Sister. "If she'd really wanted us, she would've came for us herself. Cain't y'all see that! It's 'cause she hates us, that's why she didn't come! She prob'ly won't even be there anyway!" We drove off from 2520 South Fifth Street, with Doretha having a full-blown conniption in the backseat. She was 'hooping and hollering 'bout how she hated everybody and damn sho' didn't want nothing to do with no mama named Ruby. Big Mama didn't say nothing, or try and hit her for acting fool—instead she just kept right on looking out the front window of the car. I didn't know what to do for my sister. From what I can r'member Sister was round nine or ten, which would've made me five or near to it. And I thought she knowed more 'bout everything than I did. But when it came to our mama, Ruby, Sister didn't know her like I imagined I did—as our *mama,* the woman who'd hug us an' hold us and make us feel wanted. I just sat back and let Doretha scream in my ear and kick and scratch me if she wanted to. I didn't care 'bout what she was sayin'. I was just glad to be going to see my mama.

I 'magined the reason we was able to go was 'cause Ruby had convinced Big Mama that she was done chasing them mens and dranking liquor and was ready to give me and my sister a try. I couldn't wait.

When we arrived at Ruby's she seemed kinda glad to see me and Sister, but I couldn't really tell on account I didn't r'member her ways firsthand. She was wearing what I figured to be her go-to-work uniform—a white nurse dress and shoes—and didn't seem to have a lot of time to sit and let us know how happy she was to see us.

"Here, Doretha Ann." Ruby handed Sister an empty Swanson's chicken potpie box. "There's some chicken potpies in the oven—turn 'em off in a li'l while." Ruby then showed us to the room that we would share. We had twin beds and a dresser meant for two. The room seemed fine 'nough, but I was all balled up in knots, so I couldn't say a whole lot. More than anything, though, I wanted to cry—on account that Ruby wasn't gonna be round that night—but I didn't know how to let them tears out. Instead I just held my breath for as long as I could and let the wanting pass.

At the time, Ruby was working the eleven-to-seven night

shift at the hospital—which wasn't so good 'cause we was left by ourselves a whole lot. Big Mama didn't know all that when she agreed to give Ruby a chance with us. I believe Ruby even got me into a school to show just how serious she was 'bout tryin' to keep us—I just don't r'member ever going. As I thought back to that time, I see me, Sister, and Ruby's two sons by her then-husband, Big Lawrence. Them boys was so small I don't hardly even r'member them.

I did r'member Big Lawrence. He was blacker than tar, and he didn't really live with us. He only came round when he had too much liquor on his breath and lipstick on his collar. Even then it seemed like he only came when he was looking for a fight—and that, he was sho' guaranteed to get! Somehow, nobody ever told him, but he found out soon 'nough that Ruby wasn't a woman to be messing with when it came to her mens being up to no good. I could recollect this one time when Big Lawrence came over to see Ruby, and they was carrying on 'bout him not coming over after his shift at the car dealership. Ruby only asked Big Lawrence once where he'd been all night. But by the time he was finished stuttering, talking nonsense, and wipin' the lipstick offa the side of his mouth, she'd swung a wallop right upside his head. They'd fight for what seemed like hours, leaving me feeling like my body was shaking all the way through long after they was done. And by the time they was all used up, there'd be no windows left in the front or back of his Eldorado. There'd be bricks sticking up in the hood, and his tires looked like bald hubcaps with shredded-up rubber hanging from 'em. I don't know, but I think Big Lawrence must've had a lot of money, 'cause the next time I seen him after that, he came with a new car and started all over again with Ruby.

Whenever the fights was going on, it was usually in the late night, and us kids would all be sleeping. That is until somebody called the police, and they'd come and say they was gonna take us kids away if the craziness didn't quiet down. Deep down I kinda thought that maybe Ruby really didn't want us to live with her and that's why she always fought with Big Lawrence. Maybe she wanted the police to take us from her.

I opened my eyes and looked round the kitchen, Mrs. Perez'd got quiet, and I wanted to make sure she was still there. For a minute, I watched her tear up green stuff that looked like three-leaf clovers and throw it in a bowl made of concrete. She threw in salt and little bits and pieces of onions and red peppers, then grabbed a rock shaped like a stretched-out egg and mashed it all into a pasty-like mixture. I could see the stuff inside the bowl by the way she was holding it in her arms; it was cocked the way you would hold a baby if you was feeding it. I shut my eyes again, and my mind picked up where it left off.

Sometimes I wished I could've been more like Sister, and hate Ruby, but I couldn't. I always felt like my mama was on the brim of giving me something, but right when it came time for her to hand it over, she'd change her mind and run off with it. So I always wanted to stay round her just in case there was a time when I'd get lucky. Doretha, on the other hand, was usually nowhere to be found. She was real good at finding some-body else's house to be at. From sunup to sundown, you couldn't see a hair of her. Usually, round the time for us to eat, Ruby would have to tell me to go and hunt Doretha down, mainly on account of she didn't want the neighbor folks talking 'bout her as a neglectful mama. I could hear Ruby's voice shoutin', "Go on outside and find ya' sistah, and don't come back wit'out her or I'll kick the both of yo' asses!"

When I asked Sister why come it seemed like she didn't like

being round our mama, she told me, "It's not that I don't like Ruby; it's that she don't like me, or you either. Cain't you see that she would much rather have a man or her boys up under her, than us, any a day?" I'd never looked at it that way, even though I could see some truth in what Doretha said. Sister went on to tell me how she hated Big Lawrence, mainly 'cause she could tell that he hated her. I agreed with her 'cause I sho' didn't have much for him myself, and deep down inside, from the way he'd look at me through one of his bloodred eyes, I knowed that he hated me too.

I was happy for the little bit of time Sister was round, though, 'cause she sho' was good at figuring stuff out.

"You know," she would say, "he hates us 'cause we ain't his kids. And he specially don't like you 'cause you so much lighter than him, and that's a reminder to him that you couldn't be his. And when it comes to me, it's 'cause I'm quiet and he thinks I'm sneaky. That's why he likes to whoop our asses and lock you in the closet."

Every now and again, Big Lawrence would come over in the daytime. This was not good for me and Sister. Anytime I did or said something he didn't agree with, like tell him to stop hittin' my mama, he'd haul off and punch me in the face and stomach. Then he'd tell me I'd betta' not cry. And when I did, he'd beat me up with the buckle of his belt or whatever he could find; then he'd throw me in the closet and push a dresser up to it and say, "If you squeak a sound, I swear that big roaches and even bigger rats are gonna come and eat your little mouthy ass up."

Ruby never did wanna know the truth. Most times when Big Lawrence acted fool with me or Sister, Ruby was at work or maybe even standing right behind him—with her back turned. And luckily for them, the boys would always seem to be nowhere in sight. Even when I tried to tell Ruby my side she'd say, "Shet that sissy-ass whining shit up! Cain't you see he's try-ing to be a daddy to you? Now shet up, I said!" I learned to hate daddies right there on the spot.

It was there, in the closet, I learned to hold my breath and count.

Sometimes it'd be to a hundred, and other times I'd just count till I couldn't r'member where I started from. I ain't too sure of what would happen to my sister while I was in the closet. But I do believe she'd put up a good fight. Even through the door that was closed with a thick dresser up against it, I could still hear flesh thumping up against flesh—like big hands slap-ping on a watermelon to see if it was ripe. And when I'd come out of that stupid closet, my sister would either be gone or sometimes I'd find her on the floor b'tween our twin beds balled up like a newborn baby—cryin'. Funny thing, though; I don't ever r'member Big Lawrence picking on them boys too much.

One day, while I was outside, trying to put the chain back on a bicycle I'd borrowed—a tall light-skinned man came up to me and said, "Excuse me, can you tell me where Ruby Carmichael lives?"

After giving him the once-over, I told him, "I ain't to be talking to no strangers."

He said that he was sure my mama wouldn't mind. And that he was a real old friend of hers. Then he handed me a present. "Here, I have something especially for you."

I took it and worried if he was the kind of man that I'd been warned against getting in the car with. Holding the present in my hands, I looked round, saw no car, then figured the fella was okay. I turned the gift over in my hands. It was a plastic white pen that was planted in a little flowerpot, and at the end of the pen was a white dove. "Thank you." I turned the plastic object round in my hand and wondered why he'd gave it to me. More than that, I wanted to know what I should do with it. I wasn't able to write with pens in school yet.

"Over there—Ruby lives in that there house." I pointed to the house 'cross the street from where I was standing. Holding on to my new pen, I forgot about the bicycle chain and watched as the man crossed the street. His legs was long and narrow and shaped like a wishbone. He was wearing a pair of pants with a matching coat. From the looks of him, I could tell that he wasn't the kind of man that Ruby was used to. He talked like he wasn't from round these here parts—he sounded like Dick Clark from *American Bandstand*. I watched as the stranger knocked on the door and waited. Within minutes I heard Ruby screaming and shouting. "Oh, Glenny, is that you? Where the hell have you been?" Then she pulled him into the house and shut the door. I knowed not to bother 'em, so I went on about my playing.

Later on that day Ruby called me in and sat down with me at the kitchen table. She told me she had something to talk with me 'bout. "I know we ain't never talked like this b'fore, but I gotta tell you 'bout cha' daddy." I could feel my stomach jump up to my throat and hang out for a while. For a minute it felt like I wasn't no longer sittin' on the chair, but slowly rising up towards the ceiling. In all my life I didn't even have time to think on no daddy, on account I was so busy worryin' 'bout Ruby. I wondered for a second why she wasn't talking to Sister too. Then suddenly I knowed right then and there that me and Sister didn't come from the same man, and that that man come to visit was my so-called daddy, not hers. I didn't really feel bad for Sister, though, 'cause I didn't know what either of us needed a daddy for.

"Now me and Glenn, we go way back. I've been knowing him since I was a child." I could tell that Ruby had been sipping out her liquor bottle by the way her words was starting to get deep with drawl and by her sounding like a wee l'il girl.

"Outta all the mens I ever liked, I liked Glenn, ya' daddy, the most. Hell, for all I know I prob'ly loved him. And that's why I never told you 'bout him or him 'bout you. I didn't wanna get in his way of being famous."

I was too besides myself to understand any of them words pouring outta Ruby's mouth. I didn't know how to believe a sound she said. Far as I knowed, he was another one of her men friends that she was bound to run off and leave us for. And from the looks of things, she seemed like she was stupid in love over him already. I noticed she'd taken the time to put herself together real nice-like. Her hair was softly set, then pulled into a curly 'fro puff, and she had fancy makeup on. To top that off Ruby wore her l'il halter-top outfit with the pink and red flowers. In the short time I was with her, I hadn't seen her dress herself like that for nobody. Finally she stood up, as if she couldn't sit next to me no more, and repeated herself 'bout how Glenn was not to blame, 'cause he didn't know nothin' 'bout me. And the reason he didn't know nothin' 'bout me was 'cause she'd wanted to protect him. She said he had dreams to chase, and she didn't want him to feel trapped here in Texas by no baby. Something inside me told me to go on and ask Ruby the question that was burning inside my mind and belly waiting to get out.

33

"Ruby, is that man only my daddy, or is he anybody else's daddy too?"

"Nah, he ain't nobody else's daddy, just your own—at least that I know of." Ruby sniggled as she threw in that last bit. "Don't worry 'bout nobody else, 'cause I know you meaning Doretha Ann, and that ain't none of ya' damned business." Just then, I did feel bad for Doretha, but Ruby kept right on talkin' so much that in a minute's time I seemed to have forgot 'bout my sister and her not havin' this daddy.

Ruby also told me how Glenn worked 'cross the United States, writing songs for a famous man, and that's all I needed to know. I watched her hoot and holler, but I never believed a word she said. As far as I could see, that man named Glenn was as close to a white man as they came. He looked more akin to Donna Janine than he did me. If it wasn't for that big ole natural he was wearing, and the wideness of his nose, he could've maybe passed. Plus I didn't sound nothing like him. Up to then, I ain't never heard no black people talk like him. So far as I was concerned, he wasn't real kin to me after all. Plus I didn't need to have a daddy if Doretha didn't have one.

The next day, "the man named Glenn" went out and bought me toys. I got a swing set with three seats, a seesaw, and a slide that sat in the backyard. There was also a doll that you could pull her hair out from the top of her head if you pushed her belly button. That was all nice, but I still didn't have no daddy feelings towards him. Plus, I don't recall him striking up no conversations to speak of with me.

That afternoon Ruby took "the man named Glenn" to Austin Municipal and put him on a plane back to California. A little while later, I was laying on the floor watching TV, and I heard what I imagined to be his plane pass over my head. From out of nowhere water was running down the sides of my face. I hadn't even got a chance to tell him anything 'bout myself or to ask him if he was Doretha's daddy too. Worst of all he hadn't even asked me if I wanted to go back with him. I looked up towards him in the sky and thought, I don't know who you think you is, but you sure ain't no kin to me. I didn't know much 'bout daddies, but I knew for sho' that no decent man would come and see "his child" and not even offer to take her back home with him. Secretly, I'd wished the li'l white dove could've come to life and flown me right alongside my daddy. But knowing it couldn't made me not want it no more. I traded it to the fella who'd let me ride his bike. That very next week me and Sister had to go back to Big Mama's. I didn't know why we hadda leave, but Ruby said we did, and that was that. I couldn't take the swing set with me, and the doll's head, arms, and legs was no longer hooked to her body—from what I could tell, somebody'd tore her up in a flat-out fit—so I had nothing to remind me of the man called Glenn. I never heard another word 'bout him again until the day I met Odetta Fontaine—my so-called daddy's mama.

I forced my eyes back open and returned to right now. "I think she lives round here somewhere," I told Mrs. Perez. "And if you let me use your phone, I'll call the operator and get her number."

She took the phone off its cradle and handed it to me. "Sí. Sí, mija. Ju go right ahead," she told me.

With my body throbbing to the bone, I picked up the receiver and dialed the number zero and waited for someone to pick up. Once the call was received, I told the operator lady my daddy's mama's name. After a short stall, she gave me the number. Taking my second finger, I placed it on the button that would clear the line, while letting go of the breath I didn't even know I was holding on to. I put my finger into the seven different numbered circles, one at a time, and dialed the number, willing with all my body that this woman I was callin' would still know who I was. I'd spoken to her on the phone a few times, but I hadn't seen or heard from her in a long while. But now I could recollect her voice saying, "Call me if you ever need somethin', chile." And I sure needed somethin', so here I was calling on her.

The line must've rang ten times or so b'fore Odetta finally picked it up.

"Hello."

There was a long quiet, the kind that made you wanna hang up. It felt like a prank call that left you wordless with a stranger you had no business messing with. "Hello, anybody there?"

"Uh . . . hi is this the Odetta Fontaine house?" I asked, my voice trembling above a whisper. While waiting for her to answer me, I reached up and started to pull on the patch of hair that made up my sideburn. I had rubbed and pulled it so much in my life that there was barely any hair left. Big Mama had me put Glover's sulfur ointment on the spot to help it grow back. She said it was unsightly for a girl child to be bald on one side of her head and that it made me look like a dog with mange that nobody wanted.

"Well, who wanna know?" Odetta asked after some time.

"I do," I said.

"Who is you?" she asked slowly.

"I'm Re . . . gina—you know, you came and met me and stuff. You even took me shopping once on behalf of your son, and you told me I could call on you if I needed somethin'." I hoped I had the right Odetta.

"Lawd have mercy, chile, what's the matter wit' cha? Why you callin' on me now?"

I had no answer for her. I could barely talk.

"They b-beat m-me." I stuttered and choked on the tears that tripped my words up; I wasn't meaning to say that. I don't know what I was meaning to say. It was like the words themselves needed to have somebody listen to 'em. I just wanted to be gone, and for a minute or two, it seemed like God had opened up the floor and pushed me down into a big hole and every time I stuck my hand out to grab along the sides I'd slip even further. Hearing her voice made me holler. I thought if I cried loud 'nough, somebody who'd really want to know would hear me and come break my fall by grabbin' ahold of me and claiming me for they very own. I hated that stupid Glenn for having me. And I was mad at my own self for making that stupid pact with God. I couldn't stand him!

"Who . . . ? What . . . ? Where you at, baby?" Odetta asked in a soft, high-pitched Texas way. "I come get cha, wherever you be." In all my life I couldn't r'member nobody calling me baby that I could think of. I sho' didn't feel like I was anybody's baby. I thought for sho' I was gonna break in half right there on the spot. I told her the address to where I was, and that it wasn't too far from the place she'd come to see me b'fore. Odetta promised me that she was on her way.

"Be on the lookout for a black-and-white checkered taxicab, baby. It'll be me. I'm on my way." After swearing to her that I wouldn't call nobody else, I just stood where I was, letting ever'thing work itself right on through my mind. Then it all hit me, and I could feel my body breaking from the middle.

I dropped the receiver and slid down the wall, hitting the floor with my bottom. The tears kept falling. Seemed like the harder I moaned and balled my fists, the deeper my nails cut into the palms of my hands. I just wanted to disappear. Mrs. Perez picked up the receiver and talked as best she could to Odetta. When she was done giving Odetta her address and stuff she hung the phone up.

I hadn't took notice of it until I started crying hard, but somehow Lula had cut me 'cross the neck with the Green Monster, and the salt from my tears found their way to the welt and made it hurt like the dickens. I laid a wet paper towel over the partially blood-hardened gnash, cooling it off with a quickness.

I sat on the floor next to the cabinet wall I'd slid down. My body was so sore it was the best I could do to just sit there and wait for my daddy's mama. As Mrs. Perez finished up her cooking, I sat and watched till my thoughts started chasing Odetta.

The day Miss Odetta came out to the Thornhills', she said that she'd come on behalf of her son. I wanted to know what that meant, but I didn't bother to ask her on account I was too happy to see somebody come just for me. Miss Odetta went on 'bout how 'shame of hisself her son should be, specially since I was so pretty, but that we shouldn't be too hard on him 'cause he's out in some place called California trying to make something of hisself. I already knowed that. I asked her why Glenn hisself didn't come if he was the reason she came. "Honey, that boy works real hard, and he cain't come just yet." I r'membered liking her calling me "honey."

Last time I seen her, she came to take me shopping—just me alone and not my sister. I kinda felt bad for Sister, but I didn't know what to do for her, other than to let her boss me round. I didn't understand all the particulars of grown folks' ways of who belonged to who and this and that—I just liked having Doretha as my sister, and I felt bad when it seemed like I had a li'l more than she did. Seemed like nobody ever came and did nothing nice for her like Miss Odetta was doing for me. Except not too long ago when this ole fella come to our place to give her something called a scholarship to one of them big New York schools for drawing and painting. Without nobody knowing, Sister had answered one of them contest ads in the back of one of my Richie Rich comic books, where you have to draw the picture of a dog called Dippy and send it in for money to go to school with. Well, Doretha Ann won the contest fair and square. The man told Big Mama that they hadn't seen nobody with that kinda talent in a long time. But Big Mama wasn't gonna have none of it! She flat-out told the ole fella no and said she ain't never heard of no sixteen-year-old black girl runnin' off to no big school halfway round the world to learn something she already knowed how to do. That man tried to talk Big Mama into letting Sister go, but ended up leaving Doretha right where he'd found her. Later that same night, I found Sister buried deep under the covers of our bed cryin' softly like a baby. When I asked her what the matter was she told me that she hated me and everybody else out at Big Mama's and that she wanted to die. I didn't say nothin'. I simply laid down behind her and prayed to God to let her wanna live.

I r'member when Odetta Fontaine came for me that first time I was hopping round like a box of Mes'can jumping beans. I felt good 'cause nobody told me to calm down or "act right" or anything in front of Odetta, and I liked that. I knowed that Big Mama and the grown folks would never say nothing to me in front of her on account of her s'posedly being my real kin. Anyway, I was just too happy to maybe get some new clothes. Since I was the younger of me and Doretha Ann, I always got her left-over clothes, and most of the time I didn't like nothing she had.

Odetta said that taking me shopping was the least to be done under the circumstances. Also, I learned that my so-called daddy had sent money for her to do good by me. I grabbed hold of her hard, dry hand and led her out our gate as fast as I could. I'd seen Sister walk off once she found out that Odetta was only there for me, and I didn't want her to have to see me go. We went to a nice department store, and Odetta let me look round and pick out some things that I liked. She bought me the dark blue coat, with gloves and a scarf to match. I loved them, and was so excited to wear these beautiful new things in fronta everyone I knew.

I never did have a chance to wear that coat. Big Mama'd told me to get a large size so that I could grow into it. She said the bigger the coat, the longer I could wear it. I told Odetta what Big Mama'd said, and she bought me a jacket many sizes larger that would guarantee me at least two cold spells. Once I got home, everything was fine while Odetta was there. Oh, everybody loved my pretty new coat and went on 'bout how Odetta just shouldn't have gone through the trouble to buy me such a nice gift, as they playacted smiling and battin' their eye-lashes. But the moment Odetta left, Big Mama couldn't move fast 'nough to take my beautiful coat and give it to my sister. She said that Doretha could wear it until I was ready to fit into it. Big Mama said that I was too small for the coat now, and it just didn't make sense for me to swim in it when it could be put to betta' use.

*   *   *

My sister took no pain in handing over her old funky smelly sweater jacket. I never wore the thing and hated Doretha for taking my new coat. From the way Big Mama and them carried on, you wouldn't've thought that Sister ever got anything nice, when all along it was the opposite—I was the one who had to wear other folks' clothes once they was done with 'em. I was so mad, I didn't feel so sorry for Sister anymore. I was hoping she'd wanna give my coat back without me having to ask, but she never did.

B'fore Odetta had left that day she told me that I could call her anytime I wanted. I asked her why come she was just now coming, if she knowed 'bout me all this time. And how come that time when Glenn came to see me he didn't try and take me back to California since I was his. She whispered to me that Johnnie Jean Thornhill didn't like them coming round too much and that she didn't wanna cause no trouble for me since I was living in her care. I whispered back, askin' where California and my daddy was. He was in Los Angeles, California, Odetta explained, and anybody who wanted to go would have to take a plane to get there. She went on to tell me that she hadn't been to see her son on account that she hated aeroplanes and if God had meant for mens to fly, he would have made us birds instead of men. And that birds would be runnin' the world. I tried to picture birds walking about on they tiny li'l legs telling folks how it was gonna be. I laughed. Deep down, though, something inside me secretly wanted to go to California one day.

While I was busy r'membering, a black-and-white checkered taxicab pulled up in front of the Perezes' house. I heard the sound of a car turn off its engine. As I stood up and peeked out the window, Mrs. Perez headed for the front door. Slyly, out the corner of the kitchen window, I watched as a small and pudgy, light-brown-skinned woman stepped outta the car and started towards the house. It had to be Odetta, and boy did she look different than she had some years b'fore. By now, her hair was dark brown and white, and had small tight curls circling round her head then pinned up in the back, making her head look larger than it was. Her shoulders used to be straighter, more up-right, but now they leaned a bit closer to her knees. And her forehead was even bigger than I first r'membered it to be.

Mrs. Perez let Odetta into the house. I was still standing in the kitchen, but I could hear 'em talking. Peeking out the win-dow, I saw that the taxi man must've decided on staying, 'cause he pulled out a newspaper and started to read.

"*Hola*," Mrs. Perez said to Odetta. "Ju mus be here *por* Regina?"

"Yeah, that's right. My name's Odetta Fontaine; my son is this here chile's daddy."

Twisting that li'l piece of hair that was barely hanging on to the side of my head was all my hands could do. I didn't want that pretty woman seeing me like this. I had done the best I could to clean the dried blood off my skin, but the stains was still holding on. And there was nothing I could do 'bout the welts; they wasn't going nowhere.

Odetta came into the room where I was standing and stopped dead in her tracks, just like the armadillos did when you'd shine your headlights in they eyes.

"Oh, Lawd have mercy, chile, what cha go and let them do that to ya for?" With one hand Odetta covered her mouth, which was hanging wide open, and with the other she mo-

42

tioned to touch me. I flinched and moved outta her reach, scared that she would press too hard on me. "It's okay, sugar," she said. "I ain't aiming to hurt cha now." I moved closer to the corner, wanting to disappear.

"Who in heaven's name needs to beat a chile till they see flesh? What chu do to dem folks?" I wasn't planning on answering that question again. I pretended like I never heard a word she said.

"I'm a take you on home wit' me," Odetta told me.

"But we cain't let on to nobody, ya hear, till we get some thangs straightened out," Odetta continued while looking from me to Mrs. Perez. Mrs. Perez swore that if anybody came looking for me, that she wouldn't tell 'em a word. She laid her first finger 'cross her lips and made the *shh* sound. It was nice of her, but deep down I could sense that nobody was really gonna come looking for me. There was many times I stayed gone long into darkness, and sometimes I was out way into the middle of the night and nobody never worried. Either they didn't care, or figured that sooner or later I'd be home.

Odetta and me got into the waiting taxi and drove away from the Perezes' house. I turned and waved to my friend's mother, wondering if I'd ever see her again. But more than that, looking at Mrs. Perez standing waving in her apron, I wanted to know if I'd one day have a mama of my own. Somebody I wouldn't have to leave if I didn't wanna. Or someone like Mrs. Perez, who would get mad and cuss out loud if I was done wrong. It could even be a person like Odetta, who'd run to me, and take me with 'em when things went real sour. That's the kinda mama I would want, if I ever got to choose.

*   *   *

43

As we headed down the road, I dragged my fingers 'cross my upper lip, which was now big on one side. Anytime I got real upset and cried a lot, my body would overheat and I'd get a fever blister. Big Mama said it was 'cause I was so bad and that the devil was trying to get out my body: that's what brought on the swelling. I didn't wanna help that devil by crying anymore, but seeing my daddy's mama made my insides go off like a Fourth of July celebration—I couldn't keep up with all that I was feeling, and the tears was threatening to roll. I couldn't believe that Odetta had actually showed up, just like she said. My mind kept recalling the many times my mama, Ruby, had promised that she was gonna come back to south Austin and get us. The truth is she barely even talked to us, let alone come for us. I cain't recount the Christmases, Easters, and birthdays where I'd sit and wait on her and she just didn't make it. All the other kids would laugh at me and Sister and call us names like "child of a hussy" and say our mama was a ho'. They would laugh at us for being so stupid and easy. Lula even said that she hoped that Sister and me wasn't as easy with the mens as we was with our mama, 'cause if that be the case, we was in for a world of trouble. I let them say whatever they wanted 'bout me as long as they didn't hit me with sticks or stones. Secretly, when my mama didn't come like she said, I'd just tell myself to act as if she had. That way anybody could say whatever they wanted and it didn't hurt me. Plus, I told myself Ruby wasn't to blame for not coming for us. I could tell by the way her voice sounded over the phone that she really believed she was coming. In my mind, my mama was already with me, and I was able to stretch that out and make it last for as long as I could.

While ridin' in that taxi, I wrapped the muscles from my neck down to my stomach round the crying that wanted to come and just let time and the tears pass. The checkered-cab man drove us clear 'cross Austin, from the south side to the east. As we passed the graveyard on Martin Luther King Boulevard, I knowed we was in the all-black part of town. Deep down I was a li'l 'fraid on account that Big Mama'd said that she never wanted to live round too many of her own kind b'cause black folks didn't know how to act sometimes and you never knowed what was gonna go down when you put too many of 'em together. She'd much rather be round funny-talkin' Mes'cans and them dirty white folks that wore hot pants in the snow with no shoes on they feet—at least she knowed what she was getting up front, and that's why we lived on the south side. I never did understand why come Big Mama would say the damnedest things 'bout folks when they wasn't round her, but the minute they showed up, out would come the smiles and the "Hi there, how y'all doing? Sho' is good to see ya." She could make you think you was the very person she was looking forward to seeing. I sho' didn't understand her ways.

"Come on, chile, we home now," Odetta said as she lightly touched my hand. I must've fallen off to sleep somewhere b'tween the cemetery and Odetta's. After paying the driver, she led me gently by my arm inside the covered patio deck, making sho' not to touch the sore parts. My daddy's mama sho' was a fine woman. I stepped through the small doorway and found myself standing in the middle of a tiny house that smelled like Pine-Sol on a Saturday after a good housecleaning. I wondered what Doretha was doing right now. I tried to miss her a little, but all I could think on was how much my body was stinging. I sat down on a rocking chair that had a crocheted blanket that was doubled over and laid 'cross the part where you'd put your behind—that seemed to make sitting more comfortable.

Odetta left the room. When she came back, she was carrying a pair of pink pajamas with green-and-white petals scribbled all over 'em. They was the prettiest things I'd seen yet. I moved my fingers over the raised colored thread and along the sharp edges of the front of the pants where the iron and starch had left they traces.

Odetta told me the pajamas was hers from when she was a woman of "younger days and more sinful ways." I gladly took the nightclothes and held 'em up close to my chest, while sniffing the material for Odetta's scent or any other. It reminded me of the time I'd found a picture of my mama, Ruby, and I'd sniffed it for weeks on end trying to find her smell to see if I could connect it to my mem'ry. Somehow, deep down inside, I had the notion that once you smelled a person, you would always be connected to 'em no matter what, 'cause what was in mem'ry would always be, as long as you could conjure it up. I followed my daddy's mama to the bathroom, where I was meant to change. Odetta handed me a washrag and closed the door behind her, leaving me to tend to myself.

On the wall in front of me was a mirror with old pictures stuck in the corners. The pictures was mostly in black and white, and some looked a little gold; but they was all rough and rolled up round the edges. I stood and watched myself in the mirror and let the folks in the pictures get a good look too. Where there'd once been two ponytails held together by blue rubber bands and barrettes that I'd picked out earlier that day to match my shirt, there was now hardly anything left. On one side of my head, a piece of rubber band held on to the ends of my hair and dangled as I moved about. On the other side, my hair was wide out, pushed back and stuck in midair. My face, with the leftover tearstains that had made they way to my chin, looked like dirt after water had hit it; dry tracks with li'l bits of wetness. I couldn't stand to watch me no more or let the folks from the pictures stare at me either, with they li'l beady eyes watching my every move. I laid my pajamas on the toilet lid and started getting ready for sleep. Trying like hell not to let my panties roll over the water-hose marks, I stretched the legs and the waistband out real big—my sister had taught me that trick whenever I had welts real bad on my lower parts. Then I pulled my legs, one at a time, out real slow-like. As long as I stood in one place my body didn't throb so much, but when I moved, it made my skin seem as though it was cracking and tearing all at the same time.

Right when I was buck-naked, Miss Odetta walked in on me with a bottle of mercurochrome in her hand. She said it would help me scab faster and without infection. I knowed she was right 'cause that's what Big Mama used all the time on us kids when we had cuts and sores. With the tips of my fingers, I held on to Odetta's shoulder as she bent over and rubbed the pinkish-red medicine on me. "Ouch!" I flinched the moment she touched me. Odetta lightened up her hand and put the stuff on real nice and slow. Instead of rubbing right on the hurt part, she would hold the little glass wand above it and let the red medicine fall onto the torn-up skin. I couldn't r'member when somebody had been that nice and soft with me. If Odetta was gonna be treating me like this, then I sho' could bring myself to get used to her kindness. Big Mama had been nice to me too sometimes. I mean, she let me go everywhere with her, and she taught me to plait her hair and oil the heels of her feet with

Pond's cold cream. Big Mama even showed me how to pick blackheads out her back and from round her nose. I never minded doin' these things for her, 'cause at least I wasn't being whooped or put down.

My eyes got hot, and I started feeling sorry for Big Mama the more I thought on her. She was just a li'l ole woman who'd took care of me. For all I knowed, maybe she was out looking for me now. I sho' didn't wanna make no trouble for her and have everybody mad at me. Odetta must've heard me thinking, 'cause she looked up and told me all was gonna be fine. She touched her bent fingers to my face and dragged the back side of her hand 'cross my cheek. I could feel what she was meaning; I'd felt it b'fore when watchin' mamas and they babies, when the mamas touch the li'l ones in a way where they don't have to say they like 'em or that they sorry for the hurt a child must be feeling. And now I figured Odetta must've been feeling that for me.

"Now I lay me down to sleep, I pray the Lord my soul to keep. If I should die b'fore I wake, I pray the Lord my soul to take. God bless Big Mama, Doretha, and any bad kids like me that gets whoopin's. I'm sorry, God, if I really did do somethin' wrong. And please, Lord, send me my mama." I said my prayers and climbed in bed next to Odetta. I scooted way over towards the edge so I wasn't in her way. I didn't wanna wear out my welcome.

I had learned all 'bout welcomes from Lula. She'd told Sister and me that we'd long since stayed way past quitting time. And any time we wanted to quit, she'd be happy to oblige us. The grown folks never really said anything to her, either, when Lula made fun at me and Doretha. They'd just laugh it off and tell

48

her to not be so conniving. I hated that Lula Mae got to get away wit' whatever she wanted to. I really couldn't wait till I got grown.

After closing my eyes, I secretly asked God to tell Big Mama I was sorry, and not to be mad at me for leaving and to let her know that I wasn't quittin', I just needed a break from Lula.

I looked round the room, letting my eyes get used to the darkness. Odetta's house was strange to me, so my eyes seen nothing that made 'em feel like home. At Big Mama's there was always a light left on in the bathroom so that nobody got scared at night. And I always knew that Daddy Lent was in the house at all times, when he wasn't fishing or working, keeping it protected from the boogeyman and vampires. Daddy Lent might've said three words the whole time I knowed him, but all the same I liked him being there. But here, at Odetta's, it was quiet; the kind of quiet that could only be heard in darkness. The kind of quiet that showed you something was really wrong wit' the way things was.

From the looks of things, Odetta didn't have no husband to protect us—at least not one that I could find. I'd looked on both sides of the bed to see if a pair of men's house shoes was partially hanging out, like Daddy Lent's would be, and I saw nothing. Nor was there a striped burgundy-and-off-yellow man's housecoat hung up on a nail on the back of the bathroom door that smelled like Old Spice and Bugle Boy tobacco pipe smoke.

As I laid awake, I let my mind wander on the thought that maybe my so-called daddy, Glenn, was never round me 'cause his daddy wasn't round him. But for the life of me, I couldn't figure out why my mama just liked chasing after other women's mens. Whatever the truth was for the both of them, all I

49

knowed was that I was never gonna be like none of them folks from Austin. I wasn't gonna ever have li'l kids and leave 'em in a place with people who couldn't even stand the sight of 'em. And I was never gonna have no boyfriend or husband anyway. That way I knowed for certain that I wasn't gonna have to have no kids I didn't want in the first place.

I didn't sleep too good, 'cause my skin was on fire all night long. My body tossed and turned like the sometimes working, potbellied washing machine Big Mama had sitting out on her back porch. Odetta must've had it rough with me too, 'cause she'd moved into the living room. I could hear her calling hogs from the couch.

Finally, it was morning. As I swung my legs over the edge of the bed, I could feel my clothes pulling—they was stuck to my skin. I looked down at myself and saw where the material had soaked into my welts when I was sleepin' and made the pajamas stick to me. I felt sorry for my skin and wondered if I was always gonna have scars from this. I started to tear up, but I made my tears fall quietly, 'cause I didn't want to wake Odetta. My head was pounding. It felt like somebody was standing on the inside of it beating me with a hammer to let them out.

I thought back on the other times when Lula had beaten me. Usually it was when we'd get word of my mama's whereabouts. Or, if she'd misplaced something and I couldn't read her mind to find it—*blam!* She'd haul off and hit me, like it was my fault she lost it. Once when Lula had gone on one of her sprees and used a rosebush stem to tan my hide, Sister had to put me in a tub of Epsom salt to calm my body down 'nough so she could help me take the little thorns out my skin. I kinda wished Sister was here to help me now.

I dried my eyes with the sleeve of my pajamas and slowly slipped off the bed onto the floor. I was gonna draw myself a tub and soak my clothes off. While I let the water warm up and the tub fill, I looked under the sink to try and find Epsom salt. I caught sight of what the grown folks called "clawed feet" on the bottom of the bathtub.

Out at the Thornhills' we had a claw-footed tub too, but the left front foot on it had clawed its way right through the linoleum tile and the po' thing was leaning to the ground whenever anybody got in it. At the same time, you could see what was going on under the house while taking a bath. Odetta's tub was nice and white, wit' no dirty body rings round the inside or softened turds left over from somebody getting a enema. Out at Big Mama's it seemed like all us kids was full of backed-up bowel movements, and the only way to unplug our asses was to get in the bathtub and have some long white thing stuck up our butt holes. I sho' didn't like that a'tall, but this was just as bad. I found the salt and poured it into the falling water, just like I seen Sister do.

When the bath was halfway full, I sat on one side to get my feet warm; then I put my hands on either side and lowered my body into the water. I couldn't believe that I was in somebody's bathtub that I didn't really know—I'd never been this far away from home b'fore, and I certainly barely bathed when I was home—but I was sho' glad to have a clean white tub. It didn't take long for the material to loosen up. Once I was wet enough, I started gently working my clothes away from my skin bit by bit. I'd grit my teeth down hard-like and pull the real bad ones back fast. Each time I pulled at the material, I told myself that I hated Lula's guts for what she'd done to me. And I hoped that one day the same thing would happen to her, or worse, her own kids—except baby Ella. Maybe then she'd see what it felt like to be me.

I managed to get myself cleaned off and changed without waking up Odetta. I didn't want for her to have to look after me too much, in case I needed to stay for a while. I put my own panties back on and the shirt I had worn to bed. Not wanting the water to drip all over, I wrapped the wet pajamas in a towel. While stepping on one end of the towel, I twisted the other with my hand until the water ran out, and then I wiped up the puddle I made. Realizing that most houses in the South had clotheslines in they backyards, I found Odetta's and hung the clothes out on the line to dry. Then I got back in bed to wait for Odetta to wake up.

CHAPTER THREE

TALKING TO STRANGERS

"GOOD MORNING, Miss Lady." Odetta smiled as she came back into the room after her night out on the couch. I didn't notice b'fore, but her hair was sectioned and twisted on li'l torn pieces of brown paper bag. I recognized 'em right away; me and Sister had some of our own. They was used to roll hair on when you didn't have money for the pink sponge rollers; and they was s'posed to be just as good; at least that's what Big Mama told me when I asked for the pretty pink ones and she wanted to know how I was gonna pay for 'em.

"Hi." I waved shyly to Odetta, not sure if she still felt the same 'bout me today that she had yesterday.

"Now that cha all cleant up with a good night's sleep, can you tell me why them folks over yonder was aiming to beat the daylights out cha?"

"Um, I dunno," I answered back as my shoulders lifted to help me out, all along knowing that I couldn't even explain them folks to myself let alone her.

"I just think that Lula plain ole hates me, and that's why she wants me dead. Ever since my mama left us kids out to south Austin, Lula's been mad at her. And since Ruby, my mama, ain't there to stand up for herself, Lula takes it out on me and sometimes, but not too much, my sister Doretha Ann."

"Oh yeah, that's right, ya sho' do have a sister out there, ain't cha. I wonder what that mama of yours Ruby was thankin' when she left y'all kids out there with them there people? From what I hears she ain't bit more kin to them than I am to the man on the moon. I guess she was just no more than a chile herself and didn't know what else to do wit' cha, huh? Plus yo' mama sho' was a fast one from what I hears. I ain't seen her too many times, but I know she sho' is pretty too. That's what knocked my boy Glenn off his feet, was her prettiness. They met out at the high school, Ruby and yo' daddy. I don't think they known each other too long b'fore you come along. Seem like I met ya' mama once or twice, and the next thing I known she ain't coming round no more. But, that's all right, 'cause you is here now."

I didn't know if Odetta was talking to me or herself. Seem like some of her words should've been meant for grown folks' ears and not mine. At Big Mama's I always eavesdropped to find out this stuff Odetta was telling on folks.

"Miss Odetta?"

"Yeah, what, baby?"

"What name should I call you by?"

"Well you can call me 'Mama,' or you can call me whatever sounds good, but whatever you do, call me somethin' nice."

I hated it when grown folks tried to be funny. I know she was telling me not to use dirty words when calling her attention, like "hey dog-face" or "yella-belly sap-sucker." She didn't have to worry; I knew better than to say anything bad 'bout a grown-up to their face. Since Odetta was actually bigger than Johnnie Jean, I thought she was a better fit for the name Big Mama. So I gave her the name Big Mama Fontaine. Anyway it was easier than saying just plain ole "Mama" and I was hoping to save that word in case I was to ever get one of my own.

I watched as Odetta laughed herself right into a li'l coughing spell. After nearly choking herself to death, she opened up a drawer in her bedside table and took out a ho-hound drop.

"You want one, sugar?"

"Yeah." I took it and folded it in my hand. Ho-hound was one of Big Mama's favorite hard candies; she used 'em just like Odetta—when she coughed. As my eyes wandered round the place, I seen a picture on the headboard of Odetta's bed which I hadn't given much mind to the night before. It was a man with a Afro shaped like the globes we had in our classroom. He had a high forehead, and his skin looked real high yellow, almost piss color. He had a pretty smile too, that seemed to spread all the way 'cross Austin. I let his pale face and funny-colored eyes sneak off into my head, wonderin' all the while if the stirring I felt in my belly meant he was somebody I already knowed.

"Big Mama Fontaine, is that man on your headboard your husband? The one with the big forehead?"

"For heaven's sake, chile, no! I ain't had no husband to thank 'bout for a long time. Anyway, I was married so many times I stopped countin' at number four. And that don't count the ones I wudn't even married to. And that ain't nobody's bidness, ya hear? That there photo you seein' is yo' daddy, Glenn. Ain't he somethin' just standing there? I'm so proud of him. I know he's out there in that Los Angeles gettin' famous so one day he can buy me a big house. Least that's what he says to me.

You sho' should be proud a him too, honey. You know, he working the big time these days. I thank you can hear some a his songs on the red-dio. I know he ain't done it all right, but he trying to make somethin' of himself."

My insides started moving in a way that made me wanna roll my eyes so deep into my head, I myself wouldn't be able to find 'em. I thought back to that stupid picture of Glenn and tried to r'member the first time we met to see if I could make out his face, but my mind was too jumpy, and I couldn't see him too clear. Every time I tried to concentrate, there came Big Lawrence's black and ugly face, and I couldn't keep my mind steady. For the life of me, I didn't see all of what Odetta seen in her son. And I sho' didn't want no part of my so-called daddy right then.

I thought Odetta had to be losing her mind. And as a matter fact, I wished she had. That way I wouldn't have to wrap my thinking round what she'd just said. Why would she want to claim a son who didn't even know me and barely even seen me? I bet he didn't even know my middle name. And anyway, what was there for me to be proud of in him? He never came for me when Lula Mae was tearing me up. Plus, why would he leave me with somebody who didn't even like kids? I could see that Odetta was nice and all, but she seemed to have it all wrong 'bout her stupid son—and me—if for one minute she thought I was gonna be liking him the way she did. I was almost sorry for asking her 'bout that picture.

I had come to Odetta on a Saturday, and on Sunday, she told me it would look good for us both if I was in school. Specially since she was gonna have to go to the county judge on my account and ask his permission for me to stay with her. She said that if we did everythang right, then we would have a better chance of me not having to ever deal with Lula again. Just then, everything seemed to be moving so quick. I wasn't for sho' that I wanted to stay with my daddy's mama. Like I said b'fore, Odetta was nice and all, but I didn't know her like I did Big Mama Thornhill. And anyway, she made it sound like her good-for-nothing son meant the world to her and could do no wrong, which could mean that I was no better off with her than with Big Mama.

At Big Mama's it seemed like there was always an excuse for her real kin to get away with whatever bad thing they done. For instance, one time I told her that Aint Bobbie's son Lenny made me put on boxing gloves, then beat the mess outta me while all along claiming he was trying to make me tougher. Big Mama said, "Oh, girl, he just tryin' to show you how to take up for yourself. Just hush yo' mouth and be thankful somebody wanna take the time wit' cha." But then, if I went and whooped the shit outta somebody else, I was wrong and got hit twice as hard. Not only that, but I was told that if I came home from a fight and the other person got the best of me, then I was gonna get it even worse. Yet when her gran'boys got into fights, there was always somebody wanting to put a Band-Aid on 'em and tell 'em it was all right.

Even though she tended to favor her real kin, I wanted to call Big Mama right then and there and let her know that a judge could take me away from her and she might never see me again. Maybe then she would make Lula leave me alone. I missed Big Mama, but I didn't wanna say nothing to hurt Odetta's feelings.

*   *   *

57

Monday came round soon 'nough, but instead of going to school like Odetta had said, she took me shopping for new clothes and supplies. Lord knows the clothes I came with was fit to be tied and burned. First we went down on Congress Avenue to find shoes and a couple pairs of socks. Then on to S. H. Kress five-and-dime store, and last we went to Newberry's.

Aside from that time with the too-big coat, I couldn't r'member going shopping b'fore, and now I could actually own things that I had only seen other kids wear. I bought a pair of bronze sandals that had a piece of leather that went b'tween my toes, and a smaller strap that held my big toe down. The buckle at the ankle kept the shoes on my little skinny feet. The pants I tried on was larger at the bottom than they was on top, and the shirt had puffy sleeves with little holes that looked like cut-out petals all over it, and a drawstring neck tie. I'd seen the folks on *Soul Train* and *American Bandstand* dress like this, and I'd longed for the day when I'd have my own. The shirt had to be long sleeves—Odetta said we had to hide my scabs. She said we didn't wanna give nobody reason to talk. I didn't see any harm in folks talking. Maybe somebody would talk loud 'nough for Lula Mae to hear, and she would know that what she did was shameful. I listened to Odetta, though, and I got the long sleeves. When we was through shopping I had the first whole outfit I could ever recall getting without having to beg my school's Salvation Army office for free vouchers to use at their distribution center. For now, I was happy.

My first day at the new school was like a commotion straight outta a book. The folks that really knowed me would say that I read more than the presidents did. At least that's what Daddy Lent said 'bout me. "Johnnie, you ought to watch out for that gal there; she reads more than the president I 'magine, and if ya don't watch her, there ain't gonna be nothin' left for her to read." As a matter of fact, Big Mama'd told me that even when I was little as four years old, I'd much rather read a book than eat my favorite sandwich: butter and sugar smashed b'tween two pieces of white Safeway bread. I did like them sandwiches, and that was the truth; but now I could eat the sandwich while reading the books.

After Odetta made her way through all the papers they had her sign in order for me to attend Roosevelt Elementary, I was sent to find my new homeroom. I was told to go down the hall, make a right then a left, and follow that to the end of the hallway. I did just that and made my way to the room. For a while, I held on to the little piece of paper that had 108 scribbled on it and waited by the doorway. The room was opened, so I looked round the class and started counting desks. I wondered which one was gonna be mine and hoped there was 'nough to go round.

Thirty-three chairs plus the teacher's desk was my count. As I waited, my eyes landed and stayed on a chair that was at the back of the class. It was the one I wanted. I thought if I stared at it hard 'nough, then just maybe I could make it mine by puttin' a jinx on it. What made the seat specially good was that it had a big window on the side of it—with clear glass so you could look out and see for a long ways. I loved to stare outta windows. At my old school, Molly Dawson Elementary, I wasn't allowed to sit by no windows. For years my teachers would call Big Mama and complain 'bout how my daydreamin' inna'rupted the class and my learning. Sometimes it got me into trouble. Not because anybody knowed what I was thinking, but that the teachers said it was all I did. Sit and stare. It was true.

It was all I did. Anytime I was s'posed to be going to the reading circle or standing to salute the flag, followed by three verses of "Deep in the Heart of Texas," I was nowhere to be found.

After year four, Big Mama'd grew tired of them teachers whining at her 'bout me. She finally flat-out told 'em to move the damned desk 'way from the window and stop calling her 'bout that daydreamin' mess. She also added that if they wanted to give her the job to run the class, she'd be happy to oblige them if it meant they'd stop hounding her. From that day on, I had to sit at the front of the class right next to the teacher. So here I was in a brand new fifth-grade class. I prayed I didn't have to sit next to no teacher. Anyhow, I needed to sit by the window. I needed to sit there so I could keep an eye out for my mama, just in case she changed her mind and decided to come and get me. Maybe I'd get a window seat since here at Roosevelt nobody knowed the first thing 'bout me and my staring. I crossed my fingers and wished on 'em that I'd get that window seat and my mama would come find me by it.

One by one the kids brushed by me and piled into the classroom. I watched as they found desks and took their seats. Some fiddled with opening desktops, while others pulled books out they bags and started reading. I just watched 'em while I tried to keep an eye out for the chair I wanted.

It didn't take long 'fore I noticed a long, string-bean-thin-like white woman standing next to me and softly scooting me into the room. She grabbed the piece of paper out my hand and walked quickly to her desk. I watched as she balled my note up into her fist and tossed it into the wastepaper basket.

"May I have y'all's attention please?"

I watched as the slow-mouth-moving teacher tried to get the kids to listen to her. At first everybody kept right on talking, as if that teacher had never uttered a word. But by the time she repeated herself, and snapped out "Please!" like a bullwhip, everybody stopped.

"Now that's mo-er like it."

I watched as her small pink mouth wrinkled on the word "more."

"Now, let's all start over. Good morning, class."

"Good morning, Misss Frannncisssss." All the kids repeated her words back together.

"This morning, we got ourselves here a new pupil." Miss Francis, who was sitting on the front of her desk, turned towards me, brought her hands together at her chest, and grinned. All eyes was on me.

"Sugar, why don't you go on and introduce yourself to the class?" I could feel my cheeks suck themselves in to where I looked like a fish. And at the same time my body started making these half-round twists like I was trying to mimic a washing machine.

"Hi, y'all. My name's Regina."

All the kids repeated my name back to me the same way they'd said good morning to the teacher: "Hi there, Reginnnaaa!"

Other than getting into some serious trouble, no teacher'd ever made such a deal of me in they class. At least not since Miss Schenkel, my teacher who thought I handled words real well for my age, but even then she didn't make it such a deal in front of the whole class.

"Is there anything you'd like to share with the class about where you're from, Regina?"

"Nah. Not right now," I told the teacher. By the time she was through with me, I had one foot stepping on the other, and my hands was having a wrestling match of they own behind my back.

"Well then, welcome. Welcome to homeroom one-oh-eight."

Miss Francis pointed me to a seat that was empty. It was the one I wanted. I took the chair and sat down, as the weight of my smile was almost too much to bear.

Odetta's exact words to me, as she pulled me to one side, right b'fore leaving me at the school was, "Don't go telling folks nuttin' that might let on that you a runaway." Runaway? I couldn't believe that I was now just like Jim the slave, Huck's friend. And Odetta was kinda like Huck—hiding me out so I'd be safe from the bad guys and Huck's ole drunk pap. Well then, I told myself, I should do my best to keep a tight lip and not spoil our little secret.

One thing 'bout me, was that I'd learned good to concoct a story real quick-like from scratch. Donna Janine had been good for those kinds of teachin's. So, when these kids at my new school started askin' me questions, I started spreading lies quick as a whip.

In one story, I told them that I was the ringleader in an all-girl gang and had to be put out of my school to break up the pack. Five minutes after that, I said that my mama was a movie star working in Hollywood and had to send me away so that I wouldn't get kidnapped for a ransom. By the time the kids made they rounds to try and know my business, I'd told so many stories, I couldn't tell where one started and the other ended. Most of the kids would just stare at me all bug-eyed and mysterious, but there was this one fat boy who flat-out called me a liar. Now, we both knew that them was fighting words, but I let him slide on account of Odetta trying so hard to help me out. I didn't want her to see no trouble 'cause of me. Lord knows how many times I had been put out of my old school for acting the fool. They said I was bad. This time I wanted to try and do different.

I guess you could say everything was going good until I got to gym class. It was then that things seemed to take a turn for the worse. It started when the PE teacher, Miss Marks, asked me how come I didn't change into the matching short set she gave me. I fibbed and said that the clothes was too tight, on account I didn't want nobody to see my welt marks. Instead, I rolled my pants legs up just 'nough to keep from tripping on 'em. I convinced her I was fine and was allowed to go on and join the kids on the track for a running test. Miss Marks said it was President's Physical Fitness Week and even though I was new, I'd still have to participate. No one there knowed it, but running was my favorite thing in the world other than reading.

I took the test, and as the Lord would have it, I beat everybody in the class by a good distance. At my old school, folks would've been hooting and hollering up a storm. They'd have been used to such things happening, but here, my luck had run out. After the race, the same fat boy that had called me a liar brought his mangy li'l group over to where I was and walked up on me. He took his finger and poked me in my shoulder to get my attention.

"Hey, where you be from for real?"

"None ya," I told him. I don't know who he thought he was, but he didn't scare me.

The boy looked at me with his eyebrows raised up and said, " 'None ya,' what's that s'posed to mean?"

"None of yo' business," I said back to him as I rolled my eyes and neck at the same time.

"You think you is betta' than us, jus' 'cause you can run, huh?" the boy asked, with his straggly lot standing beside him.

"Nah," I said, with my feet spread wide apart and my hands on my hips, letting him know that I wasn't scared of him a'tall. "I don't think I'm betta'. I've just run my whole life, that's all." At my old school, I was known as a bully. I would beat up any-body that sassed me or talked the dozens about my mama. Sometimes I would even take up for the little kids who couldn't help themselves. My beating folks up got so bad the principal took to sending me home from school one half hour earlier than the other kids. They said it would give me a chance to get home way ahead of everybody else. That worked fine for about a week, which is how long it took me to scout out a hiding place in the bushes in front of the school, where I would jump out and get whoever thought they could sass me and get away with it. So this boy standing in front of me, him and his friends, they didn't bother me none.

"Well you might've been running all yo' life," he says, "but I know one thang, you betta' watch yo' back, 'cause you neva' know who'll be pushing you into somethin'." Then, him and his friends busted out hollering and laughing. They just thought that was the funniest thing in the world to say.

I watched as they went on making fun at being so smart. But I didn't wanna get in no trouble so I let them have they silly fun. And I bent down to unroll my cuffed pant leg.

"Oooh! What's that on her shoulder, y'all?" I heard some-body saying, and, "Look at her neck!"

My shirt ribbon must've came loose while I was running, showing my shoulders and my upper back. Nobody noticed

64

b'fore now 'cause they was too busy laughing at themselves. B'fore I could say anything, the bigmouth girls had run off pointing at me as they made their way inside the school building. They had seen my scars and scabs. Now I was in for it.

The bell rang, and everyone that was left outside slowly started making their way back to they classrooms. I walked into mine and took my seat. I had managed to tie my shirt strings back together, so that if you tried to look you couldn't see anything was wrong. I picked up my number two pencil and started writing my name in the top left-hand corner of the paper, followed by the room number and teacher's name, just like I'd been told to do earlier that morning, but I'd got sidetracked by the big window. I printed my name perfect b'tween the two solid lines, making sure the smaller letters stayed underneath the broken-up line. As I started writing in my homeroom number, I heard the teacher call my name out loud.

"Regina Louise Ollison, could you please step outside with me for a moment?" This time her voice wasn't so slow-moving. And she looked at me straight in my eyes, as if I was staring at a picture of Jesus hisself. Oh, Lordy. I sat and watched as the teacher lady stood up and headed for the door, motioning with her hand for me to come along. I couldn't quite make myself believe this was happenin' to me, but then my body started to fail me as I half heard the other kids laughing and whispering. When the teacher had reached the square of the door she turned round to see if I was behind her. I wasn't. At first I got up slowly, like I was in slow motion. I heard the teacher call my name out again, and I realized I might be in a heap of trouble, so I left the class as fast as I could.

Outside, the teacher reached to put her hand on me, but

when I saw her motion towards me I flinched and put my hands up like I was protecting myself.

"Whoa there!" the lady said as she quickly moved her hand away and stepped back. "I didn't mean to scare you. I was just trying to make you feel comfortable, that's all." I watched as her face tightened up and she looked at me with questions running through her mind. Her voice changed, and she got real serious-like and lowered herself down to meet my eyes.

"Now, Miss Regina, this brings me to why I asked you to come out here in the first place. Is everything all right at home?" she asked me. But she sho' didn't wait long for me to answer back.

"Some of the children said that you had what looked like cuts on your body, is that true, Miss Regina?"

I just plain stared at this teacher woman, standing in front of me. Somehow I knew that if I told her anything, all hell was gonna break loose. And I didn't wanna be the one to cause it to happen. I had done 'nough already by leaving Big Mama. I would do just like Odetta had told me; I wasn't gonna tell our business. "Everything's fine at home," I told her as I put my hand to my collar to make sure the ribbons was tied tight, praying she couldn't see through me.

"Is there any truth to them welts being on yo' body?"

She was pushing for a answer, and I knew I couldn't give her one. I told myself to play dumb, and to see what would happen.

"Now, I need you to talk to me, Miss Regina. Go ahead and tell me the truth. Ain't nobody gonna hurt you." This time she was smiling a big white-woman smile, the kind that the teacher at my old school had flashed me when she tried to tell me that "little black girls" didn't ask "little white boys" out on dates, which I once did against my betta' mind. I usually felt betta' when the teaching was followed by a smile, but this time I wasn't gonna give in to it. In my mind's eye, I pressed my lips together, zipped 'em shut, and threw away the key.

"Well, since you refuse to cooperate with me, you leave me no other choice but to send you to the principal. Wait right here, and I'll get you a hall pass." Then she walked into the classroom. I stood right where I was and let my breath out. My head was beating like crazy. Ms. Teacher came back and gave me a hall pass. She pointed to the main office and told me to return to her room when I was finished, but that I wouldn't be allowed in unless the principal had signed the pass. I took the small piece of paper and headed down the hall. The back of my neck could feel the teacher's eyes staring at me. I didn't dare turn round for fear that she would know just what I was thinking. But I knew what I was gonna do. I couldn't talk to nobody. So at the moment when I should have gone inside the office, I turned the corner and ran to the first door I could find and pushed through. As I hauled tail across the play yard, I could see that there was nobody but me outside. My body felt like a firecracker that was 'bout to explode, but I kept moving.

I came to a tall Cyclone fence which made its way round the whole school ground. I put my feet into the li'l diamond shapes and climbed to the top. Making sure that I didn't touch the spiked ends of metal, I grabbed the smooth bar between the jagged pieces and swung my legs over as I jumped the fence. *Splat!* My feet landed on the ground, making my legs feel like concrete knives had stabbed through 'em. But I didn't care. I had got away without that teacher lady seeing me. And I figured that by the time they had missed me, I'd be back home with Odetta.

*   *   *

Odetta was waiting on me when I arrived. She told me the school had called and said that I'd left without permission, and that they had reason to believe that I might've been some kinda victim of child abusing. They also told her that they had to tell the police. I knew right then that I was being cursed by God. Big Mama and Lula Mae'd told me my mouth was gonna get me in a world of trouble; and here I was, trouble staring right down my throat, and this time I hadn't even said a word. I wanted to tell her that it wasn't my fault. That I had to join the other kids in a running test and that my shirt came undone. I wanted her to know that if it hadn't been for them ole stupid, nosey-ass kids, I could've stayed at the school, like the other kids. I wanted to tell her. But I couldn't. I just let my words hang close to my tongue and slide back down my throat.

"We gonna have to keep a low profile, baby." Odetta spoke after what seemed like hours of quiet. "I already called my daughter Carlene, and we'll be going to her place for a few days."

The hair on the back of my neck raised itself like a porcupine. I recollected some eavesdropping I'd done a while back when I learned that I might've had a whole slew of kinfolk livin' nearby to Big Mama's. That day I heard the grown folks talking 'mongst themselves 'bout somebody named Carlene Walker. S'posedly she was my daddy's younger sister who was on her way to making a real name for herself. Big Mama'd said, "Oh yeah, Odessa—who was her friend—you should hear what dem folks round town sayin' 'bout that Walker gal. I thank her name's Carlene or something or other. Yeah, they say she got herself into a tussle last night over some man at one a dem joints down on Sixth Street. Uh-huh, they say she received the hundredth cut, somewhere on her face. Somebody sliced her up

68

real good wit' a switchblade. Yeah, from what I hear, that gal's got more cuts on her than a li'l bit. Somebody say she even gots 'em on the bottom of her feet. Hell if that Gina don't watch that mouth a hers she gonna wind up just like her. Y'all knows fruit don't fall far from they trees now." I r'member thinking to myself that I sho' did hate it when folks thought they knowed what I was and wasn't gonna do. And just for that, I told myself I wasn't gonna be nothing like no bigmouth girl named Carlene Walker. I didn't care if she was the last person standing on the earth—I wasn't gonna have nothing to do with the likes of her.

Now I was having to go and be with the woman I'd 'magined to look like the scariest monster I'd seen. Odetta looked over at me and asked what was wrong. "You all right, honey? You look like you done seen a ghost."

I tried to move but couldn't.

"Come on now; Carlene's waitin' for my call."

Afraid of letting Carlene's name fall from my tongue, I decided not to ask nothing 'bout her, in case I got jinxed. So I asked what a low profile was, and Odetta said it meant that we had to stay away from the police. Those words I understood, so I gathered up my clothes into a brown paper bag while Odetta called her daughter to come and get us.

From the minute I met her, I kept turning my head and lowering my eyes so that I didn't have to look straight on into her face. I found things on the ground that seemed more inna'resting than the possible switchblade marks that I was s'posed have one day—if I kept on running my mouth.

"Hop on into the backseat," her voice said to me. And man did she sound tough. I did as I was told, and when she got into the driver's seat and placed her big hands on the steering wheel,

I tried to peek at 'em to see if there was scars from where she'd had stitches. I didn't see none. I turned to look out the window as we drove along in quiet.

We arrived at Carlene's house in the later part of the afternoon, at school letting-out time. Everywhere I could see there was kids with they books and bags walking on the sidewalks in all directions without a teacher or a grown folk. As we drove up to Carlene's house, my eyes liked to popped outta my head. That house was better than her own mama's. Seemed like the only place I had ever seen'd houses like this was on TV.

Inside there was as many rooms to eat, cook, and play in as there was rooms to sleep in. And all the rooms had they own door. In the kitchen was a machine that you put your dishes in and it did all the washing, while in the garage there was a real-life washer and dryer. My lands, I sho' 'nough hadn't seen the likes of this. Carlene named off all the things she owned as she showed me round her house. The whole time she talked, I was slyly staring at her to see if I could find the scars that was s'posed to be all over her body. There was none that I could see— not even on her face. Since her feet was covered I couldn't see the bottoms of them. Anyway she still made me scared by how big and tall she was. But by the time she finished showing me her house I was more inna'rested in that than them scars.

At Big Mama's we all slept in three different rooms. The whole house was no more than five rooms, and that's only if you count the bathroom that was hanging on to the side of the house by tar and a few nails. As far as a washing machine goes, we had the kind that had two rolling pins on the top, with a crank handle attached so you could wring clothes through, after you washed 'em by hand—we first soaked our clothes in a tin bucket, then scrubbed the dirt out on a accordion-shaped

70

board, then run 'em through the rolling pin part, since the washing machine itself was broke.

I overheard Odetta talking to Carlene 'bout what had happened. Carlene was asking Odetta why she was getting into "those" folks' business. She said that Ruby hadn't even bothered to tell Glenn that I was his child. And if it hadn't been for LouCinda—her sister and Odetta's daughter, who had seen me outside playing and swore up and down I looked dead-on Glenn Hathaway—nobody would know to this day.

"Hush yo' mouth right now, Car," I heard Odetta saying. "The chile might hear you."

I heard her all right. And I could see why they called her Carlene. Her forehead was so big you could lean a car on it and not even notice it. Plus, I didn't give a hoot 'bout her sorry brother anyway. Like the grown folks say, you can tell how good a man is by the way he treats his family, and so far, her brother was good for nothing.

Again I heard Odetta tell "Car" to watch her mouth. But this time I didn't hear what she said. I was too busy thinking 'bout Carlene's nickname. I made myself recall the nickname they gave me out at Big Mama's. It was "King Nappy." It sho' wasn't the kind of name you'd go round bragging about. But at least I could say that somebody took the time to rename me. Daddy Lent gave it to me 'cause my hair was so bad that the combs either got lost in it, or shot 'cross the room from the force of the naps. Daddy Lent told me I was lucky to get that name. 'Cause as the truth be told, I was also known for eating dried stray animal shit from the yard.

"Regina!" The sound of Odetta's voice brought me back. "Come in here and show your Aint Car your arms and legs, chile." I walked away from my eavesdropping post and went to her. She told me to take all my clothes off, 'cept my panties. I did as I was told. When Carlene saw me, she put her hand over her mouth.

"Mama," she gasped. "Somebody oughta go over there and whip whoever's ass that done this." Then she turned to me. "It's a good thing you ain't my goddamned chile, 'cause I'd blow somebody's fucking head off! Go on. Put your clothes on and go and watch the television in my room." I got dressed and went into the room I was told to go into. Instead of turning the TV on, I just laid down and pulled my knees up to my chest. I rocked myself as the tears rolled down my face one right after the other. But I was careful not to make noise. My mouth screamed, but there was no sound. My stomach pushed down like I had to go to the bathroom, but still I had no sounds to go with the tears. After a while, my chest got so heavy and my breath so hot that I gave in and let what little noise I could find out. But nobody heard me.

When I opened my eyes I saw Odetta sitting on the side of the bed. She told me that she and Carlene was going downtown to talk to somebody about the situation. I was to stay put until they got back. Carlene had told her that I was old 'nough to be by myself. And she was right. I had been alone many times b'fore, and I'd been just fine. I got up and went into the kitchen, where Carlene was cooking. I watched as she put a ham hock in with a pot of beans. After adding salt and pepper, she put a top on the pan and turned to me.

"Have you ever cooked before?"

I don't know what came over me, but somehow I felt that all the years of me watching Big Mama cook had somehow made me a cook. "Yeah, I can cook," I told her. "They let me cook a lot back home."

"Good, 'cause you need to earn your keep. I'm taking my mama downtown, and I'll be back in a couple of hours. And while we're gone, I need you to watch my pot of beans. I've set this here timer, so it will let you know when the beans are ready. When it goes off, just turn the fire off, okay?"

"Okay!" I told her. "Don't worry none."

I was old 'nough to cook, but Big Mama never let me in the kitchen without her. All 'cause I almost burnt the kitchen down one time while tryin' to heat up a pot of greens. I'd tried asking Sister to help me light the stove, and she didn't wanna be bothered. Sister yelled back at me from the room she was sitting in, and told me how to light the pilot. I had done just like she told me. I took the newspaper, put it to the pilot light in the oven, turned on the gas eye, and aimed the burning paper at it. Before I knew it, the paper was in flames and the room was starting to smell like gas. I got scared and ran to the sink, trying to get water on the newspaper. Meanwhile, the plastic curtains had caught fire and was melting to the window frame. I tried to holler out, but nothing came out my mouth. Next thing I knowed, Big Mama had knocked me to the floor and thrown water on the fire, all at the same time. But I didn't feel the need to tell Car all that.

Within minutes they was on they way, and I was left in a big ole mansion. I did what I'd do in anybody's house I hadn't been in before; I started rummaging through everything. I pretended I was Nancy Drew—she was my second favorite to Huckleberry—and I knowed that Nancy Drew had a way of snooping through all the evidence to find her clues to solve her cases. That was all well and good for Nancy, but I didn't know what case I was on; so I didn't know what I was searching for, but I kept on looking anyway. Finally, after I found a real thick book with pictures in it, I stopped. The outside read "Our Memories," and it had a white man and woman on the cover, sitting by a lake under some trees. I wondered what Carlene was doing with these folks' belongings, so I decided to snoop out the answers. B'fore I opened the book, I went and searched the cabinets until I found a box of Fig Newtons. I returned to the couch and started flipping through "Our Memories." Whoa! Once I opened the pages I realized that there wasn't one person in it that looked like the peoples on the front. As a matter of fact, they was all different colors of black. Some was lighter than me, and some was darker. Some of 'em had red hair, and some even had what looked like goldish hair. I kept looking through the book, but I never came 'cross those two on the cover. When I had gone through the whole book, I decided to go through it one more time, just to make sure I didn't miss nothing from the pages sticking together. The second time round I wanted to see if Glenn was in the book—I knew I'd recognize him from his picture on Odetta's headboard.

As I flipped through the pages of the picture book, I saw a photograph of Carlene standing with a man who looked some-what like her. They had the same big light-skinned foreheads. And just like the first picture I seen of him, the man who I fig-ured to be Glenn had an Afro that was sitting on his shoulders. There was another woman in the picture as well. She was way darker than them two, but the forehead was the same. The more I stared at the picture, the more I put two and two to-gether. The dark-skinned woman was the lady that lived 'cross the way from Ruby. I'd seen her a few times, had even talked with her 'bout the weather, but I never knowed her to be any kin to me. And there she was, my Ainty, right there under my own nose. Right then I also r'membered the dark-skinned woman sayin' to a friend of hers while they was sitting on her porch—"She sho' do look just like she could be kin." I never paid no mind to it a'tall.

I kept looking through the pages and seen lots of pictures with folks looking like they was having a good ole time. And I wondered why come if they knowed 'bout me they didn't come and get me so that I could be in their pictures too. I closed the book and tried to let my mind wander on what it would've been like if I'd lived with my so-called daddy's people instead of the Thornhills. Within no time a'tall I was 'sleep.

As the smoke made its way into my dreams, I caught the whiff of something burning and heard a ringing sound all round me.

It must've been going on for some time without me knowing it. Uh-oh. I threw that book on the floor and ran to the kitchen, right smack into a cloud of smoke and stink.

I opened doors and windows as fast as I could. Then I took the pot and removed the beans that was on top of the scorched part. I put them in a bowl. The burnt stuff, I scraped into the outside trash can. After scrubbing the black spots outta the pan with a S.O.S. pad, I put the beans I saved back in the pot, hoping Carlene wouldn't know any different. Lordy knows that I didn't want her to cut me up with no switchblade. Thinking it might help, I found a towel and started waving it through the air so I could get the burnt-smoke smell gone. I waited as long as I could to close the windows, and finally, when it seemed the smells'd gone away, I shut everything up to make it like b'fore. Considerin' the situation, I even put the empty Fig Newton carton back into the cupboard I found it in. I figured that if Carlene found I had burnt up her dinner and eaten all her

75

cookies she would probably try and kill me off. When she came home, sounded like I wasn't wrong.

"What the fuck happened up in here! Regina? Where my beans at? I know damned well you didn't go and burn 'em up." Carlene barged in with two li'l girls. They must've been sisters, 'cause they looked just alike.

"I know you hear me talkin' to ya. What happened to my beans? Did you burn the shit or what?"

"Uh, nah, I didn't. See, look here; they still in the pot." My body was nowhere to be found. I didn't feel like me. I felt like the burnt beans that was laying dead at the bottom of the trash can—the truth lay burning at the bottom of my belly. I couldn't say what was so.

"You take me for a fuckin' fool? I can smell that ya done burnt the shit up. Just tell the damned truth. I ain't got money to just burn, and now I gotta go and find my babies somethin' to eat. I really had a taste for them pintos, Regina."

I kept trying to convince her that the beans was fine, and that nothing wrong had happened. Her girls just sucked on they fingers, each one holding on to the side of her pants as if they couldn't stand unless they was touching her. Carlene stood in front of me, her eyes burning the meanness she felt for me right onto my skin, like a birthmark I forgot to get. I watched in quiet as she took her tongue and stuck it into the side of her cheek. It looked like she was saving a jawbreaker for later pleasures. I couldn't tell the truth. I would be beat or cut first.

"No wonder you got yo' ass whipped over yonder. It's 'cause you a damned liar, and a ugly liar at that. And God sho' don't like ugly, especially when it's a lie. I know one thing that's right, even if my beans ain't—you sho' is troublesome."

That was all she had to say to me. I wasn't gonna let no big-forehead, looking-cut-to-the-bone woman call me names. I was sick of all these folks and they evil selves. It was time to move on any damned way. One thing was for sho'; I had worn out my welcome here! It would just be a matter of time b'fore she would want to wear me out! And, I was missin' Big Mama any ole way. I wanted to go home, and I didn't need nobody to show me the way.

CHAPTER FOUR

NO TIME FOR GOOD-BYES

WE WAS DONE b'fore we could get started. I waited right good till Carlene headed out the room we was in to plan my quick getaway. Carlene told me she was gonna get her girls ready to go out, since the food she'd planned to have wasn't fit for a dog to eat. She also said she had a good mind to make me eat the burnt mess that I'd cooked, since I was tryin' so hard to convince her dinner wasn't ruin't.

The second Carlene left the kitchen I went into the bathroom and locked the door. My first mind was to worry on Odetta and how she'd hid me out from the bad guys and took pretty darn good care of me, but then I thought on it and figured if she really was sweet on me she wouldn't've left me in the hands of her nasty-mouth, bottom-of-the-feet-cut-up daughter. Plus, Odetta was on her stupid son's side anyway. That damn Glenn, what did he ever do to get me outta the mess he made in the first place? I was sick and tired of folks leaving me places and not really wanting to be bothered. Well, the way I seen it is, the time had come for me to take my troublesome self right back to where I came from.

I used the metal handle on the bathroom window to crank it open. Then I kicked out the screen, jumped to the ground, and ran from Carlene's house. I wasn't scared no more. Plus, I'd seen folks on TV plan harder getaways than me. I figured if they could jump outta skyscrapers wit'out killing theyselves, then so could I.

I'd picked a good time to head home. The sun was on its way to the other side of the world, so it wasn't as hot outside. East Austin to south seemed to be connected by one main road, Congress Avenue, but to get to it, I had to cross through the graveyard on Martin Luther King—Lord knows I must've high-tailed it through that cemetery all in a single breath.

I knowed there was only one bus that rode both the east and the south sides of town. I know this 'cause I would always go with Big Mama down to Congress Avenue, so she could do her errands. My favorite was when we would go turn in our S&H Green Stamps. Me and whoever else was inna'rested would collect the stamps and stick 'em into little green books, and when the books was full we'd turn them in for all kinds of food and supplies. Every now and again I was allowed to get somethin' sweet. But mostly we bought stuff like Ajax and Mr. Clean, to be used for Saturday housecleanings.

Running down the road, I heard somthing jangle in my pants pocket—the seventy-five cents that Odetta had gave me for lunch that morning! I was real lucky, 'cause I hadn't even thought 'bout the part of how I was gonna pay my fare, and now I didn't have to worry on it. I started to slow down when I seen a bus stop.

As I waited for the bus to come, I let my breath catch up to me and my mind wander on what was gonna happen when Big Mama caught her first look at me, after my being gone a spell. I let myself believe that she would see me coming from a ways and start cryin' 'bout how she'd missed me so. Then she'd run down the dirt road, and we'd meet halfway. After she'd hug me for a long while, like the white folks did on TV, she would tell me Lula Mae had either found a new man and run off, or had met with a bad accident and was no longer with us. Either way, I'd be relieved, and could stay with Big Mama happily ever after, like all the li'l white girls in the stories I read. In them stories, the li'l girls was loved by they mas and pas like no other. Nancy Drew and the Bobbsey Twins knowed what it was like to have they own families. They also got to be detectives and uncover the bad guys and they wrongdoings and then turn round and write a book 'bout it. Or, if they wanted to, they'd help folks out in the towns they lived in, so that it was safe for everybody to live and get along. And most of all, them li'l white girls even got to go on real TV vacations where there was snow and they could ride li'l sleds, and make snowmen, all the while never having to leave they mamas and daddies. I loved them li'l white girls, and I thought to myself that maybe one day if things didn't work out so well with Big Mama, then maybe I could find me a nice white family of my very own.

While I was letting my mind take me to places I'd never dreamed b'fore, the bus came. I got on and put a twenty-five-cent piece in. The fare was only a nickel for me, but I didn't have change. After takin' a seat on the door side of the bus, so's I wouldn't miss seeing my stop, I sat back in my seat and let my thoughts settle on Big Mama. I was happy to be seeing her soon. I always believed Big Mama when she said that she tried her damnedest to be a good Christian woman, even though I ain't never seen her go to church. She claimed that it was the things you did for other people that let you know which direction you'd be heading in the end. She said, "You should never let a dog or a child go hungry," and since she didn't care too much for animals, it made sense to her to take in and feed children and the elders. Her saying was, "There's 'nough to go round, even if it is leftovers." And believe you me there was enough of that. The only person who didn't eat leftovers was Daddy Lent. I heard him say one day, "Johnnie, I works too darn hard to eat the same cooked food twice in one week." So for him there was always new cooked food.

It was no surprise to anyone that Johnnie Jean Thornhill always had a house full of kids. And it didn't matter where they came from or who they belonged to. Accordin' to Big Mama, when my mama's mama died, from swallowing lye, the neighbors found her in the house with the body. It was Big Mama's reputation that landed Ruby in her charge. I heard tell people thought Ruby wouldn't know the difference—everybody said she was too young to r'member her mama dying and leaving her. Funny thing 'bout it, Ruby sho' wasn't dead when she s'posedly left me in that motel room.

Course, I only knew 'bout that room from what Lula Mae said—same way I learnt just 'bout everything I knew about Ruby. Seemed like folks only had bad things to say 'bout her, so I tried to play like her being kin to me wasn't such a big thing, even though secretly, I really liked her. I used to not only hear people say things like Ruby my mama was a whore, but that she couldn't stand that us girls had ruined her shape early on in her life. They said that was another reason why she didn't want me and Sister. No matter what was said, it only made me want her more. I figured anybody who got talked 'bout that bad must be somebody everybody wants.

I r'member when that song "Have You Seen Her?" came out on the radio. I would sit for days with my ear stuck to the li'l speaker on the music box, waiting on that song. It was as if the Chi-Lites knowed the questions I was wantin' to ask anybody who'd listen.

I learned all the words to that song, and I sang it everywhere I went, hoping that somebody might ask me if I was sanging 'bout somebody I knew by the way I sang it. I 'magined that if somehow it was known that I was on the lookout for Ruby and I was heard, then maybe someone would tell her.

My sangin' that song got so bad Sister threatened to cut the electric cord right off the back of the radio. She told me I sounded like I had no sense. I told her she was a ugly monkey's uncle and to mind her own business. I also told her that as far as sense went, she should use hers and help me sing the song. Then for sho' our mama might get wind of it and maybe would come back. After sucking her teeth and turning her backside to me, she'd walk off shaking her head.

The bus rolled past the Goodyear Tire Company, and then I knowed I was real close to home. I wasn't too upset 'bout it— livin' with Big Mama had been mostly all right, I guess. I got to go to Sunday school as much as I liked. Every Sunday, the church folks would come round in they van, with the Church of the Nazarene sign on it, and take me and anyone else who wanted to go. Normally it was only me. I loved to go to that church. We not only got to have Easter egg hunts on Easter and get our names picked for Christmas in order to get free presents, but we got to read the books of the New Testament. I would always compete with the other kids to see who could mem'rize the most books of the Bible. Due to my knack for r'membering words, I'd almost always win. My most favorite saying was, "For God so loved the world, that he gave his only begotten son, that whosoever believeth in him should not perish, but have everlasting life." John 3:16. I loved that saying more than anything. It was the first Bible verse I'd ever learned by heart and the only one I could say even if I was tongue-tied.

The day I decided to believe the verse, I was sitting in the church on one of the front pews, with my hands tucked underneath my bottom as my feet swung quietly back and forth 'cross the floor. I looked up and seen the white preacher man in his long red gown that was trimmed in white ribbon. He told us to turn our Bibles to the Book of John. After everybody'd found the page, the preacher man asked us to repeat after him. We started that way, simple enough, but by the end of the verse, something in me got all warm feeling and almost made me wanna cry. After turning the verse over and over in my mind, I simply got stuck on the believeth part. I had never heard such a thing of a word b'fore. It was like the *th* sound put a spell on me. I said the *th* over and over in my mind until it worked its way to my mouth. After a while, which was the end of the service for that particular Sunday, the whole saying made sense. The way I seen it was this: if God took the time to kindly put them extra letters on a already-made word, then he must've had more'n he needed of everything, and didn't mind giving away his extra son. God was a real nice man. And since I knowed the Holy Book was no joking matter, I made it my business to take it seriously.

I thought 'bout God and his book right then, 'cause as we passed the brown apartment houses on the right-hand side, where I was sittin', I knowed I was almost home. All of a sudden I could feel my belly pulling itself all tight-like.

Even though I was happy to be going back home, I was still scared of Lula Mae and what she might do to me. Come to think on it, she wasn't all I was 'fraid of. I was also worried 'bout how I was gonna get on with that crazy-ass Donna Janine and all the stuff that folks would be sho' to say 'bout me. The more I thought on these things, the more something inside of me just didn't care. I felt like from here on out, I could take on anybody who tried to do me wrong. I didn't have to stay where I wasn't wanted—I'd just be more careful runnin' away if I had to do it again.

When I recognized the 7-Eleven store out the bus window, I knew it was my stop. Pulling the cord, I told the driver that I needed to get off at the next corner. As I stepped down from the bus, my mind wouldn't let me believe that I was in walking distance of the house and people that I had run off and left without no word. I knew deep in me that I'd done bad. I'd learned in church that just b'cause somebody does you wrong don't mean you should do wrong by them. Still, as I walked the dirt trail that led back to the house, I touched my arms and r'membered the blows that slammed against my skin.

A cool wind came from inside me and crawled up my back as my skin turned to gooseflesh under my fingertips. I would never forget that whoopin'. Feelin' the scabs on my arms, I couldn't help but wonder if the way I was treated out at Big Mama's was the same way they'd done Ruby. I heard tell that my mama got whoopin's once a week, and I could only 'magine what that must've been like for her. I wondered if Ruby'd ever run off when she was my age. Or if she hit back whoever was doing the beating. Something inside my head told me that maybe that's why Ruby left and never came back. Even so, I just didn't understand why she'd leave us with the same folks that she herself'd run from.

I let the questions I had no answers for make they way 'cross my mind. I couldn't help but wish for Ruby to come and make it all a li'l bit easier. As I walked, I pictured Ruby on her way, just like when Cindy and any other of the Brady kids would cry and Carol or Alice would try and make 'em feel better. I knowed my mama could do this for me too, if she could come.

As I rounded the bend, where the grass field with the over-grown pussy willow and cattails sep'rated our property from the new apartment homes that was being built up, I seen the drive-way that led up to Aint Bobbie's front porch. Daddy Lent's old blue Chevy pickup was parked where it usually was when he wasn't working or fishing, which was in the long dirt driveway.

I also seen Aint Bobbie's Plymouth, newly wrecked, hanging out from under the carport and couldn't believe that in the time I was gone she'd already ruined another car. I like Aint Bobbie even though her kids was the worst children I'd ever laid eyes on. But if you let her tell it, they was God's gifts to the heavens. I didn't have to agree. Rumor had it that Aint Bob-bie's kids all had different daddies and that's why they was so wild. I guess it didn't matter much, as long as they had daddies. One thing was for sure, Aint Bobbie seemed to have no better luck with men than she did cars, 'cause every time you turned round she'd wrecked another one.

Since Aint Bobbie's house was in the front of Big Mama's, I went to her back door and let myself in. I found myself in the room where Bobbie kept her yellow squash-colored chester-field, still wrapped up in the plastic it came in. She didn't want nobody sitting on it, in case they was to mess it up. I never understood that. Why come she just didn't buy a plastic couch to begin with? I made my way to Bobbie's room. The air conditioner was on, and I could hear it hummin' as the air blew about the place, keeping it nice and cool. I looked closer and saw that Bobbie and her baby was sound asleep. I didn't wanna wake 'em up, so I sat down at the foot of her bed, like I had done a hundred times b'fore.

Outta all of Johnnie Jean Thornhill's natural kids, Bobbie was the nicest. She had a real quiet way 'bout herself. But lately she was always sick. Folks say it was 'cause she had too many kids outta wedlock. I didn't know what that mean, but I still liked Bobbie the best—even though I figured that wedlock was something that was like a cootie. Every now and again, Aint Bobbie'd try and act like Lula, and start whoopin' on me and then get mad if I made a sound 'bout how bad it hurt. This one time Aint Bobby hit me so hard 'cross my legs, my whole left kneecap swelled up like a water ballon. I r'member I choked my cries off into my throat and sat and rocked my knee, hugging it up to my chest like it was a child that had hurt itself. Even though her hitting me hurt more than Lula Mae's hits, I still decided to like her and wasn't sore at her for too long. I think one of the main reasons I was nice to Bobbie was 'cause whenever I wanted to know about my mama, Bobbie would tell me. She said that even though I asked too many doggone questions, she didn't mind answering them as long as I helped her clean her house as we talked. She told me that Ruby had red hair to match her temper, and that she was fast with the boys. She also said that I should watch my way with the men. I r'member thinking to myself that Bobbie didn't have nothin' to worry 'bout; I had decided a long time ago that I wasn't gonna be like my mama.

Bobbie also told me that my mama had a chipped front tooth that she got from one of Big Mama's retarded cousins. She said that one day, when Ruby was my age, or so 'bout, she was drinking a Chocolate Soldier soda water, which was her favorite, and retarded cousin Stewy ran up and slammed the bottle into Ruby's tooth just to see what would happen. Accordin' to Bobbie, Ruby beat the crap out the dim-witted boy, and that just added to folks believing she was cold-hearted. I didn't care nothin' 'bout the cold-heart part, but I sure did come to hate that Stewy fella. And if I ever got a chance I was gonna do the same thing to him. Secretly I felt sorry for Ruby on account of her chipped tooth and thought that one day I'd let her know that.

I heard the baby start to cry, and I looked up to see Bobbie waking up too. It took her a minute to adjust her eyes, and in seconds, she asked me, "What you doing here, Gina?" As I was 'bout to talk, I heard what I thought was police sirens getting closer and closer. Bobbie peeked out the corner of the window, and once the curtain was back, I could see the orange-and-red lights of the police car shining through into the room. My head started pounding 'long with those siren sounds. I got up on the bed with Bobbie and sat and watched with her as the police car came to a stop—not in the driveway, like most decent folk would know to do, but dead smack in the middle of Aint Bobbie's fresh-cut lawn. The driver got out and motioned towards Big Mama, who was cutting him off at the gate. I couldn't read lips, so I didn't know what they was saying. I just watched to see what was coming next.

It didn't take long to figure it out. My eye caught sight of a car that I had seen for the first time earlier that day! It pulled up on the grass and parked right next to the policeman. I thought I had died and gone straight to hell. I didn't have to worry 'bout reading lips no more, 'cause Carlene talked loud 'nough for the whole block to hear!

"Officer, Officer," she yelled out, as she ran to the man dressed in all black, with a silver gun hanging from a loop on the side of his belt. "I want you to go in there and get my brother's chile." I heard and watched Carlene scream at the policeman. Her hand was waving through the air as she pointed at Big Mama's house. The officer never had time to answer her before she was making her way towards the gate that separated the two yards from one another. Carlene looked like she was gonna pull out a switchblade and go to town on anybody that got in her way. I could hear her yellin' to find out where I was at.

"She ain't round here no mo'!" Big Mama screamed back at Carlene from the steps of her house, where she usually sat, chewing her snuff and wearing that faded red pocketbook round her neck. "I ain't seen her in well ova' a week." This must've sent Carlene into a hissy fit, 'cause she had to be held back by the policeman, who wouldn't let her pass by him. The policeman seemed to be caught b'tween two fussing women, not knowing what to do. I watched as he placed the heel of his hand on the rounded part of his pistol and rested. Finally he was able to get a word in.

"Now, y'all, just calm down! Ya hear?" he scolded. "Otherwise, I'm gonna have to haul your tails downtown."

That was all I needed to hear. I slipped back from the window and watched as Aint Bobbie lay, barely holding her baby in her arms. The baby started whining, and Bobbie had to turn to loosen her hold on her, and as she did, I seen that one of the things on her chest that used to feed her child was gone. All that was left was a long thick line held together by black thread.

"What you staring at, girl? Didn't yo' mama teach you not to study folks too long?" What was she talkin' 'bout? She knowed the answer to that question betta' than anybody—my mama'd barely taught me my name. My eyes caught Bobbie's as she caught mine in the act of gawking. I'd never seen such a sight. Her skin was sagging a bit, like it barely wanted to hang on to her body. In her face I could see the bones of the Cherokee that Big Mama'd told us kids 'bout, when telling where her peoples came from. It was in Aint Bobbie that the signs of Injun blood showed most. But now, Bobbie's face was gone. What was left in its place was caved-in cheeks, deep 'nough to be mistaken for small bowls. I couldn't believe that I hadn't paid much mind to Bobbie b'fore now, 'cause the last I seen her she didn't look so bad. All I could do was sit and stare.

I was so busy thinking on Aint Bobbie's cheeks that I didn't see Big Mama come in behind me. "Get under the bed, girl! Hurry up 'fo' somebody see ya!" She was panting like a billy goat and pushing me under the bed at the same time. "Cain't nobody know you here. You see what ya done gone and done?" Big Mama was talking so fast I couldn't hear all of what she was saying, but I knowed from the sound of it all that I wasn't gonna get no *Little House on the Prairie* greeting upon my return. So much for hugs and kisses wrapped in words like "baby," and "I'm glad you come home." I guess in God's plan there was things that was meant to be and things that wasn't.

The fussing in the front yard was now a bundle of nonsense to my ears; I couldn't hear nothing from under the bed. Big

Mama'd disappeared as quickly as she had come. I watched her shuffle her feet 'cross the floor, on her way to finish Miss Carlene off. As I lay in wait to be free, I couldn't help but wonder what was gonna happen to me. Was Big Mama gonna be mad that I came back and secretly plan with Lula Mae to torture me so that I would leave again? After all, they always said that I was way too much work, and that I needed more than anybody had to give. Well, the way I saw it was that if I gave just a little bit more nice, then maybe I wouldn't have to work so hard to get them to like me. No matter what happened, I was glad to be back home. And I promised to God that I would be betta' and less troublesome.

"Come on out from unda' dere, Gina. They all gone now." Big Mama was on her hands and knees staring at me. Her eyes was stuck behind glasses that made her look like she'd strapped a magnifyin' glass to her face. She grabbed an arm and started pulling me out from under the bed. Once I was out, Big Mama didn't ask no questions. She told me to be quiet and to make my way over to the other house. I did as I was told. As I got outside, I saw that the lights that usually showed the way b'tween Aint Bobbie's house and Big Mama's wasn't on. As a matter of fact, there was no lights on anywhere, making me think that Big Mama'd forgot to pay the electricity bill again. We headed round to the back door, stumbling over oak tree roots and rocks and wheelbarrows as well as anything else that got in the way. I waited for my eyes to adjust to the darkness, to give way to a shape that I recognized—but they didn't. After more tripping and toe stubbing, we got to the back side of the green-roofed house. Daddy Lent let us in. Everybody else was sleeping, so I tiptoed to my bed, trying real hard to be mindful of Doretha, so as not to wake her up. I crawled in next to my sister and settled against her flesh. I was back home. My insides was hopping all round, dancin' to the thought of seeing my sister the next day. I wanted to see if she missed me any—even though I knowed she prob'ly didn't. I was hoping that my being gone was gonna make her wanna be nicer to me. One thing was for certain—when you really think you cain't stand somebody, all you have to do is leave 'em for a while to know that the heart has a mind of its own, and mine had kinda missed my sister.

I lay 'wake on my side of the bed for a while. I was glad to notice I still had a side of the bed—Doretha must've thought I'd one day be back, and decided to leave my place in the bed open for me. Maybe in her heart she missed me. I heard the rise and fall of Doretha's breath and knew that she was dead asleep and would be madder than a bull if I woke her up. Since I had been asleep under Bobbie's bed, it wasn't hard for me to fall back into sleep again. In no time a'tall, me and Sister was breathing to the beat of the same drummer.

I woke up to Big Mama shaking me and telling me to get up fast. I couldn't move quick 'nough for her, 'cause the next thing I knowed she was pulling the covers offa me, letting the morning air steal the sleep that had been all mine throughout the night.

"Hurry up, chile, and get yo' mouthwash. We ain't got all day." Every morning before I was allowed to open my mouth and talk to anyone, I had to gargle my mouth out with the cinnamon rinse that Big Mama had bought just for me. She said my breath smelled like something had crawled up and died right there on my tongue. I was so used to hearing that I couldn't r'member when I stopped being 'shamed of it. While I was swishin' round the cinnamon, Big Mama was yelling at me to hurry up, saying that Cousin Eli was on his way to get us. Cousin Eli was Big Mama's youngest cousin from her ma's side. He usually came round when Big Mama needed to tend to business that was outta town, but not far 'nough away where you'd have to take a bus. I took the red liquid and poured a small bit into the top of the bottle and threw it into my mouth. I turned the back of my throat on, and the mouthwash started jumping round like in a washing machine.

I didn't think nothin' of getting up early and leaving with Big Mama, 'cause we did that some of the time. She loved traveling round Texas doing her business, and since she liked to keep company at the same time, she'd let me come along.

When I finished rinsing my mouth and dressing, I went back and stood by the little floor heater in Big Mama's room, paying special mind to not let the back of my legs touch the heated grates. No matter what time of year, Big Mama stayed cold, so her heater was always the first thing turned on in the early morning. One time, b'fore I knowed better, I bent my legs all the way back and scorched perfect metal lines into the back side of my knees, only to have my stupid sister say that I was 'fflicted with double joints, and that I was lucky I hadn't burned my ass while I was at it.

While I was dressing, Big Mama walked into the room and handed me a li'l vanity case. We had bought it, and 'bout twenty more like it, at a Kress's close-out sale. I held the case and thought that it was so pretty, made of off-white leather and decorated with gold rope drawn all round the edges. Big Mama said that she was glad to finally find some use for these damned cases. Somebody had told her 'bout the sale and convinced her that she could sell them cases along with Avon and make a lot of money, fast.

I opened the case. Inside was a bag of Nilla Wafers and a strawberry Cragmont soda. They was some of my favorite traveling foods. I could always tell when we were going on a long trip, 'cause of the way Big Mama'd packed the food. The more containers of Vienna sausages and sardines we had, the longer we'd be on the road. Vienna sausages was Big Mama's favorite; she loved to drink the little juice that was left over in the can.

We heard a car pull into the driveway and turn off its engine. I set my case down and went to the window to see if it was Cousin Eli, and sho' 'nough it was. He didn't bother getting out on account he knew we'd be right there. We never kept him waiting.

After our things was loaded on the bed of his truck, I climbed in the middle b'tween Cousin and Big Mama, and we was off. I really didn't know where we was going, but it wasn't important. I loved to just plain ole ride round with Big Mama. It gave me a chance to be still and listen to my own mind talk. Anyway, I knew that as long as I was with her, I didn't have to worry that she would leave me.

Halfway down the road Big Mama noticed that she had left her teeth in the jar by her bed. We turned the truck round and went back for 'em. I jumped out and ran into the old house, and without disturbing anybody, found the jar. I picked it up as gently as I could and held it out in front of me, as if I thought the teeth was gonna jump out the jar and bite me. I walked quickly back out to where Big Mama and Cousin was waiting on me and scooted back into my place. This time we was on our way for real.

Big Mama had to have her own teeth pulled right out her

gums a few years b'fore. She said it was 'cause she had py-or-rhea and that they were no good for chewing anymore. I r'member coming in from the out of doors one day and finding her slung 'cross her bed, hollerin' to the high heavens. "Oh, Lordy, why'd ya have to go and take my teefs." She cried like that for two or three days and had us draw the shades in the room like somebody had died. I guess it wasn't so bad, 'cause shortly after the doctor pulled all her teeth he gave her new ones that she cleaned and stored in a Mason preserve jar. She kept the jar on her headboard; that way the false teeth could watch her sleep at night. I held up the jar and watched the Efferdent that Big Mama must've put in b'fore we left go to work on the li'l piece of meat that was stuck in the two gold pieces that sat next to her front teeth. Johnnie Jean loved them gold teeth more than life itself.

Rumor had it that the gold was a ring my mama had given her to keep until she came back for me and my sister. And as the story goes, Ruby never rightly came back for us. Once she realized that Ruby was never gonna return, Big Mama had the jewelry man melt down the ring and put it in her dentures. She said looking at her teeth would always make her think twice b'fore she made a promise she wasn't hell-bent on keeping.

Somewhere b'tween I-35 and Ben White Boulevard, I fell off to sleep. By the time I woke up, it was clear that we was way outta the city limits. I wanted to know where we was going.

"Big Mama."

"Yes, chile, what you want?" she answered me, her gums slamming into one another like a newborn baby.

"Where Cousin Eli and us going?" There was a long silence. I got ready to ask again. "Big—"

Johnnie Jean cut me off at the gate. "Now, Gheena, please

94

don't go axing a whole bunch of questions, jus' wait and see; we almos' dere."

She always called me Gheena when her teeth wasn't in. Sometimes it sounded like she was talking with a mouth full of cotton. Once I told her that, and she slapped me upside my head and told me I didn't know nary a thing about cotton and for me to watch myself. Now I just secretly made fun of her in my mind. She couldn't tell me what to do there.

I had what grown folks called a wandering mind. I could spend hours, maybe even days, thinking 'bout what was and what was to come. I always seemed to be too many steps behind what was, being reminded only after it had left me. I stayed the most time with what was to come, like my own mama coming for me. Sometimes I seen her on a big white stallion, riding sidesaddle, her red plaits flapping in the wind. I'd see her coming from a distance, and hear the sounds of her horse stirring up the dirt under its speed. With one arm holding on to the rein, the other would be open wide, waiting to scoop me up; I'd nestle my body into hers, and off we would ride. And there were those times when she'd heard my tears and knowed that Lula had welted up my body. Then, my mama and two bodyguards would come round the way, riding in a Cadillac, ready for action. Their guns drawn and aimed at the place right in the middle of Lula Mae's beady eyes. *Pow! Pow! Pow!* Boy would she get shot up if only my real mama knew.

The sign for Cross Timbers brought me back to now. We sure had gone outta our way. As Cousin came to a stop, I read another sign pointing us towards the Greyhound bus station. Outside of five minutes we was pulling into the driveway. The windows in the truck cab was rolled down, so I could smell them fumes that only come from a bus depot. We pulled the ole Dodge into the parking lot and rolled into a spot next to some motor bicycles, and Big Mama took the jar-o'-jaws and put her choppers in. After making sure her wig was sitting on her head straight, she made her way to the rest room. Cousin Eli, who finally decided to speak, got out and stretched his legs and announced that he needed to go to the li'l boys' room. He closed one of his eyes and told me to stay put, that he'd be right back. Then he waddled off. He was 'bout as much of a li'l boy as I was. To say the truth, Eli was nothing short of huge! The man was real big, with hands that reminded me of the stretched-out-ness of a baseball glove. Not to mention that he had a big head with lips to match. So li'l boy he wasn't.

From the looks of it, there was nowhere for me to go, so he didn't have to worry none. Seemed like the worrying was up to me. For one, I wanted to know why we had to drive clear out into the boondocks to the bus station, when b'fore, all we did was drive over to Koenig Avenue. For two, how come nobody was talking 'bout why we was here? I looked in the rearview mirror and saw Big Mama coming. Her small brown body moved from side to side as her feet dragged her back to me. Right behind her came Cousin, who waited till he got good and outside before he fastened his pants up. He took the belt and pulled it way over to the other side of his body as he shook one leg, like he was trying to get something hot outta his pants.

"Come on now, girl; help me with this stuff so we can leave," Big Mama told me. She never once looked at me, and her voice was shaking. She sure seemed strange-acting to me. As Eli reached us, I climbed down and pulled my vanity case out, and he handed me my sweater. I also took the jar-o'-jaws—Big Mama would need it when it was time to take them out again.

As we moved towards the bus depot, I turned and looked back at Eli and seen that he wasn't coming with us. I kept on wondering why he'd dropped us off here. I swear, as I started walking away, I seen water hanging in the skin of his eyes. But I tried not to think nothing of it. I yelled to Cousin that we'd see him when we got back. He smiled that Gomer smile and waved as he nodded his head. By the time we reached the station door, I turned and caught the tail end of his truck as it disappeared.

We had to run to get on our bus. I handed the driver the two tickets and found us seats, like I had done many times b'fore. After everybody was on, the driver reached over and pulled the big hook handle and closed the door. I usually looked at the front of the bus to see where we was going; that way I would know how long the ride would be. This time, though, I just sat back in my chair and hoped that me and Big Mama was goin' on a trip that was gonna last forever.

"Houston. We will be arriving in Houston in five minutes. All y'all folks gettin' off here should grab yo' bags and go inside the terminal and wait for more information." The driver's voice jumped me right outta my seat. Big Mama said that we wouldn't be getting off here, so I relaxed and tried to fall off to sleep again.

"Gina."

"Huh," I answered her, bothered by her waking me up again.

"Wake up, I wanna talk to you."

I opened my eyes to see Big Mama bucking her big ole cataract peepers at me.

"Yeah, what you wanna talk 'bout?" I asked, while my stomach started bubbling up. In the whole time I'd known her, Big Mama had never talked to me 'bout much. I didn't wanna hear this.

"Gina," she said, her voice real small but straight. "'Member when I told you ya' mouth was gonna get you in a world of trouble one day?"

I didn't say one word. I watched as each word slipped from her tongue and tumbled from b'tween her lips.

"Well, chile, that day has come, and you is in trouble. You shouldn't've run over to dem damn Mes'cans, running your mouth. And if they ain't 'nough you had to go tell your daddy's peoples. Now folks is all tied in knots 'bout you, and you gots to go away."

I listened.

"I'm only going as far as Texarkana with you; then I go on back home."

"I cain't come back wit' chu, Big Mama?" I asked, as my breath started to cut off at my throat. I tried looking into Big Mama's eyes, but she wouldn't let me rest there; she kept turning her face where I couldn't see nothing but the side of it.

"You cain't never come back 'cause if you do, the authorities are waitin' on you, and they will take you into custody. All 'cause of you opening that mouth of yours."

I listened to Big Mama, but I couldn't hear the words themselves. It was like the alphabet just rolled outta her mouth all mixed up. Not making a bit of sense. I felt like hell had opened up on me and left me for dead. I couldn't make anything right with what Big Mama was saying to me.

I thought for a minute that maybe the authorities coming for me wouldn't be so bad. It could be that they'd find a nice white family for me to go and stay with. Seemed like they was the only folks that knowed how to treat kids nice. I thought I'd seen on TV where the police would come and take folks off to a betta' place. I wondered if they took kids? I also figured that maybe Big Mama didn't want me to go anywhere betta'. I kept listening to the jumbled alphabet fall out her mouth—not making any sense to me 'cause they was just letters.

By the time Big Mama was through, my insides felt like cake in a mixing bowl when you wound the beaters too fast. I held my breath in the high part of my chest to keep the tears from falling outta my eyes. I learned that from Lula Mae. She would say to me, "Shut the hell up, 'fore I give you somethin' to cry for." I'd stop my breath, and the wetness in my eyes would go away, and then she'd leave me alone. I looked again at the eyes that had rings of cataract, round 'em. I no longer seen Big Mama's face. I cain't rightly say I seen much. I wanted to break into a hundred zillion small pieces and become the air that Big Mama had to breathe so that I wouldn't have to sit and listen to no more. I could just be there with nobody seeing me.

It seemed like I held my air in forever. I hoped with every- thing I had that I could just disappear and not know how it happened. Like when you fall off to sleep and you never know you did till you wake up the next day to start over again. I sat and tried to think of where I was going. Who did I know that wanted me? There was nobody who came to my mind. Big Ma- ma'd turned her head away from me after she said what she had to say. For a while, I sat there and let the quiet rest itself b'tween the two of us. I didn't know what to do. For the first time ever, I stared at Big Mama's hands. They was small as mine. And on her left hand there was a thin gold ring that rode on her second-to-the-last finger. Her nails was jagged and kinda yellow, like she'd been cooking with mustard—but I knew it to be from pinching snuff. It was the color of her hands that made me wanna look at 'em forever. They was brown—the color of vanilla extract—with small white lines in 'em where the lotion forgot to go. I thought 'bout the times those hands would rub Pond's cold cream all over my face, leaving me to shine all day in the sun. She'd forgot to oil my face up that morning.

If a jackrabbit had any notion of what it would feel like to be cooked then ate, I'm certain he wouldn't stick round long 'nough to find out. That's just what it felt like to have Big Mama tell me I was gonna have to get on some bus and leave all I ever knowed. This was my punishment for disturbing God with my troublesome self. The truth is, he has a whole world to run and look after, so I could see how I had got on his nerves and he was tired of me. He must've sent Big Mama a sign to send me off. Now I could really see that Big Mama took more of a liking to Sister than she did me. And now that I knowed the truth, I couldn't believe I wasn't even allowed to see Doretha 'fore I left. If I'd known I was gonna leave for good, I'd at least have woke her up to say good-bye. I didn't get to say nothing to nobody, as a matter of fact. It's like everybody know 'bout my leaving except me. Well, forget them and they sorry asses anyways! My sister and them ain't so special! They all gonna get whooped by Lula Mae too! And for all they know I could be living with a nice family that didn't beat kids like you'd beat a rug hanging out on a line. Or yell at folks up in they face as if they deaf, dumb, and stupid! Yeah, I was prob'ly going to someplace where nobody was gonna know me for being troublesome! They was gonna like me and buy me pretty dresses and coats that wasn't two sizes too big or make me wear funky-smelling sweaters that wasn't even mine! I couldn't wait to get to where I was going just so I could let 'em all see how better I was than them! I was gonna be good. I was gonna be good.

Jesus, Joseph, and Mary! There he goes again! That dumb driver was at it again, yelling at folks like they couldn't understand pure talking! We had arrived in Texarkana, and he said that everybody had to get off here for all points going east and onward. Those of us who'd be departing here was told to get our luggage. I grabbed my case and sweater. Big Mama grabbed nothing. The bus pulled into the terminal and came to a quick stop. The driver said something 'bout us running late, so folks who was riding with him needed to listen for the announcements telling when to get back on the bus. After the passengers in the first six rows got out, it was our turn. I led the way, and Big Mama was cut off by a fat man who had to turn sideways 'cause his gut got stuck in the aisle. I waited for Big Mama on the sidewalk, and as soon as the big man was out, I saw her wig coming down the stairs. The driver took her hand and helped her to the ground.

"Come on, Gina." Big Mama put her hand in the middle of my back and kinda pushed me into the station, where we could check on my bus. Before she could get up to the counter, she was already talking to the man standing behind it.

"Excuse me, sir, but can you tell me when the next bus to North Carolina is leavin'?"

"Why, yes, ma'am, I surely can. You jest hol' right there." He picked up the phone and started talkin' to somebody. When he finished, he turned round and said, "The bus to Jacksonville, Narth Caralina, will be arrivin' and leavin' in about fit-teen minites outta gate fo'." I ain't heard nobody talk that back-woods since *Hee Haw*. I hated the way he sounded.

Big Mama and me went and sat down on the benches next to gate four. Lately when I got real mad and held my breath, my stomach would start pulling and stretching on the inside and I'd have to go number two. Then, instead of it being hard and needing a good push, it would fall out my butt 'fore I could get my panties down. I didn't say nothing to nobody, though; I would just try and get to the toilet faster. If not, I'd take my soiled underwear off and hide 'em under the bed or throw 'em away. This time I was lucky; I got to the toilet in time. When I came back, Big Mama was waiting right where I left her. I was glad she hadn't run off and left me like I thought she woulda. I sat down, and we both said nothing.

Over the loudspeaker, I heard the man who had helped us: "All y'all folks headin' tarwards Jacksonville, Gainesville, and Raleigh, Narth Caralina, should start lining up at gate fo'." Seemed like it took him forever to say that simple sentence. I heard the grown folks say that only hillbillies drag their words out over a week long and that that gave the drawl a bad name. We gathered up my things and headed to the line that was forming. I was walkin' too slow, so Big Mama grabbed my arm and pulled me. I kept thinking to myself, Who would Big Mama have to go on business trips with? Who would scratch and oil her scalp, or get the blackheads outta her back with a bobby pin? I know that I was the only one allowed to rub Vicks Va-poRub b'tween her thighs, when her legs rubbed together and chafed. How was she gonna get on without me? I couldn't let myself believe that I was gonna have to be alone without Big Mama.

The bus was starting to load, and our turn was getting closer. I wanted to run, but I didn't know where to go. I got on the bus, and Big Mama told me to sit in the front seat, behind the driver. She sat down next to me and started talking.

"Now, Gina, you gonna be on this bus three days. At the end of that time, somebody will be waiting on you. I ain't telling you who in case they don't show. But if you get there and no-body comes for you, here's a quarter so you can call me." She wrote the number down and put it in my hand along with the money. I already knowed the number by heart—I guess she must've forgot that.

"Now you got your Nilla Wafers and the soda. That should hold you a coupla days. Just don't eat 'em all at one time; I don't want you getting sick, ya hear me? You be good, you hear, and Big Mama will see you later now; I'll come and see you." As she stood to go she patted me on the head. "Don't forget now: stay on this bus for three days. I told the driver 'bout you, and he's gonna keep an eye out for you; just don't make no trouble for him."

I could barely hear what she was sayin'. It didn't matter—I didn't give a care to what she said.

Her mouth kept moving as she walked off the bus. "Keep to ya'self, ya hear?"

Those was the last words Big Mama said to me. Then she was gone. My chest was so full of air I could rest my chin on it. When I let my breath out, Johnnie Jean Thornhill was nowhere to be seen. She said she was gonna come and see me—when was she gonna come? Could she come now? Would she be there—wherever—when I arrived? The sun had left the sky, leaving no traces of light. There was nothing to even show me where she once stood and no sweet mem'ry worth keeping. I didn't see her wave bye-bye. Or give me special wind kisses that I'd seen people on TV throw so freely when someone they like a lot goes away. Sometimes it might be a mama sending her son off to a boot camp, or maybe a wife sending her young husband to join the army. No matter what, the women would run along-side the bus or train for as long as it was in sight. Then at the last minute they'd take they hand and put it to they mouth, kiss it, and toss it into the wind.

I never heard the bus start its engine or pull out the station. By the time I realized she was really gone, we was moving down the street.

I didn't care what she said, I wasn't sitting by this stupid driver! *I was gonna sit where I damned well pleased. And she couldn't tell me how many cookies to eat, 'cause I was gonna eat 'em all right here and now! One right after the other. And if Lula Mae's ugly face was standing right b'fore my very eyes, I would smash her upside her stupid head with that strawberry Cragmont soda and watch her bleed. Yeah, that's right! And I wouldn't even help her take the glass outta her face! Why was Big Mama leaving me? What did I do bad this time?*

I cain't begin to count the tears that fell from my eyes that night. I cried and cried and cried. And like a old cat that leaves to die by itself, I moved away from the driver and found a seat nearer to the bathroom, the ones that have three seats con-nected together. I took my body and tried to crawl into the crack that separated the seat from the back. I pulled my knees up to my bosom and wrapped my arms round my legs. I hated Big Mama! No matter what, I wasn't coming back to see her again!

Trying to quiet my voice, I put my fist in my mouth and bit down on it. I cried silently into my hand and the seat cushions. And like I always did, when I was sad, no matter what, I called out for my mama. I never understood why that was so, but it was like something inside me thought that she just might hear me.

Ruby. I kept on repeating and begging God to help me. The harder I begged, the drier my throat got and felt like razor blades was cutting me to the bone. I begged till it felt like my heart was gonna blow right out my chest. I begged till I got dizzy and it seemed like for sho' I was gonna throw up all over myself. By the time I was done pleading and begging God to help me, my head felt like somebody had split it open with an axe. I had to tell myself I didn't care and that it didn't matter and that I was gonna be all right. I pulled myself tighter and tried to tell myself I was gonna be all right.

CHAPTER FIVE

UNCLE SAM

THE SECOND DAY of my trip seemed like it might be a bit better. I'd cried myself out the night b'fore, and there was nothing left to do but wait and get to where I was going next. I say it was the second day 'cause I asked the driver, noticin' he wasn't the one I started with. I think he heard my thoughts, 'cause he answered the question I didn't even have a chance to ask: "I know what cha thinking. I got on last night while you was sleepin'." Staring at his face through the big mirror, I watched as his eyebrows danced 'cross his forehead when he talked. After a while I was sorry for speaking up. This man just kept right on talking like everybody wanted to hear how long he'd been driving and how he had earned the li'l gold greyhound dog pins he had pinned to his shirt collar—one for every year of service. He had five. I had no mind for knowing anything more 'bout him. The longer he talked, the more his voice sounded like a low hum, and in no time at all, I was back in one of my other places.

Sister was sittin' 'cross the yard with a charcoal drawing stick and a big white paper board in her hand. I knowed not to bother her when she went into one of her drawing spells, so I went on digging my deep holes in the dirt. I was hoping to break through to a hidden oil well, just like Jed Clampett had done. That way I could run off and live in Beverly Hills in a big ole castle—wherever Beverly Hills was.

Every now and again, I'd see Doretha look up and then back at her drawing paper. I couldn't for the life of me 'magine how she could be coloring anything while she was so busy looking to see what I was doing.

"Hey, girl, come over here!" Doretha had put the charcoal crayon down and cleared a place in the dirt, next to her, for me to sit in.

"Look. Who does that remind you of?"

"Lord have mercy, how'd you do that? How'd you learn to draw me?"

I watched as my sister lifted the big paper board up and tore the picture of me off.

"Here, you can have it. Now you can't ever say I've never gave you nothin'."

I took the picture of me and sat with it for a while. Doretha got up and left, but I stayed right where I was. I simply'd never seen anything like it. She had made my eyes, hair, and skin they real color. Even the dirt stains on my blue-and-white-striped seersucker dress was there. I wondered if I had special drawing powers inside me, just like my sister had, and one day they just might come out. I figured Doretha had to be the smartest person in the world other than my teachers. I folded my big picture up and buried it in the backyard for safekeeping—I marked my treasure with a God's eye that I'd made out of old thread and oak tree switches—that way nobody but me would know where it was hiding. Would I ever find it again?

We came to a stop with the bus driver's voice still ringing in my ears. I suppose listening to the driver must've dried my throat out, 'cause I sure was thirsty all of a sudden. Taking the li'l vanity case from under my feet, I laid it on my lap to steady it. I r'membered that I still had the soda water Big Mama had put in it. Big Mama. I turned to look at the empty seat next to me and had to tell myself that she was gone for real.

I went to open the soda water and seen that I didn't have a bottle-top opener. Of all the things that Big Mama had thought to put into this stupid case, Nilla Wafers and soda, I couldn't believe she forgot the most important. How could she be so dumb? I wanted to throw the bottle through the front window of the bus. But b'fore I got rid of it, I r'membered seeing my sister showing off and telling me how she had just learned to open a soda pop bottle with a quarter. I could do that! I reached into my sweater pocket and removed the quarter that I was to use in case of emergency. From where I stood, this was an emergency—if I died of thirst, I wasn't gonna use the quarter anyway! Holding the long skinny part of the soda-water bottle, I started prying the hell outta that cap. I was so busy taking the top off, I didn't realize how badly the bottle was being shaken up, and on the last tug, not only did the cap come flying off, but the red stuff had fizzled and spurted out all over my hands. Desperately trying to wet my starving tongue, I started sucking on that thing like a dill pickle with a peppermint stick in it. It almost tasted as good, and I got just 'nough to get my throat to swallow.

Looking down, my dress was not a pretty sight. I had red sticky stuff all over me, but for the first time, I didn't give a hoot. I wished that big ole red pinchy bugs would come and eat my dress off. And when they was done with that, they could eat my mouth and tongue. Maybe then, I wouldn't get into so much trouble.

We stopped for 'bout five minutes in a town called Knoxville, and a few folks got on. I took that time to go to the toilet to wash my hands. I didn't want the pinchy bugs to get my hands. Big Mama had said that one day my hands was gonna serve me good, specially if I scratched and dug in everybody's scalp like I did hers. When I got back from the washroom, I noticed a lady who'd sat down in the seat in front of mine. As grown folks say, she was light, bright, and damned near white. She wore an all-green outfit with a matching hat shaped like half a football, dented in in the middle. I couldn't help myself but to stare at her. She smiled at me, so I 'tempted to lift the left corner of my lip back at her. I didn't feel like being bothered. I took my seat, crossed my arms over my chest, and stared at the back of her head. I think she felt me looking at her, 'cause she turned round and started talkin' to me.

"How you doing, honey girl?" she asked me with a long smile.

"My name's not honey girl," I informed her. "Why you go and call me that anyway?" I studied her face while I waited for an answer. Her eyes pulled together with strain.

"Well, the way I sees it, your eyes and skin are the same honey color. So I called you 'honey girl.' I'm sorry if I upset you." The smile slowly came back to her face, showing off a set of perfect pearly whites. Folks told me I had beautiful teeth all my life, so I knew what to look for. "What's your real name, suga'?"

"Regina Louise." I answered with the names I liked best. I

'magined that by now everybody in south Austin, and maybe even further, knowed that my last name wasn't really mine. The story goes that my mama had borrowed it from my sister's daddy so that she wouldn't have to explain that she had been with two different men. But that only confused things, 'cause nobody seemed to know who Sister's daddy really was. Later folks come to find out that Ollison, the name she'd borrowed, didn't even belong to my sister's daddy. It really belonged to a boy she was dating at the time she got pregnant with Doretha. I'd overheard so much nonsense 'bout this daddy and that, I couldn't keep up with any of it. And if I couldn't keep track—and it was my own family—I felt sorry for anybody who had to try and figure it all out. So I figured Regina Louise was all anybody needed to know.

"My, oh my, those sure are the prettiest names I heard yet," the stranger told me.

Even though I had been warned not to talk to strangers, there was nobody to make me mind, so I did what I very well pleased. Plus, she was so nice and friendly, what could it hurt?

"What's your name?" I asked her.

"Oh, darlin', pardon my bad manners, my name is Private Virginia Reed."

"What's so private 'bout that?" I asked.

She let out a big ole laugh, and clapped her hand on her leg. "No, silly. My name is Virginia Reed, and I am a private in the marine corps."

"Oh, you like Gomer Pyle," I replied, happy to figure her out.

"Yeah, I guess you could say that." She was still grinning. "It's just that I don't have my own television show."

I felt betta' 'bout her already. She seemed real nice.

"Well now, baby, where's your people? Who you traveling with?"

Suddenly, what seemed real nice and friendly made me wanna kick her up and down the aisles of that stupid bus. I had no answers for her or worse, for me. I was all by myself! My mind told me not to let that nosey-ass Miss Virginia get in my business. She probably got lots of whoopin's for being so mouthy when she was little. I didn't wanna talk no more. But I knew I had to answer her.

"I ain't with nobody!" I told her as I looked straight into her eyes and lowered my voice. I was careful not to say it too loud. I didn't want anybody else to hear me.

I was trying to hold the water in my eyes. To keep it in that place where I have to count the beats b'tween every breath. Silently, I prayed that she wouldn't go on asking 'bout things that didn't concern her like all the grown-ups in my life. Miss Private Virginia must have somehow seen the prayer in my soul. I'm almost sure of it. She saw what I was hiding and musta decided not to make me speak 'bout it.

"Well, Regina Louise, you and me are gonna ride together, until whoever gets off first. And in the meantime, we's gonna have us a good time."

We rode in silence for a long while. I guess all that needed to be said had been spoke of. I stared out the window and watched as Mr. Moon only gave us a small piece of his face. It seemed as though he wasn't sure if he wanted to shine tonight. My stomach began rumblin', and it wanted something more than some nasty Nilla Wafers. I wouldn't eat another one if my life depended on it. Far as I was concerned, they was "devil's food" cookies, and I'd have nothing to do with 'em. Not only had they made me sick, but just thinking 'bout 'em made a churchgoing person want to turn on they own mama. Knowing there was nothing I could do 'bout my hunger, I turned and stared out the window again. When me and Big Mama went bus riding, I would sometimes count the streetlights from the time I got on till the time I got off. That's how I learned to know where my house was. My mind was too shaky to r'member the exact amount right then, but they was the most straight line of anything I had ever seen. It was too bad I hadn't thought to count from the time I left the house till now; maybe then I'd be able to find my way back if I wanted to.

Looking ahead, I could see that Miss Virginia had pushed her seat back and that her feet was stretched out in front of her. I'd wanted to do that b'fore; but Big Mama said that we might get on somebody's nerves, so she wouldn't let me. But without her here to see me I figured I'd do just like Miss Virginia. I pushed the button on the side of the chair arm and then used my body to move it backwards, and like Miss Virginia, I stretched my legs and closed my eyes. I could tell she was sleeping by the way her head slipped and slid from side to side. I decided to join her.

I woke up when we pulled into what looked like a rickety building posing as a bus depot. I watched as a few folks got off and headed inside the station. I seen this one woman walk smack into the arms of someone who was waiting on her. It might've been her sister or daughter. I wasn't for sure. The one who was doing the waiting came running out to greet the one who had gotten off the bus. Man was their arms open wide for one another. They seemed hungry for touching. I couldn't help but turn my head and wonder who would be waiting on me to come, wherever it was that I was going.

I turned to watching Miss Virginia, sleeping in her chair. Who was she going home to, and where was her home? Maybe she had children that also had to wear little green outfits with matching hats like she had on. Maybe she was goin' back to 'em after a long time of being gone. What made some folks keep they promises and others break 'em?

One person stood out for her habit of breakin' her promises, and that was Ruby. I took myself back to the last time I heard my mama on the phone swearing to Big Mama that she was on her way to come and get me and Sister. Nobody knowed it, but I was on the line listening. I thought of the times she'd call and say she was on her way and the ga-trillions of times she wasn't. Every doggone time she would make me a believer, though. Her voice rolled 'cross the Southern Bell line, sounding too much like rot-gut scotch and Pall Mall Reds. But that didn't bother me not one bit. I just had to give her a chance to do right every single time. After all, the Scriptures say to honor yo' mama and daddy, no matter what. I was all for "no matter what." I 'magined my mama's pretty mouth on the other end of the phone, promising Big Mama that she was round the corner; and to have us dressed so that she wouldn't have to turn off the engine of her new Riviera Cutlass Supreme—she got a new one each year, I heard. Like Snow White, I knew that my mama was gonna come and kiss me and wake me up from this horror dream.

My sister, on the other hand, she knowed betta' than to believe a word Ruby said, and she had no qualms in telling me.

"Gina, you're stupider than a hound dog. How come you

gonna go and believe somebody you barely even know, let alone see, over me your sister? Ruby ain't coming nowhere to get nobody!" I normally loved to hear Sister talk on things 'cause she was so smart, but on the subject of Ruby, she got more and more on my nerves, and I wasn't up for listening to her trash.

This one time, Ruby called and I answered the phone. "Hello, who's this?"

"Is that any way to answer a phone? This here is Ruby. Who the hell is *this?*"

All my insides gathered in the center of me, and I could barely keep still.

"When you coming for us?"

"Who's this, Regina? Girl, that's why I'm calling."

Ruby told me that a friend-girl of hers was gonna pick me and Sister up for the evening. That was all she had to say—I dropped the receiver and ran to find Sister. Me, being the biggest fool believer, *again,* convinced Doretha that "this time" we was leaving for real.

"Come on, Doretha, you gotta give her a chance. This time she gonna come—I could hear it in her voice. Plus she sending somebody else, which means it's gonna happen."

"She ain't coming! Gina, why do you keep this craziness up?"

"Just one mo' time pleeease! Just get dressed with me this one time." After what seemed like way too much pleading and promising of what I'd do for her if she agreed, and convincing Sister that Ruby wouldn't come for just one of us, she finally gave in. I started gettin' ready. I took to the rag and washed all the places that might hold odor. Starting with my feet, I scrubbed between my toes—just in case Ruby would want to buy me a pair of shoes. After paying a little extra attention to cover up the dirt rings around my ankles, I put on my folded-down white socks, reserved for special occasions, folding 'em up just enough to hide the dirt. I put on clean panties and my best outfit—a light blue dress with a rounded collar. Now the truth is, you could hardly catch me alive in a stupid dress, so for me to be going through all this rigamarole meant I was taking my-self real serious. I also threw on a pair of bottom-laced bloomers, just in case my panties wasn't as clean as they needed to be. They would also let me kick my heels up and sit with my legs open, and nobody'd say nothing.

Then, I brushed my teeth and gargled with my cinnamon rinse, and cupped my hands over my mouth and blew to be sure my breath wasn't stinky. Saving the best part for last, I started combing my hair. I loved doing hair. Making a zigzag part down the middle of my head, I put a plait on each side. Because my hair usually had so much grease in it from being pressed straight, it didn't wanna move. Since I wanted it to swing like the li'l white girls I seen, I put barrettes at the ends. Sometimes, if I really wanted a good swing, I'd use clothespins. But that was only when I was gonna hang round the house.

We sat in the small kitchen, staring out the window. Sister waited with me the first hour and asked me if I thought it was queer that Ruby's friend hadn't called yet. *Queer*, I thought to myself. I had no idea what that meant, or what she was going on 'bout. Ruby had told us to be dressed, and I had done my part. Now everything was in its place. I decided that since the best view of the street was from the kitchen window, we should take a seat there and wait. I saw lots of cars go by, but not any Rivieras. After a while I just started counting cars, and every time I got to a hundred, I gave myself a point, so that I could tell Ruby that's how many kisses she owed me for waitin'. My points was addin' up.

"You don't have to wait no more," I told Sister. I could tell Doretha was getting antsy and wanted to go.

"You will be waiting for the cows to come home before you ever see Ruby, stupid! And did you ever notice that we ain't never had any cows? Stupid jackass!" Doretha yelled, and pushed me as she left the room crying.

I still sat by that window. I kept on waitin'. After a while, my head would go bobbing back and forth. I would catch it each time, 'cause I didn't want to mess up my hair. I wanted to show Ruby how good I had combed it. I waited longer, watching as many cars as my eyes could catch, hoping one of 'em would pull into the carport. Every now and again, when I'd remember, I'd stand up and smooth the wrinkles from my dress. I sure didn't want Ruby to think I didn't try to look nice for her. The very next time I woke myself up Sister was sitting right next to me. This time, she was trying her damnedest to pick a fight with me. She was pinching me and acting crazy by saying stupid stuff. Like I was a dumber ass than she thought me to be, waiting on someone who had no mind to keep her word. As far as I was concerned, Sister was being jealous that I could wait longer than her. She just kept right on making fun. I liked her too much to hurt her, and I knew that if I really went off that I would prob'ly kill her; so I let her pick until she was tired. Just b'fore she ran out the room, she pulled one of my plaits, and the barrettes flew in all directions. I didn't care. I still waited.

When Big Mama stumbled over me the next morning, nobody said a word. She turned away from me, like she couldn't stand to look into my face. I simply got up and went to school like I had been planning on it all night.

The next stop we came to looked more like a real bus station. The driver said that everybody should get off and have dinner if we wanted, since this was a designated rest stop. Laying back in my seat, I played like I was asleep, even though I was sure 'nough hungry. I figured it wasn't nothing sleep couldn't cure. With my eyes only half opened, I watched Miss Virginia get up and straighten herself out. She was a real pretty woman with good hair that fell back in small pencil-size waves away from her face. After pulling through her hair with a wooden pick, she put on her hat and shoes, grabbed her purse, then turned towards me. I closed my eyes tightly, wishing she would go on without bugging me. Her hand gently touched my upper arm, the place right above my elbow.

"Hey, honey girl, you wanna go and get some food? I know you gotta be hungry." I played like she had just woke me up from a deep sleep. I stretched my back and legs out and yawned like an alley cat. "Yeah, I'm hungry," I answered. "But I ain't got no money." There, I had said it. Now there was nothing left to be 'shamed of.

"Come on with me then, and let's see what we can do," Miss Private Virginia Reed called to me as she turned to get off the bus. I got up and put my shoes on like I had all the right in the world to be going into a restaurant and ordering anything I wanted. I caught up to Miss Virginia as she stepped onto the ground. Somebody must have sprayed the road down where we stood, 'cause it was real wet, and I could see the steam coming up from the ground. I could tell we was still in the South by the way the air felt on my skin. It was still, thick, and sticky, just like home. Miss Virginia had made her way to the cafeteria that was next door to the place where the bus was being serviced. I turned and looked down and saw where Miss Virginia's footsteps had left wet prints on the concrete. Without a second thought, I placed my own feet in each of her steps and traveled my way to the restaurant door.

Once inside, I realized that I'd never eaten in such a place. Me and Big Mama had always brought our own food while travelin'. She would load us up with sardines, crackers, and li'l cans of Vienna sausages. On real special trips, ones that was longer than usual, we'd have Underwood deviled ham spread sandwiches. We had no reason to eat in fancy restaurants.

Miss Virginia had a tray with fried chicken, mashed potatoes, and gravy; she also had a Dad's root beer to finish it off. I got the same thing she did, except for the soda. I got a Orange Crush—my sister's favorite drink. I could feel myself starting to miss all my folks, but I knew I didn't have time to think 'bout 'em. Miss Virginia was at the cash register, and I slid up right behind her. She told me to get in front and show the man all I had. After ringing up all my goods the man told me that my total would be three dollars and ninety-five cents. I felt my face turn red-hot. I just knew he could see I had no money or peoples and that he wasn't gonna let Miss Virginia pay for me. I thought I was gonna go on myself.

"Here, ring them together," I heard her voice say from over my shoulder. As the man rang up our stuff together, Miss Virginia handed him three green cards that had words and numbers wrote all over 'em. After handing her the change, the man sucked his teeth as we went for a table.

"Hey, Miss Virginia." She looked up at me. "What was those things we paid for our food with?" I was desperate to know.

"Oh, those! They are what the military gives people who are

traveling so they can eat." She went on to say that's one of the many ways that "Uncle Sam" took care of the folks that worked for him. I didn't know who her uncle was, but all I can say is he sho' was nice to her, and I wished I had an uncle like that.

We sat in quiet and ate our chicken dinner. It was real good—but not as good as back home. After eating all I could, Miss Virginia took the rest of my food and hers and wrapped it in a napkin b'fore putting it in a bag. She told me to keep it for the next time I got hungry. Lord have mercy! How did she know to go and do that? Whoever was telling her what to do for me was sure doing a good job.

When our meal was done, we made our way back to our bus. I thanked Miss Virginia till I plumb ran outta words to say. She simply told me to thank her uncle and not to mention it again.

There was just some things in life that I just didn't have a notion for understandin'. What made this lady wanna help out a li'l girl that she didn't even know? Why come Private Reed wanted to buy me food and make sho' that I'd be all right? Or like how was rainbows really made? Did somebody in heaven have a overhead projector like the schoolteachers and shined it down whenever they wanted to make folks stop what they was doing, look up, and smile at God, as a way for us not to forget 'bout him? I tell you what makes sense to me: I believe that them same folks who was shining down them there rainbows took count of the times that Miss Virginia had looked up and smiled at God. And for that they smiled back on her, by giving her a uncle to watch out for her, and in return, she watched out for li'l girls like me. Maybe one day I could pass the favor along and do the same thing as Miss Virginia did for some other li'l girl.

The next day I lifted my head from sleep and searched the aisles for Private Reed. I didn't see her, and figured that she had gotten off during the night. I was sad that she left, but as I put my sweater on, I found a note stuck to my vanity case. That sho' was smart, 'cause my case doubles as a pillow and no one could take it without me feeling it move. I opened the envelope and read,

Dear honey girl,
I don't know where you're from or where you're going. But from the look of things, you sure need somebody to look after you. Now, I know that God has a plan for you, so I will pray that you find your way. Here is two dollars. Use it to get something to eat or drink.
Your Friend,
Pvt. Virginia Reed, USMC

I folded the note and put it back in the envelope, then placed it in my vanity case so that I wouldn't lose it. I looked out the window and smiled a thank-you into the air. I hoped that one day that smile might find her.

CHAPTER SIX

I'VE SEEN HER

WE PULLED INTO the Greyhound/Trailways bus station that was situated at the corner of Court and Chaney. I liked to watch for street signs, so I seen 'em right off. 'Cross the way from the station was somewhere called Sammy's Pool Room. I wondered how they got a pool in such a small place. I figured maybe it was one of them wading pools, for babies. Other than the "pool room" and the Southern Cleaners building, Jacksonville, North Carolina, looked like any other small town we had rode through. The only difference being, I had come to the end of my ride. Ever since we left Texas, I'd been keeping track, and as of this minute we had been driving for three days. I sat back quietly as the driver announced that we had reached the last stop. As he tilted the big mirror that let him look to the back of the bus, he caught my eyes and said, "This be yo' stop, young lady."

I watched as everybody else got up to take they bags from the overhead racks. It was then that I realized that I didn't have any other bags 'cept the vinyl case. It suddenly became clear to me that Big Mama was gonna be waiting on me to get back. Any person with common sense knew that nobody went traveling without clothes, unless they was just leaving for a short while. I wondered how long I was gonna be staying. I sat awhile, r'membering Big Mama's words, and wondered if I would have to use that quarter in case nobody came. I still had the two dollars Private Reed had gave me, so maybe if no one came, I could buy a ticket back home to Texas. I sat and waited and worked hard at not being scared. I pulled out my note and read it again as the folks fumbled with they bags and made they way off the bus. "I know that God has a plan for you." I reread them words a few more times, and finally, when the last person had left, I stood with my note and case in hand and made my way to the front of the greyhound-dog bus.

I moved slowly, wanting to give whoever was coming to get me all the time in the world to make up they mind to whether they still wanted to come. Finally, the driver stuck his big head in the door and asked me to come on. At the door, the large man offered his hand to me. I thought that mighty nice of him, considering I had only seen that done for Big Mama and I wasn't even close to half her age. I grabbed the hand and took each step with a smile.

I'd already heard the driver tell everyone to watch they step, so I took it upon myself to be mindful. Once on the platform, I felt like my body was moving in many different directions at one time. I was getting dizzy, so I walked to the nearest bench and took a seat. I looked round and saw no one, and my chest started swelling with air. I closed my teeth down hard and let my nose get wide as I let the air outta my chest. I felt the tears lining up, waiting to tell my tale.

"I cain't cry," I kept telling myself over and over. No matter what! I didn't want whoever was coming to think me a sissy if they was to find me here boohooing. I sat for a while longer gripping the paper note. After what seemed like forever, and all the others had left the station, I watched as a worker motioned a woman in my direction. With her hand, she swept the air as if something was in her way. The lady headed for me, talking loud and waving her hand.

"Well. Well. Well. Would you look a here! This gots to be my chile!" Then she busted out hootin' and hollerin' about how this was such a surprise. I laughed right along with her. Everything inside me lit up all at the same time. My heart, stomach, and even the spit in my mouth all seemed to want to get in on what was happening. Before me stood a redbone woman in a hairdo that was no smaller than a tiny mountain. Folks in the South called light-skinned women with good hair "redbone." I guess that meant they was different from being just plain black. I didn't see no difference, 'cept her hair was pulled back so tight her eyes was slanted up, making her look like the Chinese. I think she was wearing them fake eyelashes, the kind that Sister wore when she played dress-up, 'cause hers was mighty long, unnaturally so. The woman wore dungarees with silver dots running along the seams and a coat to match. Out of the corner of her mouth hung a white cigarette with no brown filter, like Daddy Lent's Tiparillos. As she talked, the cigarette moved right along with her.

"Come on over here, girl, and gimme some sugar," she yelled. B'fore I could move, her arms was round me and off again, just that fast. Stepping back, I let whatever wanted to slip out my mouth slip on out.

"Ruby, is that you?" My insides beat loudly, not knowing what else to say.

"Who the hell else you think it is? Girl, you talking stupid! Of course it's me! I am yo' mama, chile."

The tobacco stick must've been stuck in her lipstick 'cause even though her mouth opened, it didn't fall out. I kept right on staring, amazed that she could balance such a skinny stick on one lip without losing it. I could sense her voice change a bit after I asked her if she was who I thought she was. The minute I said it, I knew it was the wrong question to ask. Something in me became tight. I felt like I had been hit without being touched.

"Ruby!" I cried out again, tryin' to show her I was glad to see that it was her. I swung my arms round her neck and tried to kiss her on the mouth, like I'd seen Aint Bobbie do with her babies, but Ruby turned her cheek to me.

"Ooooh-wee, girl, we gotta get you to a store to buy a toothbrush, 'cause yo' breath sho' do stank." This time her voice was lighter, and she laughed. I laughed back, seeing that she felt better after saying that. Right then she seemed real happy to see me. As we turned to leave she asked me, "Where's yo' bags?" At the same time, she looked round the bench I had been sitting on.

"I didn't brang none."

Ruby rolled her eyes and took what was left of the tobacco stick outta her mouth and dropped it at her feet. Then, with the point of her shoe, she smashed the red-hot tip until all that was left was pieces of smoke and ashes.

"I cain't believe that the ole dog sent you clear 'cross the country without no goddamned clothes. What the fuck was she thinking?"

"I dunno," I answered, as I lifted my shoulders in wonder, not sure if she was asking me or just talking out loud. "Maybe she thought I was coming back soon and wouldn't need any," I offered, watching Ruby the whole time. I wanted to see what she was gonna do.

"Fuck that shit!" she yelled. "I know that damn Thornhill! She thinks she's slick. Johnnie Jean was gonna make sure you took nothing you didn't pay for. The way she sees it, your clothes can be used to cover somebody else's tail." I watched with my mouth hung open as Ruby went into a spin about Big Mama and her no-good ways. "She ain't shit!" Ruby's eyes grew dark and hard as she tried to light another tobacco stick. At first she tried striking the wooden matchstick on a piece of striker that she had to have torn off the original box. When that failed her, she cocked that cigarette between her lips and with the flick of her wrist, ignited that fire on the concrete floor beneath our very feet! Damn, I ain't ever seen somebody want something so bad. But the good thing 'bout it was, she stopped cussing Big Mama.

"Don't you ever let me catch you doing this! I don't ever wanna see you smoking, you hear me?" Ruby told me as she grabbed my arm and pulled me in the direction she wanted to go and didn't bother on waitin' for me to answer her back. "Come on, girl, let's get you a toothbrush." I followed behind Ruby as she made our way to a car that seemed to be waiting for us. A man was in the driver's seat, and from what I could see he was bumpin' his head and thumbs on the steering wheel to the beat of something, maybe music I couldn't quite hear for all the noise that was round us. As we got closer I could hear the last of, *Diamond in the back, sunroof top, diggin' the scene . . .*

"Get in the back," Ruby told me as she pulled her front seat forward and let me crawl into the backseat.

"Let's go to the Winn-Dixie so I can pick up some dinner and this child can get a toothbrush." The driver, a man blacker than the ace of spades, said not a word, but drove off like he was told. I guessed it was just like the grown folks said: Ruby sho' did have a way with folks.

I snuck a look at Ruby smoking up a storm in that front seat. I couldn't believe she was right there in front of me—I needed somebody to pinch my hind parts to remind me I wasn't dreaming no more. I was here with my mama. And she was real. I stared at her, takin' in as much of what she looked like as I could. A few times she caught me and told me I needed to cut the staring shit out. My heart would be a li'l bit hurt 'cause she cussed at me, but I figured she didn't know no betta' since she wasn't used to me yet. I'd give her some time.

Outta all the things I liked best 'bout her looks, her mouth was my favorite. It was wider than mine and looked softer too. Her hair was also better than mine. Hers curled in little *q*'s, soft and quiet-like, and laid at the side of her face. Mine was so tight it had a snap-back-fast way 'bout it. And when you pulled on it with a pick, it sounded like sparklers going off on the Fourth of July. But for all the soft prettiness my mama had, her tongue was fouler than a outhouse on its shittiest day. All my life I'd heard folks say some of the nastiest words that no child should have to hear, but my mama had to be the worst yet. I could see why come Lula Mae and them folks back home used cussing, on account I wasn't they real kin, and they didn't have to care 'bout me if they didn't wanna. But for Ruby to be saying the stuff she was saying round me took me by surprise. I figured that she'd wanna be nicer since she hadn't seen me in a while, but I didn't think she thought on it like that. In some way, I guess she was more like the folks back home than she wasn't, and I didn't mind as long as she didn't start putting me down and hittin' on me.

That first day, the man dropped us off at our house and left without a word to me and just a big kiss from Ruby. I looked round at the house where me, Ruby, and her two boys was gonna live. It was a street where all the houses looked mostly the same. Each house sat in the middle of a plot of grass. The back of the houses on our side of the road had a li'l creek crawling through it that was loaded with crawdaddies, bloodsuckers, and lots of other nasty stuff that I didn't concern myself with. The front yard had a porch that was attached to the house. And on the side of the house was a carport where Ruby parked her tan-colored Corvair. Sometimes a burgundy Eldorado with a beige roof was parked there too. Ruby told me it belonged to her man, Mr. Benny.

On both sides of our house we had neighbors. On the left side lived Nichelle Neil, her two sisters Carol and Deedee, and their odd brother little Ed—who I later found out was known for picking up cigarette butts and trying to smoke 'em. They had both a mother and a father, and a dog and a station wagon. I ain't never seen no black folks with dogs. The whole of they family was quiet and hardly ever talked, not unless you forced 'em, that is. After a while, and a lot of forcing, Nichelle came to be my friend. Directly to my right was Miss Ida Mason. Man, was she a big woman! She reminded me of a man. Miss Ida had a reputation for winding up a chicken by the neck until she heard it snap, then lettin' it go to run round the yard till it keeled over. I thought only mens did that. If it wasn't for the fact that she walked round half the day with hand-torn pieces of brown paper bags used for hair rollers like only women do, I wouldn't have knowned elsewise.

"Hey, Benny, you r'member Regina don't cha, my youngest girl?"

I had been with Ruby 'bout a week, and I hadn't seen Mr. Benny since he'd picked me up with Ruby from the bus station. Now he was here in our house, actin' like he lived with us or something. Why else would he be in my mama's house, touching our things like they belonged to him? He didn't seem to wanna move when Ruby first talked to him. He kept right on messing with the stereo and things. I wondered why Ruby was just now telling the man my name? I figured that was part of her own way of doing things.

Benny, the man Ruby was talking at, seemed like he had no mind to be bothered. After taking the stereo arm, and placing it halfway in the middle of a album, he finally looked up and nodded his head. "Hey now, how's it going? Ya settled in yet?" he asked as the speakers let go of one of my favorite songs.

I answered "Fine" to the first question and let the second one go on by. I wasn't real used to being round mens that wanted to talk to me and ask questions. I instead listened to "Sideshow" by Blue Magic rolling off the speakers.

Ruby moved past the man and went to her room, and I followed behind, going to mine. I could hear the Blue Magic singing from where I was. This was the first time in my life that I had my own room. I should've been happy, but I was scared 'cause my sister wasn't with me. From the time I could r'member my name, me and Sister had shared the same room, bed, and sometimes panties (the panty part only lasted till she got the bloods). My new room wasn't nothin' too fancy; it had a small bed, a nice window, and a real closet to put your stuff in. It was a nice place to "hang your head at the end of the day." That's what Daddy Lent used to say made somewhere home. I r'membered back on him more than you'd think. In b'tween the happiness to see my mama and still being buck-wild mad at Big Mama for leavin' me on that bus, I was still kinda missing south Austin and all of them. Out at Big Mama's the room Sister and me had to share was way smaller than my new one. There, we had a bed that had a ticking-striped mattress full of piss stains and springs that came out at night and bit you while you was sleepin'. There was also this big ole raggedy fan that was always stuck in the window—rain, sleet, or snow (one time it did snow). In the bottom of the fan is where we'd put a rat trap stuffed with gov'ment-issued cheese to catch the rats when they was tryin' to get in through the fan from the out of doors. Most times the smell of something dead would get us faster than we'd realize the trap got the rat. Other than the bed or the fan, there was also a ole wardrobe and a Chester bureau in our room. Sister told me that the Chester bureau is where they buried Chester, a neighbor, and the wardrobe was where his clothes was hid. I lost many nights' sleep worrying 'bout Chester coming back for his stuff. So I never went near his belongings for fear of what he might do to me.

Even though I was a li'l homesick for south Austin, my friend Theresa, and the way I could run free and wild, I knowed that I never wanted to live like them folks again. The way they sometimes treated folks out there was nothing short of being the devil's kin. And getting ready to meet Ruby's boys, I was reminded of how bad them folks could be to kids who didn't know betta' or have somebody to watch out for 'em. It happened years back when Ruby's two boys came to live with me and Sister out at Big Mama's.

If the truth was to be told, I was real doggone nervous when I set eyes on Ruby's two boys, 'cause it had been a long time since I was round boys who was s'posed to be related to me. The eldest, Dwayne Edward, was 'bout seven. His genius was discovered a few years back by a man while riding a Trailways bus 'cross the country. The story goes that Dwayne Edward started reading every billboard sign between Tallahassee and Beaumont. Nobody even knowed he could talk, let alone read. Seeing that Dwayne was only two or three or so, the man gave him the beginning of the Preamble of the Constitution to read, and Dwayne Edward looked at it one time and read the whole thing back to the stranger. Right then and there, Dwayne was offered a appearance on *The Ed Sullivan Show*, but had to turn it down on account he was still a baby. Then there was the younger boy, Dennis Roy, who was round five. Everybody figured his genius might be the fact that he was gonna be as huge as his daddy, Big Lawrence, and maybe he'd turn out to be a famous football player. But no one knew 'bout they genius parts when they came to stay at the Thornhills'.

Accordin' to Big Mama, our mama had got real sick down in Augusta, Georgia, and didn't know nobody down there. They was all livin' in a trailer park, and Ruby was unable to give the boys care. Big Mama got a call from Ruby and went down to Augusta and brung them boys on back with her. Even though their stay was real short, it was one I'll never forget.

One day that shit-disturber Donna Janine, who I already knowed to be a liar and a thief, concocted another one of her famous tales. This time it was about the boys. Now I knew right off the top that she was just green-eyed 'cause the boys got more notice than she did ('cause everyone thought it was cute how they stuck together like li'l marshmallow Easter bunnies still in the pack), and she wasn't gonna have it no way, no how! That night, while Dwayne, Dennis, and me was sleeping in our room, I heard somebody sneak in and fumble round a bit. I looked up and seen Donna Janine messing with Dwayne's pillow. Because he had a way of slamming his head against his pillow at night and knocking it clean off the bed, I thought she was being kind and putting it back under his head. It never dawned on me that the good-for-nothing conniving hussy was up to her usual tricks.

The next morning her "kindness" turned out to be nothing short of a mission from the devil hisself. Donna Janine had placed a butcher's knife underneath Dwayne's pillow. She had run and woke Big Mama up, swearing on the Bible all the way that Dwayne had put the knife under his pillow 'cause he wanted to kill his brother, Dennis, while he was sleeping. Now, I knew she was a lie, but them stupid-ass grown-ups, they swallowed every cotton-picking word Donna Janine said. When she was asked how she knew what his plans was, she said she'd overheard him talking to himself. The truth of the matter, if anybody really wanted to know, was that the boy could barely see his way out of a paper bag, even if you gave him directions! And all you had to do is see that he couldn't hold his own eyes steady, let alone a butcher knife!

Big Mama beat them poor kids bad. She threw Dennis in just in case whatever it was that possessed Dwayne Edward might've rubbed off on him, seeing how close they was. I don't r'member what happened after that, but I do know that the boys became my responsibility. Every day b'fore I went to school, they was to be put outside the house. Big Mama believed that there should be no demons in the house when no one was home. An old wrecked car sat in Big Mama's yard—her daughter Aint Bobbie had it towed there on a promise that she would have it fixed by her then-mechanic boyfriend. My duty was to get the boys to the car and get 'nough food to last 'em all day. Most of the time they was only wearing a pair of old dirty drawers and a T-shirt. I wasn't let to give 'em clothes in case they would try and hide something on they bodies. Big Mama said that if you gave the devil an inch he would take a mile, so it was best not to tempt him.

Once they was in the car, I'd have to bring 'em their food. I'd mix powdered eggs with water and stir in some potted meat. Most times the meat would be so hard that the spoon I used would bend till it took on the shape of a question mark. If there was bread, I would get 'em some to soak up that nasty mixture and help push the stuff down they throats. And the eggs I had to serve them babies was cold, watery, government-issued eggs. I knew what they was 'cause I'm the one who stood in line to get the free vouchers. Big Mama said that I was good with people, so I'd be the best one to ask for the free coupons. She also believed that free food was God's way of helping her out, and since she was doing some of his work it was the least he could do. By the time Ruby did come and get them boys, they stomachs was poking out in front of 'em real big-like, and they tongues had what looked like white ringworms all over 'em. I had prayed for God to send our mama for them kids, even if it was to mean that I couldn't go wit' her. I was glad when she came.

*　　*　　*

I'd been scared to see them boys now, in case they r'membered me to blame for they bad treatment. I recognized them right off as they came tearing through Ruby's living room the day I got there.

Each of 'em looked at me and kind of smiled.

"Is you our sister?" The older one talked for the both of 'em.

"Yeah, I guess so," I answered, not certain if I even had a right to be part of what they already had, not to mention that I was being unloyal to my sister for claiming them, since I knowed how she felt 'bout Ruby not choosing us. Laughing like baby hyenas, they kept right on moving back to where they had come from, outside in the backyard. I just stood and watched, r'membering those bad times.

"Why don't you go on out and play with the boys?" a voice asked me. It belonged to Benny, who was standing at the door eyeballin' me.

"That's all right," I told him back. I didn't wanna look at the boys just yet in case they could tell what I had been thinking 'bout, even though something inside me told me that if they hadn't r'membered by now, they prob'ly never would. "I'll go in a li'l while."

"Suit yourself," he said as he moved away from my door.

I looked round in my mind to try and find somebody as black as Benny. Big Lawrence came close, but Benny took the cake. His skin was as smooth and dark as midnight. He had a nose shaped like it had been pinched in a clothespin, and his eyes was dark. His lips, which he referred to as "soup coolers," was brown on the outside, like he'd used one of Ruby's Maybelline eye-pencils round 'em, and a lighter shade of red on the inside.

And he had a tongue that was pink, like he'd licked raspberry Kool-Aid straight from the package. And as dark as he was, he sure did have good hair. It was jet black and real shiny. His waves was wide and soft, making his hair lay flat up against his head all along the sides and back, but longer on top. He was wearing a green outfit with black and brown spots smudged all through it, with a matching hat. His pants was tucked into his boots, making him look like a pirate. Round his waist was a belt, holdin' a gun and a police stick. I think I even seen some handcuffs. I wanted to ask him what all that mess was, but something told me not to be too nice to Mr. Benny.

After he left my doorway, I went and brushed my teeth, then was off to find Ruby, knowing she liked it when my breath smelled nice and sweet. Her room was kitty-cornered from mine. Walking over to her door, I stood and waited for her to notice me. She was puffing on a cigarette and talking on the phone. I was happy she was by herself. While I stood by and lis-tened to Ruby talk, I watched her feet. I loved feet and was plumb stumped at how something so long and narrow could hold up a big person all on they own. It was a true mystery to me. Ruby was wearing the flip-flop house shoes that she seemed to love. I liked when she wore 'em 'cause I got to see her toes, and they sho' was pretty the way they was painted red and filed to be perfect—they looked just like mine 'cepting for the filed-down, painted-red part. I was happy to see that Ruby and me had the same feet. It made me think that maybe mine would be able to wear beautiful shoes like the ones that Ruby wore to parties. And maybe one day, my feet would take me to all the fancy traveling places Ruby'd already been.

"Come on in, Miss Lady," Ruby called to me as she hung up the phone. I loved it when she called me Miss Lady. I felt like it took a li'l extra to call me that than just plain ole Regina. I made myself believe that I was becoming special to Ruby. "And take that hot-ass sweater off; you making me boil just looking at ya." I did 'xactly like I was told. I took the sweater off and had a seat at the foot of Ruby's bed. I couldn't bear to sit too close to her. As it was, I felt like I was only dreaming.

"What's that on ya' arms there?" Ruby asked, balancing that cigarette b'tween her lips. I looked down at my arms. I r'membered how I had held 'em up in front of me, trying to keep from being hit in the face. I studied Ruby's face for a minute. Even though she was twenty-nine, which I figured out for myself since I knowed she had Sister when she was thirteen and a half and me when she was eighteen, I could tell that she had seen and heard too much hard stuff in her life. Her eyes was sad by the way they hung at the corners. I sho' didn't wanna bring no bad news. So I let all the stuff I'd saved up in my heart and mind melt like icicles in the sun.

"Oh, these old things," I said as I picked the last of a old scab off my arm. "I fell in some bushes after tripping over a tree root." It felt real nice to be able to say whatever I wanted to, whether it was real or not, just to see what would happen, just to see how it could change the way something turned out.

"Oh, girl, you still a tomboy, I see. And I betcha that didn't stop you either, did it? I bet you just got up and kept right on moving, huh?"

Nodding my head and laughing right along with her, I watched them eyes of hers lift from they lazy corners and grin at me. I liked it when she was happy. And it seemed like she found some things in me that made her that way. Whether it was my breath or my wild ways, I wanted to be the one who could help lift all the corners of her face into a smile—eyes, lips, mouth, ears, and all. Ruby took a minute and thought 'bout what she was fixin' to say.

"Guess who's coming to live with us in a little while?" I had no idea what Ruby was talking 'bout.

"I don't know." I couldn't 'magine who.

"Your long-lost sister, Doretha," Ruby said with a lack of care as she sucked the smoke back in her mouth and let it blow out her nose.

"When she coming?" I wanted to know right then and there! Not seeing my sister for what seemed like forever, even though it'd been a coupla weeks, was a li'l hard for me. Although we wasn't that close, when I didn't see her, seemed like my heart wanted to play tricks on me and make me miss her.

"Oh, hell, I don't know. I ain't gonna say. I don't want you holdin' me to nothing in case it don't come out right." Since Sister was coming to live with Ruby and us, I thought it'd be a good chance to ask her something that I'd been holding on to for a while.

"Ruby."

"Um—uh!" From the way she answered me, I could sense that she might've been tired of talking to me. I could just feel it.

"Can I ask you a question?"

"Not if you gonna keep asking 'em."

"Will you get mad at me if I ask?"

"Hurry the hell up and say the damn question, Regina, 'fore I change my mind!"

"Are you Doretha Ann's real mama?" There, I'd asked the question that'd sat in my belly for a long time. Now it was up to Ruby to set the record straight.

"Looka here, li'l girl, I'm a grown woman, and I ain't up on lettin' some child of mine go round asking me dumb questions. Ain't nobody but Johnnie Jean done started that shit 'bout me not being Doretha's mama. I'm a tell you one time and one time only, I'm the girl's mama—period. You prob'ly already know too damned much 'bout me being thirteen when ya' sister was born. And that's none of nobody's fuckin' business, you hear? If ya' gonna tell the story, tell it right! That old witch Thornhill made me leave Doretha when she was a baby. Every time I tried to get her, she threatened to call the police on me and say that I was a minor and a unfit mother. I hope I set the record straight and you ain't got no more childish questions 'bout who's who to what. Now go on outside and try and be a child."

"All right," I replied, and left it alone as I swallowed hard to make sure I could still breathe. I didn't feel so right pushing her for more, and she wasn't gonna have it any ole way. Plus, the way I seen it was, if she wanted to talk more 'bout Doretha or any of us, she could in her own good time. Just from sitting and listening, I knowed I could never tell Ruby 'bout what happened out in south Austin or ask her why she left me there. I knowed it was too much for her ears to hold. Her eyes had seen too much already.

"And r'member this, Regina, I'm the one that gets the last word."

My days was filled with getting to know my new home and the folks round it. Since it was so close to summertime when I came to Ruby, she didn't even bother putting me in school for the last coupla weeks. She said it would be a waste of time, so she gave me a extra early vacation. That was fine by me. I got that much longer to play on my own, and I got to read new books that Ruby bought me by Laura Ingalls Wilder and Louisa May Alcott whenever I wanted—Ruby brought the books for me from a li'l white girl's family she worked for, and I sho' was happy for it.

I learned most of my neighborhood information out from my next-door neighbor Nichelle and her daddy, Kenny. Nichelle told me, "Now you can go on and say hi to whoever you want to, but leave that Miss Ida 'lone. 'Cause she don't care much for folks meddling in her business, specially kids." I not only heard that Miss Ida could kill off a chicken, but that she was the meanest lady on the block. I wasn't worried 'bout nobody being mean after knowing Lula Mae. Plus I'd learned in Sunday school class that all of us had a piece of nice in us somewhere, so I was to look for it, no matter what.

I got my chance to meet the old crotchety neighbor Miss Ida first hand while I was picking pecans off her tree branches that hung over the fence which divided our yards. Since I didn't want to dig round in that sorry li'l creek for tadpoles, I thought I could gather and bag pecans and sell 'em, figurin' I'd make some extra money to buy the sweets that I so loved to eat.

"Hey now, what you thinkin' 'bout there? Those is mine, and I don't remember saying you could have some for yourself."

Man, did she look like Wilt "the Stilt" Chamberlain. I wondered if she played basketball too. 'Cause from the looks of her she could've been a whole team by herself. "Are you a basketball player?" I asked her.

"What kind of nonsense is you talkin'? Have you ever seen a woman as old as me play basketball before?"

I hadn't really thought 'bout how old she was.

"I know what you're doin'. Yeah. You trying to fake me out,

so that I cain't see that you stealing my nuts. I'm on to ya all right. And as far as picking goes, if you wanta pick so you can make some change, you ought to join me and the others on the weekends, and go on down to Masie's blueberry farm. There you can do all the picking you want and get paid for it. And furthermore, you can call me Miss Ida. Everybody does, and it specially don't sound right for kids to be calling grown peoples by they first name." Miss Ida seemed to growl when she talked. Like the words had to fight each other to get out her mouth. I didn't mind that. Even though she came off like a real tough one, I could take whatever she had to dish out, mainly 'cause she wasn't calling me names or making me feel bad 'bout myself. She said what needed to be said and still was wanting to be my friend.

"Well, since you already at it, why don't ya go on and pick yourself a few more bags this time—just next time ask me first. You ain't from round here, is ya? Where'bouts ya from? I can tell from ya' accent you from up Narth, ain't ya?"

"Nah, I'm from Texas." Seemed like she was barely gonna let me get a word of my own in.

"Who's you kin to in that there house?"

"The lady Ruby's my mama."

"Uh-huh. She been living here a long while. How come I haven't seen you before?"

"I don't know." I pulled my shoulders up towards my ears and let 'em fall back in place as I answered Miss Ida.

"Here ya go; this is a double pecan and might just bring you twice the price." Miss Ida handed me a nut that looked like it was a Siamese twin. I put it in my bag and said, "Thank you, Miss Ida."

That was the beginning of our getting to know each other.

Most folks thought that Miss Ida paid way too much mind to other people's business. She knowed everything 'bout everybody. Nothing could cross her way without her knowing. But all that was just fine by me.

When summer finally did come, and the boys was home with me, I had to find ways to keep us all busy. Even though the boys had lived in Jacksonville for a long while, they wasn't let to run the streets like me, and didn't know 'bout the goings-on in the neighborhood. After I'd been there awhile I'd take 'em with me to Masie's blueberry patch, and we learned to pick as many as four dollars' worth of blueberries in one day. Since the boys was pretty good when they went, I would give 'em a li'l something to keep 'em happy. They was really too small to be standing in the hot sun, so I let 'em run round the bushes in a attempt to cool themselves off after we'd get the baskets started. If they was good and didn't cut up a ruckus too much, I'd give 'em a portion of what was made. That way everybody got what they wanted: money to shop at the candy store. If we wasn't out picking berries and spending our earnings on candy, we would hang out with the other neighborhood kids and run up and down the streets pretending we was all track-and-field stars.

I couldn't believe it, but it took three times straight for me to beat everybody in the neighborhood running. It didn't take long for word to get round that there was a new girl about who could "smoke you in yo' tracks." Seeming like every time I turned round somebody was knocking at our door and I was being put up to trying to outrun the fastest they had. It was all going good until Phyllis came along. Man, she had to be the prettiest dark girl I'd ever seen. She didn't look like the black folks I was used to setting eyes on, with her long wavy braids that flapped behind her as she left you in the dust. Her plaits was so long, they made me wanna climb right up one of 'em and just take a seat on her shoulders while she ran.

Anyway, Phyllis and me had to race each other. I can still hear li'l Ed's voice screamin', "Runners on yo' mark!" Here, me and Phyllis bent down on one knee while the other was stretched out behind us. And we leant forward on our fingertips. "Get set!" We lifted our behinds in the air and leaned a li'l more forward. *"Go!"* We was off! I'd learned to never look behind myself when runnin' 'cause it would only slow me down. But with Phyllis, I didn't have to worry 'bout that 'cause she was the one doing all the looking back. By the time she busted through the string that Ruby's two boys was holdin' on each side of the street, I was barely halfway behind her. And nobody was holding no string for me by the time I did cross the pretend finish line. For weeks I had to listen to, "Ooh, you got whooped by Phyllis." And Phyllis this and Phyllis that—it took a long time to live that one down, but it was okay, 'cause nobody could beat her; and I was just the latest fool that proved it! Plus I got to hang out with her sometimes, but not for too long 'cause she was way older than me and didn't want li'l folks taggin' round her too much. But every now and again she would come over to our side of the street, and we would do relays and other kinda runnin' games.

When I wasn't hanging with Nichelle, and li'l Ed, or any of the other kids in the neighborhood, or listening to Miss Ida tell me more than any child needed to know 'bout lost womens and the ill-willed mens they kept, I was up in Ruby's face. That is, when I could catch up with her in b'tween her two jobs and parties. Not only did Ruby work for the Springfield Hospital doing her LVN duties in the intensive-care department from eleven to seven, but she also worked in private home care where she'd go to a ole white man's house and clean his bedpans and wipe his dirty ass. Ruby complained that the ole man was a sorry case for the way his grown kids would let the shit cake up on his back till Ruby came and scraped it off with a rubber spatula. Ruby said that she didn't understand why whites like to have other folks come and take care of they own. In this case, though, she s'posed it was 'cause the old man's kids could stand him 'bout as much as they could the smell of his shit. Ruby would just go on and say how she 'magined she'd be no betta' off than the white man for the way she'd treated us. "I know y'all are gonna just let me rot in my own piss when I get old. I can just see it now. But I guess I couldn't blame y'all for how you'd treat me since I ain't never been that good a mother to you."

I just listened to her. There'd be no way that I could change her mind to think different, so I'd let her go on and on, which she usually did while pouring herself just one more drink to keep her fire burning. But secretly I promised myself to never let shit get caked on Ruby's back, no matter what.

When Ruby wasn't b'tween them jobs, I'd spend my time watching and helping her get ready for some function. It didn't matter what was going on in town—Ruby seemed to be able to find herself caught right up in it. And if nothin' was happening round town Ruby was either going out to the base with her friend-girls or inviting folks over to our carport for a cookout. Now the barbecue part wasn't so bad, it's just that it usually meant that there would also be card games of spades and gin rummy, too much scotch and Annie Green Springs wine, and fights 'bout who messed with whose man. Me and Nichelle and li'l Ed would hang out with the grown folks as long as we could.

But it wasn't no time a'tall till the cuss words started flying through the air along with fists, food, tables, and finally even the threat of guns. No doubt, Ruby was always in the middle of the mess. From where I stood I could see why Ruby had a hard time keeping her word to folks like me and Sister. And I'm for certain she really didn't mean no harm. It's just that my mama said too many things to too many people when she was liquored up, and by the next day, she wouldn't r'member a word she'd said and expected life to just go on like she the one in charge of making it all happen.

There was this one time when Ruby accused her best friend-girl Lola of wanting to do the nasty with Mr. Benny. I overheard the whole story and thought it was real stupid. Now the woman Lola had been round our house on several occasions, and each time Ruby was certain something was going on, 'cause she was picking fights with everybody in the house; but she never said a word to Mr. Benny. That is until she got full as a tick real quick-like on that scotch.

"Hey, Gina, go call Lola and tell her to come on over, I wanta talk to her."

I didn't bother to ask Ruby why; I just called. "Hi, Lola? Ruby needs you to come right on over." I hung the phone up and stood where I was, staring at Ruby as she drank a li'l bit more.

"Why don't cha go on outside and play with the boys?"

"Cain't I stay here with you?"

"Nah now, go on out from under me, shit. Don't start gettin' on my nerves."

Seemed to me like I was already on her nerves. I felt myself getting hot in my throat, 'cause I didn't wanna show her that what she said hurt my feelin's, and I didn't wanna get her going;

so I left well enough alone—specially since I knowed she was drinkin'. I was also starting to see that Ruby wasn't a'tall what I'd hoped for her to be: a nice woman who wanted to dote all over me since she ain't seen me most of my life. But I don't think Ruby cared that she hadn't seen me. I don't think it'd even crossed her mind. As a matter of fact, I didn't talk with or to my mama that often. Seemed to me that Ruby was betta' if you just did stuff for her, then hurried up and got on outta her face. As long as she was getting somethin' from you things was fine, but if I wanted to "sit up under her" as she put it, that wasn't all right. So when she did tell me to go and do something, I did it without asking too many questions, even though she hurt my feelings a lot. I went outside like I'd been told to do.

I found the boys sitting out back near the creek with play fishing poles. They looked like they was aiming to catch whatever came they way. I sat down next to 'em and picked rocks out the grass and tossed 'em in the water. When the boys yelled at me and said I was scaring the fish away, I told 'em that the fish would think the rocks was food and come to see if there was more. They believed me. I didn't bother to tell 'em that there was nothing close to being a fish in that silly creek.

After hearing what I thought to be gunshots, I ran in the house to see what in heaven's name was going on up in there. What I thought was shots turned out to be folding chairs flying through the air and landing on walls and floors or whatever they was aiming at.

"Get yo' nappy-headed ass out my house now! You loose-lipped hussy!" I heard Ruby throwing stuff and cussing Lola like nobody's business. But the difference was Lola wasn't just standing there like some of the other folks I seen Ruby take on, no siree; Lola was throwing stuff and cussing right back! I couldn't believe it. I'd figured ever'body was too scared of Ruby, like I was, to stand up to her—I might've been right 'bout ever'body, 'cept for Lola. That wasn't all. I seen pink rollers flying past my face with the hair still hooked on to 'em as Lola and Ruby was beating the daylights outta each other over some jet-black man who wasn't even round to see it to believe it.

I didn't wanna get into Ruby's mess, so I waited back outside with the boys till they was done beating one another. There was a time when this kinda stuff would make me wanna hide and not come out. But by now, I was so used to it, I just waited round to see who came out looking the worst; then I'd know who won. Most usually it was Ruby who came out looking un-scratched—that is unless she'd had way too much liquor, in which case she could look more whooped than not. And more than likely it would only take a day or two for Ruby and her friends to get back on speaking terms. They would act like nothing ever happened—black eyes, bald spots, and all. Deep down inside of me, I wondered if my mama'd ever wanna fight somebody like that just to keep me.

I went from picking blueberries in the heat of summer with Miss Ida to picking wigs in the quiet of Ruby's bedroom, in a walk-in closet that she had turned into her li'l beauty parlor. In-side the parlor was what she called a vanity. It was a dresser you could sit at, and there was a mirror connected to the desk part. It sho' was the prettiest thang I'd seen yet. I told myself that one day I was gonna have a parlor for beauty too. On the desk was white foam, shaped into doll heads, that had necks that was stands to help 'em from toppling over when the wigs was on 'em. There was also a glass tray that held a lot of good-smelling stuff. Ruby called it perfume. And said that maybe one day I could get a job and buy some nice things for her. I couldn't wait for the day that I could do something nice like that for my mama. I loved the way she said "perfume." She made it sound like it smelled, sweet and soft. Her favorite ones was Charlie, White Shoulders, and Chanel No. 9. I liked the White Shoulders, 'cause that's what she wore the most. That other stuff gave me a headache whenever I got a whiff of it.

Outta all the things I did in Jacksonville, spendin' time with Ruby was the best. I'd waited a long time to see her. As a matter of fact, it seemed like I'd waited the whole of my life to be with her day and night and not worry on if she was gonna come or not. Now I was here with her, and I was gonna do all I could to make it easy for her, so she could see that I was no trouble a'tall. Before I got to help Ruby for real with her wigs, I'd stand outta the way and just watch her go to work on combing out, setting, and styling 'em. She had what was called falls; they hung from a ponytail that was attached to the top of her head by a snap-shut button sewed to each side of the hair. She reminded me of them dolls where you push the button on her stomach while pulling on her ponytail and watched it grow. Ruby also had a bouffant made outta pin-curl–shaped pieces stacked on top a one another. That's the one she wore to pick me up in that looked like a small mountain. At first, she wouldn't let me help her with the wigs. Instead I was in charge of keeping her supplied with her necessaries, as she called 'em.

"Here, child," she would say after handing me one of her cigarettes, "go to the stove and light this for your mama."

I loved it when she asked me that way.

"And try hard this time not to explode the end, like you did the last one!"

It was true. I was guilty of making the end of the tobacco stick look like a firecracker had gone off in it. I couldn't figure out why for the life of me. I had done exactly how Ruby had told me. I let the stove coil heat up to red-hot. Then I took the tip of the cigarette and rolled it on the fire till it caught. Once I seen there was smoke coming out the end, I'd run and give it to her. Secretly, I blew on the cigarette myself just the way I'd seen Ruby do. I figured that's what made it look so bad. I was always careful not to let her see any wet lip prints—that would give me away. So I rolled my lips back inside my mouth and used the exposed part of my skin to blow with. I loved it if I had to go back and light it a second time; that way I had a chance to put my lips where my mama's had been. Right where her mouth had left a wet spot. I would place my lips right on it and play like it was a kiss meant just for me. I also loved when she left a small bit of her slobber near the hole of her Coke can. I would take it up in my hands and sip the bit she had left, wantin' to have a piece of her with me at all times. That way no matter what, I knowed she could never leave me again.

Sometimes when Ruby wasn't combing her own hair she'd hard-press mine for me. Just like Big Mama'd do, she'd have me wash my hair, then pull through the knots and plait it into small sections all over my head—that way it'd be easier to pull through later. After my hair air-dried half the day, Ruby would take the comb with the teeth that got hot, and work them naps right on out my head. When Big Mama used ta do my hair, she was all gentle-like, and let me sit between her legs on pillows while she plaited. Now Ruby, on the other hand, she wasn't for all that sitting-b'tween-the-legs stuff. No siree. Ruby liked it when I sat on her bed as she stood over me, pullin' my nappy hair to its freedom. I figured she stood 'cause it was easier for her to get to her cigarettes and drinks. Plus, she prob'ly didn't want them ashes getting in my hair, with me sittin' 'tween her legs. She was kinda rough, but she was still with me, so that was okay.

When I wasn't exploding Ruby's cigarettes or fetchin' her fresh ice-cold bottles of Coca-Cola, I'd sit huddled close by, watching her go to town on whatever it was she'd be doing. Sometimes Ruby was putting on them fake eyelashes, using a stick pin to spread the glue on. All I could do was watch. I was scared to touch the lashes, 'cause I thought they was peeled right offa dead people's eyes.

At other times she'd be applying Lee Press-on Nails, the ones that was already colored to match her outfit and already-polished toes. And since I never did get the cigarette thing right, I wasn't let to touch 'em anymore, so Ruby moved me over to combing out wigs. I liked this best, 'cause I could take my time and didn't have to leave the room that often. That way I got to be with my mama longer. From time to time my mind would wander off and fall on stuff that Big Mama and them had said 'bout Ruby, and I'd look to try and figure out all their dislikes for her, but I just couldn't see what they saw. Sometimes though, I picked up what the grown folks called a li'l temper problem. It came out specially when stuff didn't go just the way she saw fit. But all in all, my mama was fine by me. If I secretly had anything bad to say, it would be that Ruby seen no wrong when it came to men; or her boys either, for that matter. And I learned that no matter what, don't ever try and tell her anything 'bout her mens. The fight b'tween her and Lola shoulda gave me the good sense to know betta', but it didn't. I thought that was just the way Ruby was with her friends—I knowed for certain she'd never go flat-out ape shit all over her child. How wrong I was. I found out the hard way.

CHAPTER SEVEN

MR. BENNY

MR. BENNY TOLD RUBY that he didn't wanna live on base any-more, and asked if he could come and stay with us till my sister moved in. There was no way this side of hell I wanted that man to come and stay with us. For all the time I'd waited, I barely got to see Ruby as it was, and with him laying round, I knowed I was gonna see her even less. At first Ruby seemed dead-set against it. She hemmed and hawed 'bout the house not being big 'nough for all of us, and the fact that she had girls runnin' round the place and how it would look having a man she wasn't married to living with her. But that didn't last too long, 'cause that ole sly dog Mr. Benny convinced her that his living there would help everybody out, specially her, since she had more bills now that I had arrived. And he made sure that Ruby saw that there'd be only more mouths to feed with Doretha's com-ing. By the time he was through reminding her of what trouble we was gonna be to her, Ruby had reached under the sink and pulled out her bottle. Out the corner of my eye, I watched him come up behind Ruby while she was pouring the drink and wrap his arms round her waist. Then he'd bite her on the ear and tease her and tell her how much he thought of her and how lonely he was being on that base. He even went as far as promising to help with "the kids," telling her how he thought we was left by ourselves too much.

"I don't know, Benny," Ruby told him. "They seem to be doing just fine. Anyway, when I'm not here they're sleeping, and by the time I get home they all run off to play."

"Come on now, girl. These kids need a li'l daddyin'. They need somebody here to protect them."

I didn't know nothing 'bout no daddy, and sho' wasn't gonna be calling Mr. Benny something I couldn't even let crawl out the back of my throat for my own daddy. I called my own mama by her first name, so if he was countin' on me calling him daddy—that was outta the question!

Within a week, Mr. Benny had moved himself right into our house. One green army bag after the next came piling up in our living room. And whatever stuff he couldn't fit into Ruby's closet, he put in with the boys. Seemed like he didn't care what or where he moved into as long as he was in. At first, he was on his best behavior. He helped us keep the house clean and made sure we had food to eat. He even helped me learn a new favorite food: Tony's pepperoni pizza topped with black pepper and Tabasco sauce, cooked to a crisp. And when Ruby went and bought me the canopy bed I had begged her for, he promised to help put it together and paint it white for me, with frosted gold rings wrappin' themselves round the poles. I'd always wanted a white bed, but we had to order the natural version since it was more affordable. We left that bed in the carport too long, and a mongrel dog came and chewed off one of the knobs that was to keep the canopy from falling off the poles. Mr. Benny knew how to fix that too. We all worked good together for 'bout a month or so—that was, right up to the time my sister came.

We picked Doretha up from the same bus depot I had arrived at. When she arrived, I ran up and put my arms round her. I had never done that before. I wasn't so used to touching folks like that, but it was the first time she and I was away from each another that I could recall. Her and Ruby, well, they sort of grabbed each other's shoulders and leaned forward, creating something that looked like the roof of a house. The whole time we was all standing there in that station, looking awkward and stiff, Doretha never took her eyes off me. Seemed like she was more concerned with seeing me than she was to see Ruby. I could tell she was playacting, 'cause as long as I'd lived she ain't never been that sweet on me.

"Hey there, Gina girl, how're you doing?" she asked as she pretended to punch me in my arm. She said hi to the boys by waving her hand from the middle of her waist, makin' it look like she didn't wanna be bothered. I wondered if she r'membered 'em like I did. I knowed that sometimes when bad things happen to me, my mind will tell me it ain't so. That it ain't as bad as it seems. That way, I can keep on hoping that what is bad really ain't true. It's like my mind would play tricks on me, letting me get on with my business. I hoped that was true for the boys and Doretha.

When we all finished sayin' our hellos, there we all was, all together. Just like my next-door neighbor, Nichelle, and her family. It would've been just right except for Benny being there. I wanted to know how long us being together was gonna last. I knowed one thing for sho', the thing that made us different from Nichelle and her folks was that all Ruby's kids except her boys had different daddies. It was clear to all that could see that Mr. Benny was no one's daddy, 'cause he didn't look a thing like nary a one of us. He had two daughters of his own, but they didn't live with us. Anyway, I 'magined him not being any kin to Doretha was gonna be a problem. I r'membered from Big Lawrence how Doretha could act—if the man don't like her, she wasn't gonna play to like him either. My sister was almost seventeen and had lived most her life with Big Mama, the only mama she had ever knowed, so I figured that she was gonna have a hard time with Ruby, specially since she didn't even be-lieve that Ruby was her real mama. And the only daddy she had was Daddy Lent. From where she stood, they was all that mat-tered, even if they wasn't "real kin." Deep down I could feel a storm a-brewing.

When we lived out at south Austin, nobody really bothered Doretha like they did me. She was always the one that was smart and never made no trouble for no one. If the grown folks asked her to do somethin', she'd do it with no back talk, so that way everybody'd think she was "a real nice girl"—unlike me who was too boy-ster-ous—whatever that meant. Not even Lula Mae messed with Sister too much that I could see. There was only once that I can recall Lula and Sister getting into it. I believe it had to do with Sister starting somethin' called a pe-riod. I was outside stirring up mud pies in a ole black kettle that sat b'tween two oak trees in our backyard, and I heard 'em start.

"What's that smell? Who forgot to take the garbage that had them fish guts in it, outside?" I could hear Lula's big mouth all the way outside. I didn't hear nobody answer, so I tried to keep on with what I was doing. I didn't like emptying no garbage cans on account that I hated looking at them maggots that crawled round the bottoms of the cans. And I knowed that Lula Mae was gonna start getting me involved if she learned that I was listenin'—so I ignored her.

"How come every time I pass your room, Doretha Ann, I smell somethin' dead?" Then I heard two people going back and forward 'bout who should be able to tell who what to do. I started hummin' to drown them out.

"You have gots to be the nastiest thang I ever seen in my life!" was the next thing I heard. Then Big Mama, Sister, and Lula Mae was all in a tizzy. Sister was cryin' and yellin' 'bout how she didn't know, and Lula was telling her how a girl on her period should know better than to hide 'em under the mattress for months. I didn't know what they was going on 'bout, and I didn't wanna know. I did hear my sister yellin' at Big Mama and Lula, asking them why didn't they tell her if she was doing it the wrong way. She threw a fit that I think scared everybody. After that folks went round saying, "Y'all should be careful wit' them quiet ones; they'll sneak up on you and cut ya' throat from behind." My sister had it in her to go crazy if she had to, and I wagered either Mr. Benny or Ruby was gonna be the ones to set her off.

It didn't take long for hell to break loose from wherever it was b'fore and find its way to our home. Like a thief in the night, it snuck up on our li'l house and robbed us all of any chance to be more than we was. It sort of started when Doretha thought that Ruby liked me more than her. It didn't help when Ruby thought Sister was being fresh with her man. I ain't for sho' which hurt more; I just know it started.

"Why does she hate me so much and like you?"

Those was words I hadn't figured on ever hearing. I'd

thought that Sister was happy with having Big Mama as her own, so it never come to me to think on the fact that she might be jealous of me and Ruby. Suddenly, it seemed that Sister hated me to the core.

"And how am I s'posed to live in here while you've taken all the room up?" Now Sister was mad 'bout the room we was sleeping in. Seemed like I didn't know who she was no more. Seemed like nothing could keep her happy or her mouth from telling us how mad she was for having to be round Ruby and "her men," as she put it. And if that wasn't enough, she caught sight of my dog-chewed-up canopy bed under the carport. That had to be the last straw, as the grown folks would say.

"Why is it that you gets to have your own bed that you asked for and I don't?" They was questions I would've answered if she'd let me, but Sister didn't wanna hear nothin' I had to say. "I know she likes you betta' than me! And it's 'cause you her li'l light-eyed yella baby! You ain't nothing but a li'l white girl!" I stood and watched as my sister plumb lost her mind. Outta nowhere she was throwing a conniption over nothing. Doretha reminded me of one of my teachers who'd use a pointing stick to show us all the wrong answers we'd got on a test. Something inside me felt like it'd been stepped on. I was all wrong in my sister's eyes. I wanted to tell Doretha that I was happy to see her, but I couldn't when all she did was make me feel bad.

Matters only got worse when Ruby would leave Doretha in charge of the whole house when she wasn't home. That was all well and good at first. But when Mr. Benny started workin' the opposite times that he was s'posed to work, things started getting hot. For one, all of a sudden Mr. Benny needed to sleep all day so that he could do his military police job at night. Which meant that all us kids had to creep round the house like we had

155

no business being there in the first place. For two, Mr. Benny
needed the house to be spic-and-span all the time whether he
was there or not. And that's why the creeping round part
b'came real hard—who in they right mind was gonna walk
round on they tiptoes to clean a house? And if that wasn't
'nough, Mr. Benny started bossing Doretha round like she was
his own. And Sister sho' wasn't gonna let one of Ruby's men
treat her wrong. No way.

"I don't know who you think you are, but I'm here to let you
know, you ain't no kin to me, and I ain't about to wash no
damned dishes that I didn't dirty," she told him all in one sentence. Flash! Mr. Benny jumped over the couch and slapped
Doretha upside her head so hard you could've heard it on the
other side of town. Ruby wasn't home then, so she couldn't take
up for Sister. Now me, on the one hand, I was trying to stay
outta other folks' mess 'cause I'd seen from Big Lawrence what
can happen by running off at the mouth. But she was my sister,
and I couldn't hold back for long.

"Don't hit her no more!" I screamed at him. I didn't even
know where that came from. Everybody stopped where they
was; Sister standing there, holding her face in her hands, and
me with my right fist balled and ready for action. As for Mr.
Benny, he slammed the door, closing himself in Ruby's room.

"Just wait till your mama gets home," he yelled back at us.
"We'll see then who's the boss."

We sho' didn't have to wait long. Ruby was home in two
snaps and a crackle. We figured the ole crybaby, Mr. Benny, had
called her and told on us—"his" side of the story, that is. When
Ruby thundered through the front door, me and Sister was sitting on the couch watching Dark Shadows. I had straightened
up the kitchen so there'd be one less mess to speak of.

"Shut that goddamned TV off!" Ruby yelled as she walked through the kitchen, into where we was, on her way to her room. As I moved to push the on/off button in, she moved past me, almost taking my arm with her, and smashed the button into its hole, knocking the dang TV off the table.

"I don't know who the fuck you think you are, Doretha, but I'm the only bitch that rules this roost." Ruby's face was ugly. It was all drawn up like she had ate a whole pack a Sweetarts at one time. Her curly hair was all matted up in tangles. I never knowed somebody so beautiful could look so bad. "And as for you, Miss Regina, you need to take your little narrow ass and find some kids to stand up to, 'cause my man ain't the one! The problem with you is you think you already grown, and that may well be, but not in my house you ain't! Furthermore I cain't believe that I work almost twenty-two goddamned hours a day and I cain't get the fucking house cleaned!"

"Why you hate us so much, Ruby? Why'd you bring us here if you wasn't gonna take care of us, but leave us with some man that even you hardly know?" Doretha was standing right up to Ruby. Asking her things I couldn't dare to think 'bout, for fear that Ruby would know I was thinkin' on 'em and would try and get rid of me.

"I know one motherfuckin' thing, Doretha." Ruby's face looked like a tornado hit it. "You ain't got no goddamned right to stand in front of me and ask me shit 'bout what I do. And I know somethin' else, you betta' watch yourself, before I blow your fuckin' brains out."

"*I hate you!*" Doretha screamed, and tried to run out the room. But Ruby caught her 'fore she could run, and they was beating each other all the way down to the living room floor.

I thought my mama would be different. For all this time, I let my mind convince me that if Ruby had the chance, she would take up for her babies—specially me and Sister. I'd thought that she wouldn't let some no-'count man treat us any kinda ole way. But instead, here we was watching her in full-blown sight take sides with that no-good Mr. Benny, without even tryin' to hear what was going on for real. Not to mention beating up my sister—her own child—b'cause of him! I heard that dog-faced man come outta Ruby's room and try and break them up. You should've seen his sorry ass play like he wanted them apart. "Come on now, y'all; there is no call for all this mess. C'mon now. Ruby, leave the girl alone." He looked like he was trying to pull 'em apart, but when Sister almost managed to hit him, he dodged her punch and sat on the edge of the couch arm, a place where Ruby told us never to sit. From there, he slouched with his arms folded 'cross his naked-ass chest, chewing gum and watching Ruby and Doretha go at it. Even with all the fighting, I couldn't help but watch him. Each time he chewed, it forced his lizard tongue to snap out while he made popping sounds. It looked scary and mean. Finally he said, "All right, y'all break this shit up." Mr Benny jumped in and pulled the two of 'em apart. But that fight was just the beginning.

What was meant to be a coming together of a mama and all her kids turned out to be a time of bad beginnings. Miss Ida, who I'd talk to over or through the fence sometimes, said it all had something to do with the way folks lived they lives in the past and how it was all coming back to bite 'em. "You should try and keep a right mind 'bout what cha do, child, 'cause what goes round will be back again to greet cha." I didn't know what she was saying by that; but it sounded smart, and I thought maybe it'd make sense to me someday.

I knowed Sister was doing her best to make good with Ruby, but it seemed that no matter what she did to try and please our mama, Mr. Benny had a way with making it out to be wrong. And he'd convince Ruby that his way of looking at it was the right way. Like the time he found what he said was a dirty plate in the dish rack and slammed it on the floor. When Sister tried to explain her side, Benny cut her off and called her all kinds of lies, then told Ruby that Sister had dropped the dishes on purpose. I knowed that Ruby would never believe us girls, so I didn't even try to change her mind from his.

There was many more fights to come. If it wasn't Ruby and Doretha, it was Mr. Benny and Ruby, and more often than not it was Doretha and Mr. Benny. It got to the point that the neighbors would shut they windows and doors—all of course 'cept Miss Ida—when they saw a car pull up in our carport. 'Cause they knowed that sooner or later all hell was gonna break loose.

Somewhere in all of it, my twelfth birthday came and went. Ruby had told me she would take care of me later. She also said that if she didn't r'member, it would be all right for me to remind her. I didn't know how to remind her and was too scared to try and figure it out. The only present I r'member from me turning twelve was the scar that I got when I tried to shave my legs like I had seen Sister do. Accordin' to Ruby, I was to be more grown at twelve than I was at eleven. So I thought to see if she was right by shaving my legs. I did it just like I'd seen Doretha do. I wet my leg down with water and Ivory soap and took a pink razor and run it straight up the middle of my leg— right on the bone part. It took all of two minutes for me to see my leg turn from brown to a white then pink bloody stripe. The

159

line moved from the front of my ankle to my kneecap. Figuring
that Ruby was a nurse and she'd know what to do, I showed her.
I shouldn't have done that—not only did I have to hear her go
on 'bout me trying to be "grown" before my time, but I also had
to have rubbing alcohol dabbed into the bone, to keep it from
infection. I figured that was more than 'nough to let me know
I didn't wanna be too grown-up too soon. Specially if it'd mean
I'd have stripped-up legs. When I was no longer inna'rested in
razors, I decided to try on Sister's makeup. Doretha'd once told
me that I didn't need to use the Maybelline black eye-pencil
'cause my eyes already looked like they was lined. So I laid some
pink glitter stuff 'cross my eyelids like I'd seen her do.

"Oh no you don't! Get that black mess offa your eyes. *Now!*"
What was Ruby going on 'bout? I didn't have nothin' black on
'em.

"I ain't wearing nothin' 'cept eye powder. What black stuff
you talking 'bout?"

"I've told you, Regina, that you ain't nothin' but a child.
Shit! Don't rush yourself b'fore your time."

I went and wiped off the pink powder and showed Ruby the
difference. For a full week she swore I was wearing makeup and
threatened to beat me if I didn't stay outta hers. Her words got
me to thinking: I wondered if Ruby'd ever really looked in my
eyes b'fore now. It was a question I couldn't answer, and I didn't
wanna bother her with it, so I decided that if she hadn't seen
'em by then, it would probably take her another twelve years if
a'tall.

My fightin' with Ruby and Doretha wasn't my only problems. Seemed like no matter where I went, mens was gonna try
to get fresh with me. At least when I was back on Big Mama's

property, when her gran'sons came in the night to try and take
what didn't belong to 'em by trying to stick they things in me,
they used the window. One at a time, is how they did it, till all
of 'em sat crouched at the foot of my bed. I didn't know how
many it was for sho' 'cause I tried to play 'sleep by squintin' my
eyes. By what I could figure out there must've been at least
three. The oldest gran'son, Lenny, pulled down my panties to
just above the thickest part of my leg, and that's when he'd put
his thing right up to my you-know-what. Then he tried to push
it inside me. I opened my eyes up fast and started pounding his
nasty self offa me. And since I caught him off guard he stumbled over my body but managed to put his hand round my
mouth. "You betta' not say a damn word, or I'll tell 'em you told
me to come and get some," he whispered in my ear. "You betta'
lay your fast ass down and let me take it!"

I pulled my legs together tight and decided I would die trying to keep 'em closed b'fore I'd let that low-down dog stick hisself in me! I knowed that Big Mama was right in the other
room, so if I fought hard 'nough they'd get scared and leave.
Strong as Lenny's mangy ass was, I still kept my legs closed
tight, 'cause I was strong too. Since he was the only one doing
all the holdin' it wasn't hard to work against his pulling and
tugging. It was dark, and I couldn't make out who else was in
the room, but I could hear small sniggles and figured they was
the younger boys. I don't know what was going on for Sister, but
she must've not knowed or was acting like she didn't know
what was happening. After a second or so, Lenny tried to stick
that nasty thing inside my hind part. I squeezed my butt together real tight like a board until he finally gave up. Then the
dogs left the same way they came. As they was leaving they

started calling me names like prick-tease and cocky wench, promising to get and tame me next time.

Here, in North Carolina, I didn't have to be 'fraid of folks using windows and sneaking in during the night like long, black, flying cockroaches whose wings are too big to go into small places. Here, he came right through the front door. As bright as day and sure as midnight is pitch black, he stood tall and proud like the oak tree on Big Mama's property.

Aside from Mr. Benny being a bully and asking us to do everything when Ruby wasn't 'round, he started actin' real strange and saying stuff that I know a grown man shouldn't be saying to no girl. The first time he got fresh with me, I didn't say nothing to Ruby or nobody else, seeing that there was so much going on already. I knowed he was being fresh 'cause I'd seen how him and Ruby acted right b'fore they'd go in her room. And I don't know what he was thinking, but I wasn't planning on doing nothing like what he did with her.

One day Ruby told me I needed a bra-zear. She said my chest was buddin' and it was time for me to act like a girl and strap 'em down. "I'm too young to be a gran'mama now!"

When she told me this, I looked down at my chest and saw that my shirt stuck out in front of me a bit. I hadn't really no-ticed b'fore. Plus, why'd she have to say that thing 'bout being a gran'mama? What was that s'posed to mean? Sometimes Ruby made me madder than a wild pig with a firecracker up its ass, the way she'd just say whatever came to the front of her mind.

Of course Mr. Benny had been tellin' me as much. I just didn't understand at first what he meant by the way he said it. Folks had called me perky b'fore 'cause they'd say that I was full of spirit. But there was something in the way that Mr. Benny said the word that didn't sit right with my mind.

"You sure are looking real perky these days," Mr. Benny would say as he chewed and popped that stupid gum. At first I had no idea what he was talking 'bout. I'd been a li'l down in the spirit ever since Mr. Benny moved in. So what was this perky mess all 'bout? He sounded like a damned fool.

"Won't you come on over here and let me touch them li'l titties of yours?"

"What you mean by touch 'em?" I asked that black-as-midnight dog, until it b'come clear to me what he was on 'bout. Then I couldn't think of 'nough bad words to call him. One good thing 'bout hanging with Ruby was that she never ran out of bad words to say. There was many a day that she called Mr. Benny out his name, and now I see why. He was nastier than a dog full of mange. I knowed good and well what Mr. Nasty wanted.

"Come on over here, girl, and let me pull on them nipples. I know you'd like it if you let me." He moved his thumb and second finger together to look like one of them crawfish the boys got out the creek.

I don't know who he thought he was talking to, but I wasn't gonna give him a chance to think on it twice. I turned right round and hauled ass out that house as fast as I could. I pretended I was back at Big Mama's and one of her oldest gran'sons was teaching me how to run by throwing bricks at the back of my feet. He claimed it would help me move quicker if I thought I was gonna get hit by a piece of concrete. I wasn't for sho' if Mr. Benny was after me, 'cause I didn't look back. And I didn't stop till I came to Miss Ida's yard. I knowed he wouldn't come over there on account that Mr. Benny was well aware that Miss

Ida wasn't gonna take no stuff from any mens. I didn't know if Miss Ida was home or not, but I didn't care. I ran up to her screen door, yanked it open, and acted like I was gonna go straight inside. Mr. Benny never bothered to chase after me past the backyard. But I could see him standing in the carport looking through the trees that our two yards shared. He was tucking his undershirt into them ugly green pants he had to wear to work. Finally he turned and went back towards the house. I listened for that gum-popping sound to get farther and farther away. When it was nowhere in earshot, I felt all right.

I sat down on Miss Ida's porch swing and waited. I ain't for sure how long I was out there, but I'd say an hour or so later, I seen Ruby's headlights as they turned into our driveway. The lights shined right in my eyes as they woke me up. Once I heard her car door open and shut, and the sound of her slippers slapping and dragging on the concrete, I made my way back home. I decided right then and there that I wasn't planning on telling Ruby nothing.

I cain't rightly r'member if I was dreamin' or if it was real, but I r'member feeling like I was in both places at one time, but nowhere long 'nough to know for sho'. I was sittin' in a car with a man. He was wearin' a tan-colored suit with green bar pins on his shoulders that had li'l tiny gold stars on 'em. It was only me and him in the car, and we was just riding. There was no talking going on b'tween us. The road we drove down had rows and rows of trees on each side, and if you looked out straight ahead, you'd think you was riding into the tip of a arrow that you could never reach. All of a sudden I was real antsy being with this fella. The longer we drove, the more fitful I become. I can hear a man's voice with no face saying to me, "Have you ever touched one before?" I try to think what "one" means. Again, the voice says, "Have you ever seen one?"

My heart is telling me that it ain't right what this fella wants to know. Slowly, I start raising from the seat like I'm on one a them magic carpets. I'm real light, and I cain't feel nothing. I wanna open the car door and jump out. I heard once that my mama had done such a thing before when she was fighting with Big Lawrence, and she came out all right. They say she landed on her feet. I tell myself that since me and her have the same feet that maybe that'll help me land on the ground like she did.

The voice says, "Come on, who're you kidding? A cutie pie like you gets hit on all the time, don't you?"

Now he wants to start hitting me? I'll hit him back! I swear 'fore God! I'll hit him back! I ain't afraid no more, not of him. It's like I'm moving in slow motion and I cain't lift my arms or hands, and nobody can hear me saying, "Let me outta here!"

"Give me your hand." I cain't lift my hand. He takes my fingers and pulls me down while he puts 'em on the bump right below his belt. He's got one hand on the steering wheel, and the other is holding my hand down on the bump. *That don't matter,* my mind says to me. *That hand don't belong to you no more.* I don't care what it does 'cause it ain't mine. My mind is telling me how things is gonna be. It says, *It's all right now; don't worry 'bout nothing.* I go along with it. The longer the fingers stay on the bump, the bigger it gets; it goes from nothing to a big ole hard something in no time a'tall. My mind says to me, *Don't think on it; it ain't really there.* I think 'bout Ruby's feet. And wonder 'bout how they got on the dogs that is now chasing me. I'm running and looking back, and the dogs with the red-painted Ruby toenails are gaining on me. I wonder if this is what it was like for all li'l girls. My mind comes back to me. I'm no longer in a car driving down a long road. And the dogs stop in the middle of the road as I go higher and higher in the sky. Now I'm in my bed, and my panties and pajama bottoms is 'cross the room on the floor by the door.

My sister had been trying to tell Ruby something for a while 'bout Mr. Benny, but Ruby wasn't hearing her. "You need to keep a betta' watch on your children and stop paying so much attention to that man!" When I'd ask her what she was meaning, she'd just say, "You're too young to understand." The fights between him and Doretha got so bad that he would chase her down the street and grab ahold of her while nearly beating the mess outta her with anything he could get his hands on. Sometimes it would be a plastic bat that we'd use to play stickball with or one of Dwayne Edward's fake bowlin' pins. After he caught Doretha and whooped her, he'd drag her back in the house, where she'd end up doing whatever he wanted her to do in the first place. I would watch from a distance and made sure the boys or me was never caught in the middle.

Ruby never quite heard Doretha till the day that white woman from the county came over. Doretha had told the folks at school what was going on in our house. She told 'em everything there was to tell. About how Ruby left us kids in the company of Mr. Benny, and how he would make us work for him, and then he'd beat her and sometimes me, if we didn't do it his way. She had bruises on her skin and pain in her voice, and they believed her.

Ruby stood and listened while the woman brought the counts against her and Mr. Benny. There was something said 'bout child endanger and this and that. I couldn't understand all that was said for all the screamin' and hollerin' Sister and Mr. Benny was doing in the background. But I could see that Ruby wasn't gonna have it for too much longer by the way her face stretched itself out. When Ruby had all she was gonna take, she just went off and cussed the county lady and Doretha out like they was dirt. She called Sister all kinda lies and told her she was a good-for-nothing ingrate. Ruby yelled that after all she'd done to bring Sister here so that we could all be a family, if her only repayment was to be accused of neglect it would be best for Sister to get to steppin'. Ruby said, "If you thank it ain't easy to leave now, it sho' ain't gonna be any easier with your ass loaded with lead. Now get the fuck up out of my house, before I have to use my pistol. I brought you in this world, and I can take your ass straight on out." I didn't know if what Ruby said was true, but on the other hand, I thought that maybe God did give mamas a special power to send us back to where we came from.

When Ruby was done with Sister, she turned her mouth on the county lady and told her that she thought it to be in her best interest to get fire in her ass and move on out her yard, otherwise she wasn't gonna be responsible for what happened. That was all she had to say; that white lady bolted outta that front door quicker than a matchstick could catch fire, with Sister bringing up the rear.

A coupla weeks after the gun-threatening act, Doretha come and moved her stuff out. Ruby had made Mr. Benny put up the canopy bed by that time, and I saw how it was all the more reason for my sister to go and lose the rest of her mind. Right b'fore she left the house Doretha pulled a steak knife out the kitchen drawer and put it to my throat. "I fucking hate you! How come she likes you more? If it wasn't for you I'd be special to her. She's got you and all your cutesy-ness. She don't need me. Why? Why come she didn't choose me?" Doretha held the knife right against my throat while she screamed and cried real hard.

It was so bad that I started crying back. "I'm sorry, Doretha. I didn't mean to do nothing!" I shouted back at her, making sure not to move too much. I could feel the knife digging in my skin, and I didn't care what happened. "Go on and kill me, I don't care!" And right then, I really didn't care.

After crying and screaming and telling me how much less than shit I really was, Doretha grabbed my bedspread and wiped black eyelash stuff all over it. And if that wasn't 'nough to satisfy her, she blowed her nose in as many places as she could. Then she dared me to say a word. The last thing she said to me b'fore she tore outta the door was, "Watch out for that motherfucker Mr. Benny."

Doretha leaving was kinda good. I mean if you had a mama like Ruby, that is. Ruby was nicer to me and would give me more of what I asked for. But I still had to deal with Mr. Benny. At least when Sister was round, he'd get to her first. And only after he wore her down did he turn to me. I don't r'member him fooling with them boys too much. Plus, I think if he had, Ruby would've blown his cotton-picking brains out.

I guess I hadn't noticed so much when Sister was round, but now that she was gone and it was a li'l quieter, seemed to me like ever since Mr. "Nasty" Benny moved in, Ruby spent more time in her room with him than she did with me.

Anytime Ruby came home from working, she would get us kids all cared for with food like Kentucky Fried Chicken and then set us up in front of the TV, then she would take their plates into the bedroom. From the corner of my eyes I could see her getting his stuff ready and carrying it to him all pretty-like. I hated Benny and wanted to know how come I couldn't eat in her room with her. I told my mind that when I got older I would make a man do all for me what they made a woman do for 'em.

For what seemed like hours, I could hear Ruby and Benny making crazy noises that sounded like cats being choked. I came to understand 'xactly what was going on; they was doing it. One time when I was s'posed to be watching the boys, I heard them cat sounds and wanted to go and listen more up close. The boys really didn't need no watching 'cause they was sound asleep on the couch. I threw a cover on 'em just so they wouldn't wanna wake up from the cold and come looking for me. I waited till the sounds was good and loud; then I tippy-toed to Ruby's door. It was open a li'l bit.

There was a smell. I'd never smelled nothing like it b'fore. It brought to my mind what cigarettes, alcohol, sweat, and per-fume might stink of if they was all put together and shook up, then spread round a dark room. It made me scared. I could see my mama. She was spread out all wide, and her sheets was hanging on for dear life at the edges of her bed. She made small sounds like she was hurting, and her arms was holding on to her headboard. Where pretty had shined 'cross her face, ugly now took its place as I seen her eyes and mouth all drawn up. I don't think she was liking whatever was being done to her. I could see a black spot moving round on top of her while the sound of gum popping was mixed in with the baby cat moans. I froze in place for a second but closed my eyes and scrunched up my nose 'cause I didn't wanna know anymore. Not the smell nor the sight. I wanted to wash it offa me, but somehow I knowed that was a scent I would never clean from my mind.

What was they doing? Why did she let him do that to her? Was these the things Lula Mae was accusing Ruby of? Was my mama really a woman who'd just lay down with some ole nasty man? Did that make her a ho'? It couldn't be true. Ruby would never let nobody do nothing to her that she didn't want 'em to do. I thought to myself that it was Mr. Nasty who was forcing hisself on her. He was no betta' than Big Mama's ole nasty gran'sons, who tried to force themselves inside of me. Was he hurtin' her? My mind was going haywire trying to figure them two out. All I had to say was, if that's what Ruby did to get me and Doretha, then doing it was out. There was no way I was gonna let no man climb on me and pop gum and make my room smelly and ugly. I was never gonna do it! I wanted to know if all pretty folks had to do this with mens, and if so, did they get less pretty each time they did it? 'Cause from the looks of Ruby's face, it had to be true. And then I figured that's why Ruby hated her girls. Maybe she hated us 'cause folks called us pretty, and she was scared that mens would want to do those things to us and not her b'cause she'd used all her pretty up. I opened my eyes and placed my hand on the doorknob and turned it slow as I pulled the door closed.

After that night it was hard for me to look at Ruby. I didn't want her to know that I'd learned the secrets of what her and Mr. Benny did at night in her room. The truth is she'd prob'ly hit me and say that I was too fast for my own good and that I should take my "wanna-be-grown ass" out her face. Lately, that seemed to be all that she had to say to me.

From that day on, I played like I didn't care that Ruby would rather be doing the ugly with Mr. Benny and not be with me. It was coming easier for me to 'magine that Ruby really wasn't my mama anyway. I'd told myself that I was more than likely somebody she'd borrowed from a neighbor, like a cup of sugar. I figured that maybe one day she'd have the good mind to give me back to my rightful owner. In the meantime, I'd made a way to be with the part of my mama that I liked the most. It wasn't 'xactly the same as being with her directly, but it made me feel betta' all the same. I would wait right good for Ruby to leave the house; then I'd sneak into her room and start to play with her wigs. I'd pretend like the wigs was on Ruby's head and she wanted me and only me to comb 'em up nice for her. It was here that my mama told me that I was her favorite li'l girl and that nobody could ever take my place. In this time I'd have with her there'd be nobody else to bother us, and I could take care of all her necessaries, and she would smile out at me. For a few hours I'd get my time with my mama like this, in my own way. The more I 'magined I was with her, the longer it would last me when I wasn't, 'cause she'd be in the room with him, forgettin' 'bout me. I figured I was lucky, though, to have her in my imaginin's, and I'd come to see that nobody could take her away from me when we was there. Also, Ruby got to stay pretty when she was in my mind. There she'd never have to do what she didn't want to, and she could be the way I wanted her to be: all mine and nobody else's.

CHAPTER EIGHT

CRAB BALL

IF I'D KNOWED I was gonna get caught at it, I wouldn't've done it in the first place. But somehow I had to show that big-mouthed tattletale Dennis a lesson. For the record, Ruby's boys and me got on rightly fine for the most part. But there was days when one of 'em in particular worked my nerves. Dwayne Edward, he was nice all the way round. All he ever wanted to do is play golf, bowl, and read. All you had to do is tell him once, maybe twice, and he'd know when to get on out the way. Now Dennis was just as nice a boy, the only difference being, he kept a secret like a baby who ate Ex-Lax kept her bowels. I got so tired of him promising he wouldn't tell, just so he could come along with me, then turning round and blabbin' anything he could r'member, that I had to do something 'bout him.

This one Saturday, a couple of us neighborhood kids was playin' doorbell ditch—that's where you ring a doorbell and run—a few streets over from our own house, and we came to a yard that had a package from a place called Hickory Farms layin' beside the mailbox. I figured the folks didn't want the box no more since it was left outside, so we took it with us, forgettin' all 'bout ringing the doorbell, and found a place to open it. For a minute we all stood wide-eyed, wondering whose house we was gonna take our new treasure to.

After nobody could make up they minds, we ended up at the back of our house, out near the creek. Once we was all situated I opened the box and found all kinds of food inside. There was cheese shaped like a baseball then rolled in some kinda nuts, and big ole sausages, with li'l mustard jars to dip 'em in. We went to town, Dennis included, throwin' out the ball-shaped thing first, then eating the rest of the goodies. But when we went back inside our house and Ruby asked us what we was up to, Dennis goes and say, "I didn't wanna eat that stuff they stole in the first place, but Gina made me."

I could've beat him down right then and there. I narrowed my eyes at him like a hawk on its prey. "Shut up!" I mumbled at him, and moved to pinch the daylights outta his arm.

"You betta' stop it," he said, cryin' and holdin' the place on his arm where he was feeling the fire.

"What the hell is goin' on here, Regina?" Ruby asked me.

"I don't know what he talkin' 'bout," I said, with my arms crossed behind my back and my face turned to Dennis as I said the words slow, to show him he betta' not say another thing.

"Dennis, now you betta' tell me what is so, and I mean real quick-like. I ain't got time for all this shit." Ruby's face looked just like she said, like it didn't have time for no shit. Her eyes, mouth, and eyebrows was pulled towards her nose, sayin' she was not to be played with.

He told the whole story. Dennis also told Ruby that I said I'd beat him up if he spilled the beans. For being a yellow-bellied mama's boy, Dennis got off without being cussed at or told off, and being the youngest didn't hurt either. Ruby told me that I was the oldest and should've knowed betta', so I could expect a ass whippin' when she could get round to it; but in the meantime, I was to stay in our yard only, with no kid visitors. "And furthermore," Ruby told me, "if I find out you touched that boy in any way, I'm gonna whip yo' ass twice." That was fine by me. I didn't mind hanging with myself, 'cause it gave me time to make a real good plan to get that blabbermouth back.

Everybody knowed the meanest boy on our block was Ernest Thurgood. He was a bully who'd beat the crap outta anybody for no good reason. I also heard he'd beat the crap outta folks for a good reason, if the price was right. This is where my plan came in. One Monday morning I ran out to get on the school bus, a full five minutes ahead of the boys. Me and the boys rode the same bus even though we didn't go to the same school. I got on, told the bus driver that the boys was comin', and spotted Ernest right off. Man, was he a big sloppy-looking boy. He still had that pus-looking stuff in his eyes from just waking up and was twice the size as both my brothers put together.

I asked the fat bully-boy, who was nothin' close to cute, if he would beat the mess outta Dennis the minute he stepped on the bus. When he asked me why, I told him 'cause Dennis had talked 'bout him behind his back, and if that wasn't 'nough to make him wanna go off on him, then I'd be willing to give him some money, to do it just b'cause. He asked me how much, and I told him thirty-three cents—it was all I had. It was a deal. I adjusted myself in my seat like nothin' was goin' on. As I peeped out the window I could see 'em coming. There they was, Dwayne Edward in the front and "Li'l Bigmouth" bringin' up the rear. I couldn't keep myself still waiting to see what was comin' next. Up the stairs they came, and as Dennis took his sit, Ernest walked over and hit him in the eye, just like that. B'fore anybody could say one thing Dennis had run back off the bus and into the house, hollerin' like a ninny all the way.

Quick as a flash, Ruby was out the door and on her way, with Dennis's sorry ass in tow. She was draggin' him right back 'cross that lawn and straight onto that bus.

"Who the hell is Ernest? And I wanna know now!" Ruby was not playin'; she had that pulled look on her face again—the same one she wore the last time there was a problem with me and Dennis. All the kids pointed right at Ernest, and Ruby walked right up on him. "Who the fuck you think you are hittin' my child? Who told you you had the right to touch him?"

Ernest looked like he was gonna go on hisself. Ruby grabbed him by the collar of his shirt and was 'bout to ask him again when the boy screamed out and pointed right at me. "She did. She told me to beat him up 'cause he talk too much."

Ruby's eyes turned to where his point landed—right smack in the middle of me. "Regina, I know you didn't do what he just said." She must've frog-leaped over the seats to get to me.

"Get yo' ass up and let's go." I looked at the bus driver, praying she was gonna do something, but she didn't. "Come on, you rotten li'l thing. Get yo' ass up now!"

Ruby had her hand round the back of my neck and was slapping on me all the way off the bus. I could hear all them stupid kids laughing at me as the door closed and the bus drove off. Ruby was still slappin' me as she pushed me 'cross the street.

"I thought I told you not to bother Dennis, and you have to go and get that boy beat up, your own brother at that." She never took a breath as she hit me all upside my head with her fists. I just kept telling myself, *That didn't hurt—that didn't hurt.*

Ruby's hittin' wasn't as bad as Lula Mae's, plus Ruby didn't use water hoses and extension cords. She used fists and if necessary guns. But I wasn't worried that she'd shoot me on account I wasn't Sister.

"Get yo' grown ass outta my face. I don't wanna see you no time soon." She pushed me outta her way as she walked off. I stood where Ruby left me for a minute, right on the grass in the front yard. I put my hands up to the places that really did hurt and rubbed 'em. I wasn't gonna let her know I was cryin', so I kept the tears inside and let 'em pile up in my throat. As Ruby left my eyesight, I headed for the li'l creek in the backyard of my house. I let her words stomp 'cross my mind again. "Get yo' grown ass outta my face. I don't wanna see you no time soon." Those words wasn't news to me; plus, I didn't care if I ever seen her again. I plopped down on the green grass, which was wet from the mornin', and just sat there cryin' quiet for as long as I could think. I knowed that something in me changed for Ruby right then. I still loved her and wanted her for my mama, but I saw how she could really be. Far as I could tell, this was just one of the many times she picked one of her boys or a man over me. I thought Doretha's leavin' had made it betta' for me, but I could see that Ruby just wanted to be with boys; they was the ones she stuck up for. Now I don't feel so sorry 'bout those eyes that seemed so sad 'cause I thought they'd seen so much that was hard. I could see that she prob'ly brought hard on herself for sticking up for the wrong folks. I didn't wanna worry 'bout Ruby no more. I felt sorry for my own head and heart.

It took a while for the story of my mama whoopin' my ass to die off a bit on that stupid bus. I had to clamp my teeth down on many a day, just to keep from kickin' somebody's tail for pokin' fun at me. "Boohoo, yo' mama beat you. Boohoo, yo' mama beat you," them mangy li'l kids would say to me. Finally I told 'em that the next one who reminded me of that whoopin' was gonna get whooped themselves. I guess they came to see that anybody crazy 'nough to get they own brother beat up was somebody not to fool with. Shortly after that, all the boohooin' stopped.

The only thing that made riding that stupid bus all right was knowing that it was takin' me to school. I loved my new school. I specially loved Physical Education, 'cause I got to play a bunch of sports that I never heard of b'fore—like climbin' ropes that was connected to the ceiling of our gym, and doing basketball. I was real good at both of those. I don't ever r'member doing nothin' like that back in Texas. The only sports I ever did there was runnin'.

It didn't take long for me to fall hard for my PE teacher, Ms. Peterson. She had to be one of the nicest people I knowed— even though she looked just like a fella. That didn't bother me a'tall. Miss Ida looked like one too, and she was my friend. I was keen on Ms. Peterson 'cause she paid more attention to me than I could ever r'member getting, without me being in trouble. She said that I was real good at all kinds of sports, but specially good at crab ball.

Crab ball was a game that had two teams. Each team was on either side of a line. The idea of the game was for all us girls to get our hands in the back of us, feet in the front; knees bent, and our bottoms on the floor. We was to crawl round like crabs, kicking a ball to the opposite side of a line that was taped to the gym floor. You got points after the ball flew over the marked line, and the first team that got to ten points won. The ball was a gigantic beach ball that floated in the air when you kicked it, so it wasn't all that easy to make a score.

"That's it, now, Regina, you've really got the hang of it. You are a real pro at crawlin' on that floor!"

Ms. Peterson won me over right then and there. I had never heard words like that 'bout me. Lord knows she should have never said a thing to me, 'cause after that I became a super tomboy. There wasn't a sport I didn't do, specially if she was round, 'cept maybe swim. I was a li'l bit scared of water on account of the things you could swallow without you even knowing. I got really good at basketball. So much so that Ms. Peterson told me 'bout a camp in Raleigh, at the university.

"Regina, why don't you apply for the basketball camp at the University of North Carolina? I think it will help you hone in on your skills. Check it out with your parents and let me know. Plus, I think you'll get a kick outta living on campus with lotsa other girls your own age."

I ain't never heard of no university till then, and I couldn't wait to get home so that I could let Ruby know what my teacher said.

The first thing I did when I seen Ruby that night—I stayed up till eleven-thirty to talk to her when she got off work—was tell her what Ms. Peterson said 'bout the camp and living in a university. She said, "I'll see what I can do. But you know money don't grow on trees." That was good comin' from somebody who complained a lot 'bout not having no money. Maybe Ruby was wanting to be different with me.

One day, not long after asking Ruby 'bout the camp, I was out on the porch talking to Nichelle and her sister Carol when

Ruby called me in to talk on the phone. She told me it was somebody I didn't know but that he wanted to talk to me, and for me to never turn down a man who was interested in talking, specially when you was the one wanting somethin'.

"Hello."

"Well, hello there. How are you, Regina?"

The man on the other line sounded like a white. I couldn't for the life of me figure out how he knew my name.

"I'm fine, thank you."

"Your mother tells me that you would like to go to a basketball camp. Is this so?" Who on earth was this man?

I could hardly understand him, with all that proper talking. Plus, why was this white man asking me questions 'bout my "mother" and camp? I let him go on.

"Yeah, I want to go to camp. My teacher say I'm good."

"Do you know who I am, Regina?"

"No, sorry, cain't say I do," I replied.

"My name is Glenn Hathaway. I am your father. Do you remember me?" Jesus, Joseph, and Mary! I sho' didn't ever think I'd hear from Odetta's son Glenn, and I wasn't sure I wanted to. But on the other hand, if he was calling to do good by me for a change, then maybe him calling was a good thing?

I was quiet, caught by a mem'ry—I could see it as clear as water: Ruby sitting down and telling me 'bout the light-skinned stranger. . . .

"Hello, Regina. Are you still there?"

"Yeah, I'm here. Is you gonna send me the money for camp? It costs two hundred dollars." The way I saw it was, if this man wanted to send me money to go to camp, that was fine with me. That didn't mean I had to like him.

"You waste no time driving in your point. I'll see what I can do."

"Bye now. I gotta go back to my friends—they's waiting on me." I didn't wait to hear what he said. I handed the phone back over to Ruby and went back outside.

I just couldn't believe it when the money came. I was even more surprised that Ruby used it to send me to the camp. With Mr. Nasty runnin' things and all, there was no tellin' what could go down. Maybe in her own way Ruby knowed what her dirty-dog boyfriend was up to and she was trying to get me outta his sight. Whatever the reasons, I didn't give a hoot. I just wanted to go and be away from home and have some fun.

After riding on a bus for several hours we arrived at the University of North Carolina's girls' basketball camp. I couldn't believe it! I was on a real college campus. All the yard surrounding the school was green and cut short, nicer'n Aint Mae's back home in Texas. I knowed I was gonna love it here. The counselors told me I was gonna stay on campus for five days and live in what was called a dormitory. I ain't never seen somethin' so big and clean as them buildings the dorms was in. I wished right then that I could live there. The next thing our counselors did was set us down and let us know what to expect for the next couple of days. I wondered how they would be able to know what was gonna happen every day we was there. I thought they was real smart. One thing they said made my belly jump all over the place: they told us to invite our families to see us in our last game. Somehow, I knew betta' than to even think 'bout it. It was one thing to ask Ruby for money for a camp; it was another to ask her to come and watch me play some game. I didn't let myself believe one minute that that was gonna ever happen. Instead I tuned them words "invite your families" right on outta my mind.

Within the first day of camp I learned that I was a forward. I had no idea what that was. But quick enough, I understood that my job was to snatch the ball in rebound from the backboard, the air, or the other team and get it to the first person on my team that I could see. I liked playing basketball, but I wasn't as good at it as I tended to be at crab ball. Plus my PE teacher didn't come to the camp with me, and I guessed that's why I wasn't betta'. I always seemed to do mighty well when somebody I liked was rooting me on. But even though I was by myself, I took a liking to being at the college with all the counselors and kids. We was all happy and had a lot of fun.

One thing I noticed quickly was that nobody tattletaled on each other. And you didn't have to worry 'bout no pesky li'l boys having to hang out with you all the time. We got along fine, just like the folks on the TV shows. Plus, we could have anything we wanted at camp without havin' to feel shame for asking. Not like at Big Mama's, where I'd ask for somethin' as small as a nickel and have to hear 'bout how ain't nobody was paying for her to take care of me and my sister and if I wanted anything then I should find my mama and ask her for it. At camp I loved the pizza and soda pops. I was told that *soda water* was a word used by folks from the sticks and made folks see that I wasn't from North Carolina. And if I wanted to be cool, I should say "soda pop." So soda pop it was.

At camp there was always 'nough food to feed everybody.

We could eat as many times a day as we wanted, and nobody yelled at us for taking the last of anything. I never even had to worry that somebody had put they name on a piece of chicken with an invisible marker like at home, when Mr. Benny would cuss at me 'cause I ate it without knowing he'd put tabs on it. One of my favorite times at the university was when we had a talent show and I sang a song called "Doctor's Orders." The counselors helped me make myself up like a real singer, with a feather scarf to go round my neck and high-heeled shoes to match. Since the song started out with a clock ringing, some-one gave me a clock so I could mimic the singing right to the tee! I came in first place, and I got to have a pizza of my choice. I picked pepperoni and shared it with my roommates. I woulda done it for nothing, I had that much fun, but if I could win food to eat with my singing, then maybe one day I could stand up in front of folks and sing for my food all the time.

Aside from singing, eating, and goofing off, we learned games that taught us how to trust each other. There was this one game that I forgot the name of, but really liked. The coun-selors told us the object of it was to fall backwards and believe that the person in the back of you was gonna ketch you. And when they did, you knowed you could trust 'em for always. I got to be good at that game. At first I was betta' at ketchin' the folks, but by the end I was also good at trusting I'd be caught.

I could say from deep in my heart that being at this camp with all them rich kids and counselors made me think that maybe I could go to college too one day. When I listened to the other girls talking, I overheard some saying how they parents had already told 'em that they was gonna go to the same schools they parents had gone to. One girl said that at least four people in her family—her brother, cousins, and daddy—had already been to the very university that we was standing on. I couldn't believe that. Right then and there, I promised myself that I would do all I could to come back to a place like that.

On the last day of camp, we had play-off games. We was to bring our families to watch, so that they could see how good we'd got, and cheer us through our last game. All the other girls at the camp was white kids except me and one other black girl. I'd watched and listened to all of 'em line up behind the pay phones and call they families to make the arrangements. I didn't bother to feel bad; I just started running round the phones making stupid noises while the girls was trying to talk. That is until the counselor told me to cut it out and act like a lady. I made it seem like I didn't care that they was calling folks. Anyway, I'd already spent most of my life without nobody coming to anything I did—whether it was running or playing basketball, nobody I knowed had ever showed up to watch me. I figured that the only reason Ruby really sent me was 'cause my so-called daddy gave her the money and she needed me out her face for a while.

Even though there'd be nobody in the bleachers rootin' for me, I didn't let it bother me too much. Instead of getting bent up 'bout it, I just told myself that it didn't matter anyway, and that's just the way that some folks' lives was. Anyhow, I imagined that Ms. Peterson, my PE teacher, was gonna be there for me, shoutin' my name out all over the place like she did when I played crab ball. "Go, Regina! Go, number fifteen!" It was all I needed.

During the first ten minutes of our play-off game I was fouled, which meant that I got to go to the free throw line. Oh, Lordy, did I feel scared having to stand all by myself in front of them people, trying to make a basket. I stood there, at that free throw line, like I was told, dribblin' the ball in front of me the way I'd learned all week. I prayed to heaven that the ball would go straight in and that everybody would jump out they seats and shout, "Yay Gina!" Yet at the same time I was happy as hell that nobody was there to watch me, in case I didn't make it. As I held the ball above my head, resting it back in my hand, r'membering what the coach had taught us 'bout flicking the wrists and aiming, I talked to God. I made a deal with him that if the ball made it inside the basket, that meant I was 'sposed to go to a university one day.

Being at the camp all week, I could see that I could get away from folks that made me scared. At college I met girls who talked 'bout they families and how much they loved 'em and the plans they had for the future. I never knowed that the future was something I could really plan for. I'd only thought that if you wished on something hard 'nough, then it would one day come true. These same girls didn't seem to be holding secrets 'bout they mamas' boyfriends and worrying whether or not they should close they eyes at night. I wanted to go to college so I could be free.

I dribbled again, aimed at the backboard just above the net, bent my knees, and jumped in the air as I let go of the ball. *Swoosh!* I made it in! I couldn't believe it. I figured God must've been talking to me. I could hear folks was cheering for me—I was going to college. On the second ball, I asked God if my PE teacher could tell I liked her and if maybe she would want to take me home with her so I could be her child. Dribble. Aim. Shoot. The ball flew over the backboard, never coming close to the net.

The way I saw it, I was glad that Ruby never came. If she

had've, I might've tried to make the shots for her, and I would've never found out that I should go to college.

Back home, things with me and Mr. Benny wasn't getting no betta'. At first I thought that him and Ruby spending so much time together would make him wanna forget all 'bout me, but it wasn't too soon that I come to learn different. Whenever Ruby would leave for work, Mr. Benny'd lay in bed till he heard the sound of her car start and roll out the driveway. We'd both learned to listen for the same thing; we just had different reasons for listening. It started out where he would call me in and ask me to walk on his back. He said that I was prob'ly good with my balance and heavier than the boys, but not as heavy as Ruby, so I should be a pro at back walking. When he put it that way—that I could be good at it—I decided it might be all right to do it for a while. I cain't say why I wanted to help him out other than the fact that he wasn't being real nasty for once and that he'd let me take his blackjack weapon to school for show-and-tell, where I became a instant hit with all the tough boys who wanted to join up with the army one day and b'come military policemen. And if that wasn't all, out of nowhere he started giving me money for no good reason.

I think I must've walked miles on that man's back. And for some reason I never told Ruby that I walked on his back and he gave me money. Something inside me said she'd never believe me anyway.

"You're 'bout the best back walker I ever had," Mr. Benny told me one morning as he asked me to step off so that he could turn over and face me. "Lean down here closer so I can see your eyes. What color are they anyway?"

What was this crazy man talking 'bout now? He knowed damn well what color my eyes was. I started feeling nervous in my belly. I turned myself towards the edge of the bed slowly. "I gotta go to the bathroom," I told him. Mr. Benny grabbed ahold of my hand, and my skin went colder than a Sno-Kone.

"Ooh, look at how them nipples are perking up now! Lord have mercy, child. I know you want me to touch 'em, don't you? How'd you like it if I told you I wanted to fuck you too?"

I pulled my arms closer to my body and stepped back from him. "You black-ass bitch!" I howled at him, not knowing where the word came from. "Do you say that to your own child? Do your li'l girl walk on your stupid back too?"

I quickly dropped to the side of the bed and slid off.

"What! What'd you just say to me?" He reached and grabbed me by my arm, swinging me round.

"Let go of me!" I yanked free and grabbed his wrist and twisted his skin, trying to give him a rug burn. I had learned that at camp. It never fazed him.

"I'll show you something. Don't you go talking back to me with your little cocky ass. That shit might be cute with your mammy, but it ain't working here."

He tried to put one hand round my neck, but I moved out his reach b'fore he could. I did the only thing I knowed to do; I ran. Since the back door was never locked I blasted through it and didn't care that all I was wearing was my night slip. Out the corner of my eye, I could see Mr. Benny coming for me. "*Help!*" I screamed. "*Somebody help me!*" I didn't care that the rocky driveway was hurtin' my bare feet, I just kept on moving. I got right good to the end of our yard, and damn me! There he was.

"*Let me go!*" I screamed. "*Help me!*" He got me by the tail end of my slip. After he'd picked me up, he tried puttin' his hand over my mouth while dragging me back inside. I kicked and hollered the whole way.

"Sit yo' ass down and shut the hell up," he said all quiet-like as he threw me on the couch. I started kicking him and fighting back with all I had. I caught sight of the boys looking on. Dwayne was rocking back and forth in the hallway, and Dennis sat right beside him.

Mr. Benny threatened to slap me with the same blackjack he'd let me take for show-and-tell if I didn't shut up. The boys watched everything.

"*I'm gonna tell Ruby on you, Benny. I hate yo' ass!*" I screamed, and scratched at him. I'd seen him beat my sister up and tell lies, and I was not gonna put up with no more of him and this crazy shit! *Goddamn it! Why was I having to go through this everywhere I went!*

"You just wait and see. Ruby's gonna put yo' ass out!" I screamed at him.

"Oh, yeah? Well, that's what you think. We'll just see about that!" Mr. Benny yelled back at me.

Ruby showed up just as Mr. Benny was backing out the driveway to leave. I later found out that it was Miss Ida who'd called Ruby down at the hospital and told her what was going on. From the minute Ruby walked through the door, she started yelling at me and asking me why come I was dressed like I was, and what the hell had I gone and done this time. Mr. Benny had already called her and told her that I hadn't listened to him when he asked me to clean up, that instead of doing the dishes like he'd asked I flat-out refused and got sassy on top of that. He said that therefore, he was left with no option but to kick my ass.

"I cain't believe that I leave the goddamned house and everything falls apart. I ain't at work a whole fucking hour before the nosey-assed bitch next-door neighbor has to call me and tell me you running down the street hollering. What did you do to piss Benny off? And why didn't you mind him? I gave him permission to treat you like you was his own! I'm the mother in this here house, not you!"

I didn't know what to say to her, but I tried for the one thing I knowed she'd hear. "Why don't you ask the boys what happened?"

"They're babies, for heaven's sake. How they gonna know what was going on?"

"Just ask 'em and see! Just ask 'em."

"I ain't got to ask them a goddamned thing!"

"Fine, then! Mr. Benny tried to do this to me!" I held up my middle finger and showed her the sign.

"He's been making me walk on his back and giving me money. He also said he wanted to pinch my titties." I told her everything all at one time, hoping and praying that she would believe me.

"Is that so?" Ruby said, standin' in front of me with both hands on her hips and now a cigarette stick stuck b'tween her teeth. The white nurse dress she was wearin' and her hair all crazy made her look like she had just finished workin' on bringin' Frankenstein back to life.

"Well, you don't say? If I know you, and yo' fast ass, you prob'ly brung it all on yourself, trying to be grown and all. Now get that crazy-talking shit outta my face."

Staring at her mouth as those mean things came falling out

was more than I was gonna take. I gathered up all my strength, and in a hot second, I let her know what was on my mind.

"I don't know why you had me anyway! Everybody knows you didn't want me or Doretha either! I hate I was even born!" I screamed at the top of my lungs and didn't give a good goddamn what she thought. I'd come a long way, for a long time, to be with a mama that just didn't have no mama feelings for me. I was tired and mad for wanting somebody who didn't want me!

"I hate you!" I couldn't believe I'd said it. I'd gone and told Ruby what was laying at the bottom of my throat for so long. No matter what happened now, I'd said it—no taking it back.

I think I can recall the hard of her fists slamming into the left side of my face, knocking the wind clear out me, and all my sense right along with it! And even though I don't recollect pickin' myself off the floor, I do know I fell to it. I also don't ever r'member Ruby ever askin' 'bout the story of Mr. Benny wanting to do what the middle finger stood for to me. All she said was she'd heard all she needed to hear, and it was clearly a misunderstanding on my part.

I believe it was then that I first felt the hate of being a girl. I hated being a thing that folks called pretty and that gave mens the notion that pretty much they could do and say whatever they wanted and nobody would do anything to 'em. I hated light brown eyes and a smiling face that told the world "Look at me, look at me—do what the middle finger sign means anytime you want." All I could think of was what it must be like to be a boy, or a man. They was the things that made Ruby smile and know she was wanted. She had to fight for 'em and let it be knowed to all that they was the ones she loved. Far as I could see, you didn't mean nothin' to Ruby 'less she could take up for you and pretend like nothing ever happened. I could see how she just let me and Sister move out to Big Mama's. She must've did it by saying, "They never happened. They never happened"—and I knew she believed it too.

I could finally see that Ruby was never gonna hold me in that place where a mama's s'posed to hold her baby. Deep in the warm where we one time breathed the same air and took in the same food, a place where God watches over the two and keeps them as one. I was never gonna be one with my Ruby, the mama I'd 'magined, loved, and waited for all my life. Now I could see what my sister saw: that only a fool would sing a song to find somebody who didn't wanna be found. Somebody who could only see mens, not girls. Right then I wished I hadn't wasted all that time singing that song "Have You Seen Her" at the top of my lungs. Far as I was concerned, I didn't need to see her no more.

"You going to stay with ya' daddy in California. I already talked to him 'bout it, and he agreed that it's time for you to go and see what it's like to live with him. I think you gonna like it just fine."

I didn't know what to say to that. My mind, body, and breath was all trying to be in the same place at the same time, and it wasn't coming together too well. "Why I gotta go, Ruby?"

"'Cause I said so, and he finally wants you."

"But"—by this time the tears was hauling ass down my face—"I don't even know him, and what if he ends up not liking me, then what?"

"He's ya' daddy; he's gotta like ya."

"If he liked me so much, then why come I ain't ever lived with him b'fore?"

"You sure is a sassy li'l girl. You should try and mind ya' manners and not ask smart-aleck questions. You didn't live with him 'cause I didn't say ya could!"

It was planned that I'd leave my mama in less than a week's time. I was told that I'd be riding a big airplane, and it would take 'bout five hours to get 'cross the whole United States. Ruby'd told me all 'bout the time changes and how North Carolina was three hours ahead a California, so if it was gonna be four o'clock in Jacksonville, then it'd be one o'clock in California. That didn't make too much sense to me, so I didn't give it too much mind—I had other things to concern myself with.

To keep my mind offa the time changes, the pains that stabbed through my chest, and the too many times I'd have to run to a commode to keep from shittin' on myself from the runs, I wondered how airplanes stayed up in the sky. Whenever I could, I'd lay out near the barely running creek in the back of our house and watch to see if I could spot a airplane movin' 'cross the sky and maybe see how the folks fit inside. For the life of me none of it made a lick of sense. Outta nowhere I could hear Odetta Fontaine telling me 'bout how God'd made birds to fly and not people, and I again 'magined if she told me that 'cause she was as scared to get on that plane as I was myself. I wondered how it was for Odetta when Glenn left her. Did he go on his own, or did she make him go on account that she didn't want him anymore? And maybe if that was to cross his mind, then maybe it could make him want me a li'l more.

Hughes Air West, Flight 716, leavin' Jacksonville, North Carolina, to San Francisco International was gonna arrive on time, despite the heavy fog problem, the captain of the plane told us. He went on to say it might get a li'l bit bumpy, but for us to just relax and we'd be on the ground b'fore we knew it. I looked up as the FASTEN YOUR SEAT BELT signal went on and thought it was best for me to stay put. Earlier on, it had taken two air hostess ladies to hold me in my chair as the plane was taking off. They had to work real hard on account I was screamin' all over the place. I hollered for what seemed like forever as our plane pulled away from the place where I could see Ruby standing and waving good-bye. I stared at her till I couldn't make out her face anymore. The next thing I knowed I was dizzy and puking up and crying all at the same time. B'fore long folks was leaning over in their chairs and stopping in the aisles asking me, "What's wrong li'l girl, you gonna be all right?"

"I . . . want . . . my . . . mama." I couldn't get the words out my mouth in one full sentence for the life of me. All I could do is hiccup, cry, and try and answer folks' questions. As people kept coming round to ask me what the matter was, I watched their faces as I repeated to each one that I wanted Ruby, and each one would move past and say things like, "You'll see her again soon." Or, "Don't cry like that. The two of ya will be back together in no time." Person after person said the same things over and over again, till finally I let myself believe 'em and fell off to sleep.

When I opened my eyes I could see that I was not dreamin'—it was all real. I was in a plane, high up in the sky, surrounded by folks I didn't even know. It wasn't even like the Greyhound bus ride I took from Big Mama's to Ruby. There wasn't a bus driver looking out for me who would pass on to the other drivers that I needed watching, and there wasn't a Miss Virginia Reed who made time all but disappear. No, I was by myself with the kiss that Ruby'd left laying 'cross my face. As the tears started sliding out my eyes again, I unballed the toilet paper that one of the air hostess ladies had gave me, and I was careful to only pat round the place where Ruby had kissed me.

On one hand, I was beginning to see that my mouth was real bad—every time I opened it somethin' was sure to go wrong. On the other, I didn't see what was so bad 'bout telling my own mama that her nasty man wanted to do what the middle finger stood for. What was wrong with that? I didn't understand how kids could do stuff like lie and other things they not s'posed to and when they get caught, there'd be hell to pay. But when grown folks did stuff like talk nasty to kids, or even worse— touch they titties, or leave 'em, or whoop 'em for nothin'— nobody says a word. I wasn't gonna be nothin' like that, when I got grown. As far as my mouth goes, I had to tell Ruby the truth, even though she'd said in so many words that I was the one that made him wanna touch me. Deep down though that hurt me real bad, I was glad my mouth told on him. At least that way he might not wanna do things like that to other folks' kids.

After Ruby stopped denyin' Mr. Benny could do any harm, she'd started to tell me 'bout the great life I was gonna have with Glenn—my new daddy. Ruby said that Glenn was rich and worked for a Mr. Barry White—I knowed who he was 'cause all the women in the South talked 'bout how they'd only throw they panties at him, Isaac Hayes, and Teddy Pendergrass. Them women made me wonder if Glenn got panties throwed at him. For all I knowed there was gonna be panties layin' all round Glenn's house. I was sure I'd find out soon 'nough. The PLEASE BRING YOUR SEAT FORWARD sign was on as the air hostess ladies went 'bout the plane telling folks we was 'bout to land. I looked out my window, which I'd been 'fraid to do b'fore, and watched the clouds rush past us as the plane moved closer and closer to the ground.

Nadine, Glenn's wife, was s'posed to pick me up from the airport. I'd asked Ruby how'd Nadine know who I was, and she'd guaranteed me not to worry 'bout it. And now that I was here waitin', I was worried, even though if somethin' did go wrong, it wouldn't surprise me.

"Regina Ollison, could you please pick up a white courtesy phone."

I thought I was hearing things. I couldn't believe that some-one knowed who I was and was calling me over a intercom. Again, I heard the message repeat itself. I stood up and went to a information desk and asked them what a white courtesy phone was, and they showed me. Apparently, Nadine'd gotten the time I was coming wrong and was having trouble finding me. I agreed to stay where I was till she arrived.

"Well, hello there. It sure isn't hard to see who you belong to." A white woman walked up and stood in front of me. Her skin was the whitest I'd ever seen up close, and her dark brown hair lay against her shoulders in soft curls. Even though she was a li'l pretty, I didn't like the clothes she was wearing 'cause they made me feel funny inside. I couldn't figure out why, but her pants, that was three inches from her ankles, didn't look so good—they was high waters in a bad way. It felt like there was somethin' in her being so white that made me feel "real" black all a sudden.

"Hi. Are you Nadine?"

"Yes, I am. And you, no doubt, have to be Regina?"

"Yeah. Where's Glenn?"

"Oh, he's working. You'll see him later."

"Oh."

Nadine helped me go to the place where you claim your suitcases. I picked mine up and struggled with it as I followed her out the airport. We walked a short way and took a elevator to get to her car. And when we reached it, I had to let the words fall outta my mouth and have they say.

"This sure is a ugly car you drive. Is this the best you got? My mama, Ruby, she drives a new car every year, and they look way better than this." I didn't want Nadine to think she was gonna get in too good with me right off the bat. Anyways, Ruby'd already told me that I didn't have to like Nadine if I didn't wanna. She'd said that just 'cause Glenn decided to marry her, that don't make her shit to me. Nadine just helped me put my bag in the trunk, and we drove off.

"Sounds to me like you already miss your mom," was all she said, real quiet-like.

I didn't say a word. I hated the way she used "mom." It sounded real white to me, and what did she know anyway? And where was my so-called daddy? My belly was flip-flopping all over the place as I thought on seeing Glenn.

CHAPTER NINE

GLENN AND NADINE

I DIDN'T SEE GLENN the night I got to Richmond. As a matter of fact he was out of town then, and Nadine had a hard time getting hold of him. I knowed that she was trying with all her might to play like it wasn't pulling on her mind that he wasn't round, but I could tell by the way her eyes watered up when she talked 'bout him and how she didn't look at me head-on when I asked 'bout him again that it was hard on her.

"He's in L.A. right now working with Barry White, and he just can't get away; but I assure you he is happy you've arrived and will be looking forward to seeing you." How did he know I'd arrived if he wasn't to be found? Later I heard Nadine calling round Los Angeles at all hours of the night, asking folks if they'd seen him.

"Hi Ruth, it's Nadine, Glenn's wife? Fine, and you? Well, I just wanted to know if you've seen Glenn this evening? Yeah, he told me he'd be working late. I just figured that maybe he and John might be together. Okay. Very well then, Ruth. Bye now!" I watched as Nadine played like she was happy to be talking to her friend, but once she said bye, her smile slid from her lips while she stared down onto the receiver. Far as I was concerned, Nadine didn't have to go through no trouble finding Glenn on account of me. I figured if I'd waited this long to see him, a few more days wasn't gonna kill me. Anyway only a damned fool wouldn't be able to see that Glenn was up to no good. As far as I was concerned, him not being home was no big thing, but I felt sorry for Nadine.

It wasn't till I got to Nadine and Glenn's house that I'd met their kids—they had two girls. One was six and the other four. When she'd come to pick me up from the airport, her sister Rose had stayed with the girls. As we walked into the house the two girls kept they distance from me. As a matter a fact they hung close to the walls like moving pictures as they slowly made they way towards Nadine.

"Candace, Delia." The girls stood as close to they mama as possible, the whole while never takin' their eyes offa me.

"This is Regina, the one I was telling you about—she's your new half sister. Do you remember me telling you about her?" The one girl, Candace, who looked the oldest, pulled her bottom lip in with her teeth as she nodded her head up and down to answer her mama, while the younger one bucked her big green eyes at me and stared like she'd never seen a somebody with black skin color b'fore. All my life folks'd told me I was light-skinned and even went as far as to call me outta my name for it—like piss color and half-baked—but these kids took the cake; they wasn't light, they was as white as they mama. Not only that, but they had the worst hair I'd seen yet. Unlike my hair, that was pressed out and pulled into two braids, they had what looked like long nappy ropes growing straight out their heads. It looked like they'd never seen a pressing comb let alone a regular comb a day in their lives. I decided to try and be nice, so I let Nadine know I'd help her out with them girls of hers if she wanted.

"I'll help you comb their hair if you want me to."

"That would be really wonderful, Regina. As you can see, I probably need all the help I can get." The girls turned their faces into Nadine's body and hid for a while.

"Okay, it's time for Auntie Rose to leave now."

I watched as Rose kissed the girls and Nadine good-bye and said "Welcome" to me as she walked out the door. I s'pected that a "Auntie" was the same as a "Ainty" and realized that I was really round white folks. I was fine with that. Anyway, Miss Rose reminded me a li'l of that teacher Miss Francis at Roosevelt Elementary School—so she seemed all right by me.

"It's time for bed, girls. Let's get ready to settle down." I couldn't believe that folks really talked to kids the way that Nadine did. She was real nice like that. I hadn't heard her raise her voice once. She sho' was different from my mama.

I quietly cried myself to pieces as I laid on the sheets and blankets Nadine'd set out for me on the living room sofa and I listened to her put those kids of hers down for the night. The way she kissed 'em and said good night really tore me up inside. I ain't never in my whole life seen nothin' like that for real, 'cept for maybe in the movies. I was sho' missing my mama, even though she never kissed me good night b'fore.

Glenn and his family lived on a street called Downer, in the town of Richmond, California. Most of the houses on the street seemed real close to one another, and the road appeared narrow; it was only wide 'nough to let one car pass at a time. Glenn and Nadine's house was the smallest on the block. It had two rooms for sleeping, a kitchen, a bathroom, and what they called a family room. There was barely any furniture. The best thing you saw when you came into the family room, which was the first room of the house, was a piano. And on top of that was a big ole picture frame of Glenn and Nadine. They was all dressed up in they wedding clothes and feeding each other from the same piece a cake. And next to them was smaller pictures of they li'l white girls. Although Nadine looked all nice and stuff in her white gown, I thought my own mama would've looked prettier, and I wanted to know why Glenn picked Nadine over Ruby.

Next to the piano was a small couch that had worn-out arms covered by li'l sleeves. Next to that was a organ, and next to that a phonograph, with records underneath it. I figured that was Glenn's music-writing stuff. I wanted to know who learned him to play the piano and if he'd passed it on to me since he was s'posed to be my daddy. Maybe I could play too, but I just didn't know it.

The rest of the house wasn't much to speak of. As a matter of fact, I couldn't believe that this man my mama thought was a li'l bit famous would live in such a place. B'fore I left Jacksonville, Ruby made me believe Glenn lived in a big ole house with people carrying trays round to serve me. I had already pictured what my bedroom was gonna look like, with its canopy bed, just like Ruby had bought me, only difference being I would have all the other furniture to match. And it would have been delivered already painted, without the "dog-gnawed-off" pole. And I thought I was gonna have folks driving me round and pointing things out to me, showing me how lucky I was to be Glenn's li'l girl. Now, I was thinkin' maybe Ruby'd tricked me again.

It would be two days later that I finally met up with Glenn. I didn't actually see him at first, but I did meet his voice. I was sleepin' on the couch in the living room where Nadine had put me, since the house only had two bedrooms and they was occupied by her and Glenn in one and they two girls in the other. I heard a car pull up in front of the house and park. Then the key was turning in the lock all quiet-like—seemed like Glenn didn't wanna disturb us. I listened to the sounds of Nadine getting outta her bed all hurried up. She shuffled her feet 'cross the wood floor that kept the hallway from the living room, and then when she crept onto the carpet the wood creaked underneath. Since the room we was all in was mostly dark, I didn't trouble myself with trying to see what was goin' on. I just laid there and played possum.

"Hi, baby," she whispered to him, not leaving a whole lot of time for him to say much back.

"I missed you." I could hear Glenn and Nadine's mouths touch, and her sayin' something like "uhmm" then pulling away, as they leave li'l sucking noises in the air. Then they moved closer to where I am.

"There she is! She's every bit of you, and I assume, a small piece of Ruby."

I could hear 'em tryin' to whisper over my back while I kept playin' like I was 'sleep. Glenn and Nadine was standing over me, looking at me from over my head like one might stare at a sleepin' baby in a crib, not wantin' to wake her up 'cause of the racket she might cause. Nadine went on to say to Glenn how there was no denying that I was his, on account of how much I looked like him. I could feel his hot body and breath move next to me, to maybe get a up-close look. I kept holdin' my own breath. Finally, after what seemed like forever and a day, he moved away and I took new air in. I smelled cigarette smoke and thanked God that he hadn't touched me or woke me up. I cain't rightly say why, but I just knowed I wasn't gonna like him too much.

I saw Glenn the next day. Not in the way where you all sit down to a table and introduce yourselves so that everybody knows who you is, like at a new school. Nor did I see him like the kids on TV when they run up to a long-lost relative and show 'em just how happy they is to see 'em. No, I seen Glenn as he was leaving for the airport! It was clear to me that the man had only come home just to see my back when I was sleepin', 'cause Lord knows he was 'bout to miss my face, again.

There they was, him and Nadine standin' there by the door staring at each other like they didn't have no sense. She looked like she was holdin' on longer and harder than he was. His head was down, and she kept lifting it up with her hands, begging him to just stay a li'l while longer. "Come on, she's only been here a few days, and you haven't even heard her speak. Can't you just wait till she wakes up? And what about the girls? They'll die if they knew you were here and didn't see them. What's goin' on, Glenn?"

From where I was layin' I could hear and see the whole commotion. At first I wanted to listen, so I didn't let 'em know that I was awake.

"I really need to get back to L.A., sweetheart. We're getting ready to launch this new project, and Barry is really antsy. He really had a hard time with me leaving in the first place. Look,

I'll call all the girls as soon as I land, but I really do have to leave, sweetheart."

Through the slits in my eyes, which was narrower than a blade of grass, I looked him over good. There was that wide forehead that you couldn't miss if you tried. And his nose seemed wide enough that he could put his whole fist in it if he had to dig for a booger that didn't wanna go nowhere. And he sure did have a head full of hair. His hair was narrow at the sides and got round on top, in the shape of a new kind of Afro. He didn't look too different from the picture Miss Odetta had on her bed. And what laid on his head was also layin' 'cross his face, from one ear to the next. It looked something like wall-to-wall carpet, thick with no spotty parts.

I was 'bout to turn away but I didn't. Now that Nadine had moved her body out the front of his I caught sight of somethin' that looked swelled up in the front of his pants right where you cross your legs. It was nasty. I couldn't believe that he could act like that. Lord have mercy, he should be 'shamed of himself for wantin' to let that happen. I couldn't help but wonder if that was the way it was when he went out with Ruby. I could see the two of 'em as if they was right before my very eyes. On one of my snooping fits while I was living with Ruby, I'd found some of Mr. Benny's dirty magazines and read a couple of them so-called love stories in the back of it, so by now, I was able to figure out just how grown folks treated one another.

I'd wrote one of them love stories for Ruby and Glenn in my mind. I 'magined that Ruby and Glenn had just finished "doing it" with each other and Glenn had rolled over and let his mind wander off to faraway places. And there was Ruby, wanting to know if his mind was on her and how they was gonna be together for a long time to come. I see him wanting to leave—

wanting to go and make his songs with the famous Barry White in Los Angeles so that he could get real rich and go back to Texas one day and buy his mama a big ole house. I also saw Ruby wanting more for him than she could ever need for herself and not caring to stop him from having his way. Then Glenn leaves both Austin and Ruby behind. But he don't know that she got me from them being with each other, and she thinks having me is the same as having him. But one day she saw it ain't the same, and having me ain't so special to her anymore. I reckoned that stupid ole snow white Nadine must've come along while Glenn was getting famous. And I saw how she must've got in the way of him wanting to go back to Ruby and buying his mama that house and learning 'bout me.

I 'magined that Nadine wanted Glenn all for herself and them li'l Vienna-sausage–colored babies they had. And 'cause of Nadine wanting Glenn so bad I could understand that he didn't know that my mama had to be with big black vampires and mangy dogs who played like they was men, but wasn't. He didn't know that Ruby had to work two jobs and clean white folks' shit off 'em just to try and have some spare change to buy frozen pizzas while Nadine got called sweetheart and treated to a nice house that wasn't haunted by men's wanting to touch her girls in places that'd be hard to talk 'bout.

My mind broke off from the story—it couldn't work as no love story no more, 'cause what 'bout Ruby? Didn't she need somebody to take up for her, to show her that she was special and that she didn't have to give all of her prettiness away? She needed to know that no matter what, there was always gonna be somebody in the world who was making sure that she got her share. Maybe I had to be that somebody. I told myself to give Ruby another chance.

* * *

I looked back up at that white woman who was still stand-ing staring into Glenn's eyes. Finally, Glenn let go of Nadine's hand and opened the door. As he was just 'bout ready to turn the knob to go, I drew up from that couch and started talking to him.

"Hey, where you going?" I could feel my heart beatin' like somebody was skippin' stones 'cross it.

"Oh, hello there. Good morning." Glenn moved closer to me and put his hands on his hips. It seemed like he was scared to touch me. But that was okay with me, 'cause I was scared to touch a real daddy too.

"I'm on my way to the airport, Regina. I'm sorry I won't be able to be with you until I get back from Los Angeles. I just wanted to come and make sure you arrived okay, but I don't have time to stay. My album is due out in a couple of weeks, and I have to go and move things along."

When his words reached me, I could have sworn that Dick Clark had gave up on being at the beach and was standing right in front of me—and gettin' ready to leave. Lord knows I ain't never been that close to a black body that sounded like that.

"When you comin' on back?" I didn't know what else to say.

"In no time at all. And when I return, we'll spend some time together. But for now I want you to listen to Nadine and help her where it's needed. Will you do that for me?" Glenn had moved away from where I was and had the door closing behind him.

"Bye." I waved to him.

I didn't even know him, so wantin' to do something for him was hard for me to just say yes to. But then I thought 'bout how

Big Mama helped folks out all the time and how Ruby was a nurse and helped other people, and I thought, yeah, I might be able to do that for him. Even if it mean I gotta help Nadine out too. Before he left, Glenn had come back in from the car and handed me a package. He told me not to open it till he was gone, sayin' it was a record him and Barry White had been working on, but the difference was, it was Glenn singing on it—his very own record. He said that if everything went well while he was gone, then in no time, I would be hearing his songs on the radio. I played like I was smiling and watched my so-called daddy leave.

I don't know why, but as he left out the door, I wanted to cry. I told myself that it didn't matter and to let him go on his way. There was no need to be cryin' over somebody I didn't even know. Seemed like I had spent most of my life doing just that. If I wasn't cryin' for folks who was leavin' me, I was cryin' for folks who didn't want me round and made me leave.

Maybe it was 'cause I was so much older than them or simply 'cause I didn't care to be round kids too much anymore, but I never did take a liking for Glenn and Nadine's kids. Right from the start, it seemed them girls really didn't have a mind to see that I was half they sister. I think they was scared to be round me. When I told Nadine what I was thinkin'—that mouth of mine just couldn't stop itself—she said it was 'cause the girls didn't know me too well and for me to give 'em time. I didn't know nothing 'bout no time. I just wanted to be nice to 'em like I was with Ella, and I wanted them to like me the way she did. But them girls, they didn't wanna be bothered. They'd

rather be with Nadine than touch a stranger who had no reason to be in they house. There was many days that I'd watch
them run past me, like they was spooked, into they mama's
arms. I ain't never seen firsthand until then that a mama's arms
is where you go when you scared, and that she is meant to hold
you. That's what Nadine did for her girls.

Every now and again, I let myself 'magine that Nadine could
be my mama. That she could do the things for me that she
seemed to love doing for her own girls. But whenever I thought
our chance had come, something or somebody came right down
the middle of it. If it wasn't her whiny girls wanting her all to
themselves, it was that Glenn had lied to her again and pissed
her off to where she shut herself off from me, like maybe she
couldn't stand the thought of me being round her. I cain't recall
a time when Nadine touched my face soft, like she did with her
own, or dried one of my tears after I fell and hurt myself. I
knowed she could never sit me down b'tween her thighs and
comb my hair till I fell off to sleep—I knowed that 'cause of
how her own girls' hair looked like thick nappy ropes matted
right to they heads. I 'magined that them days was gone for
me—getting my hair combed didn't matter no more. Anyway, I
figured that if God wanted me to have Nadine as my mama
then he would make a way for us to be.

I made myself believe that Nadine's girls and maybe even
Nadine herself was scared of me 'cause I was a different color
than all of them. After all, I felt the same way 'bout Big
Lawrence and Mr. Benny. They scared me partly 'cause they
was so dark and partly 'cause they was plain ugly. And from
where I stood it was clear that I didn't look like I was kin to
anybody in that house—if color had anything to do with it. My
so-called daddy was real light-skinned, like the color of the

government-issued applesauce that came in them metal cans and that Big Mama used to make applesauce cake. Not to mention that from the way things looked, Glenn was trying to pass for not being black. Specially by the way he talked and all. Then there was his wife—she was white like the powdered-sugar icing that Big Mama used to make to spread on the applesauce cake after she'd baked it. And they kids was as white as the flour I'd use to dust the pan so the cake wouldn't stick. That left me. And if you put me up next to anybody in that house, I was the only one that didn't fit into the cake. I was as black as tar, just like Mr. Benny and Big Lawrence. I was starting to hate black.

There was this one time that me, Nadine, and her two girls was out doing some shopping at the local Kmart store and we ran into a friend of Nadine's. The lady stopped us and started being nosy by asking all kinds of questions.

"So Nadine, how are these lovely little ladies of yours? Aren't they the cutest things since ponytails? Their skin is so pretty and bright. And what wonderful hair they have." Nadine just stood there, smilin' at the woman. The woman didn't say a word to me. I played like something had caught my attention, making me look off into the yonder. Then "Miss Nosy" turned her head in my direction.

"And what do we have here?" My breath got caught in my belly. I waited to see what Nadine was gonna give her.

"Oh, uh, this is my husband's, Glenn's, other daughter, Regina."

"Oh, you never mentioned to me that he was married before."

I watched as the two women rested they eyes on the other. The woman gave me a fake smile, the kind that Howdy Doody wore all the time, and continued to talk with Nadine for a minute. I turned my head the other way. It seemed like whenever I was with a grown folk that had to explain me, they had to scramble for words and take what they could, like roaches when the lights was turned on 'em. I couldn't wait for the day that a stranger would ask who I was and somebody would return with, "Oh this here is my pride and joy." I knew it might happen one day, if I was good.

While Glenn was gone, Nadine signed me up for school. Downer Junior High was located in San Pablo. I really didn't want to have to go to another school and get to know more stupid kids that I'd prob'ly be leaving any ole way. I'd been to more schools than I wanted to let anybody know 'bout. The lady who was helping me wanted to know 'bout my ole school. I decided to not be too helpful.

"What's the name of your last school?"

"I cain't recall on account I been to too many."

"Oh, I see." The lady looked at Nadine over the top of her glasses and gave her a small, tight li'l grin.

"If you want the name of the first school I went to I can give ya that."

"Oh. And what would that name be?" The lady sucked her teeth at me like Flo did on Alice's TV show. I told 'em the name of the first school I went to so that they could send for my records. I figured the folks at Molly Dawson would know me a whole lot betta' than anybody in the schools of North Carolina.

I was given a readin' test and afterwards, the school people told Nadine I was smart and that I tested way higher than my grade level. I overheard that I was to be put in a class for kids who could do their work without a lot of help. They also said that I would need some work on the way I said things, but that that would come in time, with extra reading at home. They talked to Nadine like I was nowhere to be found or as if I couldn't understand a word they said just 'cause I had a backwoods-sounding accent. If they thought I was so smart, why come they didn't think I could hear? I was twelve years old, not some li'l baby, and I was sitting right there, listening. They should've just flat-out told me that I talked country. That way I would've understood 'xactly, and tried to do somethin' 'bout it.

For the most part, I came to like being in my new school. I was in some special kind of program. The counselor explained that the program was designed for kids who s'posedly learned at a faster rate than other kids. We got to take field trips to the Standard Oil refinery and learn how oil was made. I also got to learn how electricity was discovered and the way it was put together so that stuff could run—like cooking and lightin' up a house. I s'pose I was real glad to learn that the word *electricity* was good for something, since it had made me lose the spelling bee contest in my old school, Molly Dawson, when I forgot to connect the *city* part to the rest of the word. I also learned how to make a transistor radio with my own hands, which I got to keep and take home. There was nobody to show it to there, but that didn't matter so much anymore. Nothing really mattered too much. Not only did I make stuff and learn a lot, but I got to read whatever books I wanted to. Mostly I'd just read the same things over again, like *Huckleberry Finn* and *Tom Sawyer*. I liked them the most—it was like they was old friends who made me feel like I wasn't all by myself.

*   *   *

209

I made two friends at Downer. One was brown—the color of the Topaz perfume that Big Mama liked to wear. Her name was Anica. And my other friend was Italian, which accordin' to her really wasn't white. Her name was Marlena Ballentino. When I asked Marlena how come she got to be Italian instead of plain ole white, she didn't have a good answer for me. She told me to ask her folks.

"Why cain't you tell me?" I asked her.

"Why are you so worried about it?" Marlena answered.

I couldn't find a reason other than wanting to know if I was something other than black. The way I seen it was, if Marlena was the same color as any other ole white person, but she didn't have to claim white, then maybe I could claim something else, even though I was s'posed to be the color of black.

When I told Marlena 'bout my thoughts, she told me that wasn't possible: "Everybody knows that black is just the color black, and it can't ever be anything else." When I wanted her to tell me why, she told me that black was black and that was that. And that her father said that she could have black friends come over as long as they wasn't boys. I didn't even waste my mind to tell her that Nadine and Glenn had kids that was white even though they was black, and that made them something else. What, I didn't know, but they was definitely something else.

That night I went home and took off my shoe that had a black bottom and held it up to myself while I stared in the mirror. I also got a black crayon and put it to my face. I didn't look nothin' like either one. My own mind could see that no matter what Marlena said, I wasn't just black. As a matter of fact, my skin was as far from being black as Marlena was from being Italian. No, I wasn't gonna let her make me believe that I was black like the rubber sole of a shoe that was only good for shuffling bodies to and fro—and for leavin' dirty scuff marks nobody wanted on they clean floors. I was more than just that. I was brown-skinned with pretty eyes, just like my mama. I was also good at crab ball and knowed that there could be somebody somewhere who was gonna one day want me. And even if there wasn't, I was meaning to be somebody on my own. One day I was gonna be something else more than just a color.

I spent most of my time at Marlena's, 'cause she had a big family and I just fell in with all the noise and commotion that was already going on. I think it took many whole weeks 'fore her folks ever knowed I'd come round. Lord knowed I didn't wanna be with Nadine too much. Mainly 'cause it seemed like we felt the same way for each other. More and more her girls was the centerpiece of her life. Like when Big Mama used to put a lace doily on the table for company, and tell us that if we got something on it she would kill us. The doily was only for the company, not us, and we had to guard it with our lives from getting dirty. That's how I felt when I was with Nadine, like her girls had to be guarded with her own life.

Nadine read stories to her li'l ones, right after she'd put 'em down to bed in they room with the matching beds and sheet sets, and curtains and dressers that had piggy banks shaped like a goose. She read 'bout Cinderella and the Little Red Ridin' Hood, and each night finished one story and started the next— sometimes reading the same page over and over 'cause somebody loved the way it sounded. For a while I'd sit and wonder what it would be like to be treated that nice. I convinced myself that those was the ways of the white folks. And I couldn't stand that Nadine's girls was half being black and the other half white and they got the white mama like the one I wanted so bad. Some nights I'd just watch her girls and wonder if they would ever know what it felt like, not to have the same mama love them or want them for the rest of they lives. Even though Nadine didn't treat me like I thought she would, I told myself that at least I should be happy that she never wanted to hit me or feed me the remaining parts of picked-over food, like Big Mama and them sometimes did.

After a while, I stopped wonderin' 'bout all the foolishness that Nadine did for her girls and just started hanging out with my friends. I told myself that I ain't wanting no mamas, white or otherwise, 'cause as far as I can see they all is the same: good for nothin' but the ones they choose for they favorites. And that favorite wasn't me.

On Sundays Marlena's family loaded up they kids and went to visit her daddy's mama. Marlena told me I couldn't go with her family to visit the woman who lived in a place called Sonoma. Marlena told me it was 'cause her gran'mama hadn't seen a lot of colored folks, and it might upset her to know her grands kept company wit' the likes of 'em.

I didn't know the word *colored* was something that I could be called. In all my natural-born days nobody'd ever called me such a word. Plus, what did it mean? How could I be colored and black, and something more than a color? I didn't know how to put my mind round that. So I just said that was fine by me. I knowed that Marlena's gran'mama was prejudice and she just didn't know how to say so.

I was learning in school 'bout prejudice. We learned 'bout

Martin Luther King and slavery. I'd heard of folks who hated people like me 'cause we was dark skinned. But then I didn't understand why they put a white baby with brown skin and a white bottom on a bottle meant for white folks to use so they could get dark. I seen it in Nadine's bathroom under her sink. It was called "Coppertone Sun Tanning Lotion." I asked Nadine what it was, and she said it was to make folks with pale skin look betta'. When I asked her why folks who hate us wanna look like us, she told me that a lot of times people hated what they couldn't have, and that not all white people hated dark skin. I figured white folks was mad at God for not givin' them they fair share of dark skin, so they had to mix up some color of they own.

I decided right then and there that it was the color part that Marlena's gran'mama hated and not me, and I was never gonna act black or colored, whatever that meant. Even though I secretly wanted Marlena to take up for me and tell her gran'mama 'bout me and how I was different than just a color, I decided that it was all right that she didn't stick up for me, as long as she didn't act too much like her gran'mama.

On the Sundays when Marlena was gone, I'd just hang out wit' my other friend Anica. She was never my first pick of friends, but I figured she'd do when Marlena wasn't round. Anica was a girl without many friends to call her own, and she really got on my nerves in no time a'tall. I thought her to be selfish and greedy—she ate up all my food on any given day wit'out thinking two times 'bout it. I guessed that was why she was so fat. Plus, her mama was "a foot soldier for Jesus" and didn't seem to care too much for kids who didn't know the whereabouts of they own peoples. But at least being with Anica and her strange mama wasn't as bad as being with Nadine—they always included me in they conversations and showed me it was all right I was with them.

One day ole Miss Bushfield the "foot soldier" asked me how come I was always at they house, and where my folks was. When I told her I didn't know, she kinda looked at me all bug-eyed and spooked, like she had seen the dead. "What kind of folks let their children run the streets anytime they wants to?"

I dodged her questions like they was meant for the air. Then she'd start recalling Bible verses that damned sinners to hell, as she put it. I'd just laugh her off as funny, not realizing, till way too late, that she was a stone-cold monster 'bout the word of God. On occasion, I was invited to go to church with the two of 'em. Anica told me it would be a good idea since her mama thought me to be a li'l bit strange. She said going to church would show her that I was from good stock. Anica's mama said that all that came into her house needed to be clean. And standing before the Lord was the best way to clean the spirit. I didn't mind so much, seeing that I used to go to church most Sundays back home.

My first visit to the Church of God in Christ had the dickens spooked right outta me not outside of five minutes. I ain't never, in all my natural-born days, heard nothin' like the stuff those folks was going on 'bout up in there! This is how it happened: First, we'd get inside the church building and find us some seats—we had to be right up under the preacher's nose. I think ole Miss Bushfield had something going with the preacher, the way she flashed her teeth at him the whole morning. After taking our seats, we'd have to get some hand fans so we could cool ourselves off, in case the Holy Spirit made you too hot, in which case he might want to jump on you to clean your body of sins. This was news to me. At the Church of the Nazarene, they never talked nothing 'bout no Holy Spirit jumping on you and burning your sins outta you. Sometimes, while I was sittin' there in that pew, I would start repeating the books of the New Testament, just so my mind would be busy with other things, in case Mr. Spirit thought he was gonna pay me a visit. I would try and r'member the names of the books startin' with the ones I knowed well. Matthew, Mark, Luke, John, Acts, and Romans were 'bout all I could recall. So I'd say 'em over and over again.

Then there was the music. The organ, piano, drum sets, and tambourines would join the choir and start warmin' the souls up so that the Spirit wouldn't have to work that hard to get in them. Now you knew when the Spirit had jumped on somebody 'cause of the way they shot outta they seats and run round the whole church full speed, whooping and hollering Jesus' name at the top of they lungs. Many times they would hop on one or both legs and look like they was stepping in sticker bushes, or like Jesus hisself was beating the daylights outta 'em with an ex-tension cord. On a good day, if the Spirit had got all the demons out they bodies, they could then start speaking some words that nobody but the Lord hisself could understand. Miss Bushfield told me it was called speaking in tongues. After all the cutting up was done the poor soul would fall down on the floor like Donna Janine did when she had one of them fits. That's when the minister and his deacons would gather round the fallen soul and ask them to turn they life over to the Lord. It took as long as needed, 'cause the preacher wasn't gonna take no for an answer.

I was used to the Church of the Nazarene, where Jesus was

quiet and didn't run round beating the sin outta folks and forcing 'em to speak words that only him and his daddy understood.
He just hung over the pulpit on his cross, and on the windows
keeping watch over us. I kinda missed the Church of the
Nazarene. There they told me that Jesus loved me and that I
could be whatever I wanted, if I wanted to. And they never
held me down to no floor while smearing oil all over my forehead, tryin' to force me to turn my life over to Jesus.

When me and Anica wasn't draggin' ourselves to that tore-
up church of her mama's, we would either be making our way
over to Wild Cat Canyon, looking for the wildcats that the
boys in the neighborhood told us 'bout, or figurin' out and
singing the words to our favorite songs. Sometimes we even
played doorbell ditch; but that didn't last long 'cause Anica's fat
behind couldn't move too quick, and she got us caught a few
times. And the people threatened to call the police on us if it
happened again. I figured Anica wasn't all that fun, but again,
she was betta' than being with Nadine.

Livin' with Nadine just wasn't working no more. I didn't
know how to be when I was round her and them kids, and
whenever I was round 'em, all I wanted to do was be someplace
else. I figured that it was up to me to try and find myself a new
place to live. I guessed that if I was real nice to Anica's mama
and pretended to like the Jesus she liked, then I could maybe
live with them. And if that didn't work, I could try Marlena. I
tried Anica first, since she was seen as black like me.

I told Anica's mama that Glenn was a famous music person
and was rich and lived in Los Angeles.

"If he so rich, how come you ain't with him?" she wanted to
know.

"B'cause he ain't got time to write records and be no daddy," I answered her.

"See looka here!" I showed Miss Bushfield the record Glenn had gave me, and how he signed it and all. "To Regina, with all my love," it read. I thought to myself, All what love? But I didn't let on to the Jesus freak.

"Well, if he loved you that much he should have his God-fearing tail here to take care of you."

I told Miss Bushfield that Glenn also gave me a signed record from Barry White and one from Love Unlimited. He'd actually sent them to me from Los Angeles. Each time he was s'posed to be home I got a record instead. I was glad he'd sent 'em though, 'cause I loved that one Love Unlimited song: "Walking in the rain with the one I love." I'd rather spend my time listenin' to that song than be with Glenn.

After many days of going to that church and helping her round her house with her chores, Anica's mama finally told me that I was welcome at they house anytime. She say she loved Love Unlimited, and Barry sho' did remind her of some good ole times. She said that Barry was the kinda man that made the womens want to do the work of the devil. I offered the record to her to listen to for a while, but she said that the Lord wouldn't let her listen to no worldly music, 'cause it made her wanna wrongfully sin, and she needed to be able to tend to her flock—unlike my daddy and his wife. Miss Bushfield even went as far as to say she'd talk wit' my daddy if I needed her to. She told me she could have her whole congregation gather round his and Nadine's house and clean the bad spirits out! For a minute I thought I'd like that just to see what that ole Nadine would do when the spirit of Jesus was upon her, but instead, I told her no thank ya.

I taught "Walking in the Rain" to my friends, and we would walk to school arm in arm, singin' it loud as we could. I was always the one wit' the biggest mouth, and I liked that. Whenever I could, I'd be as loud as I wanted, and the good thing 'bout it—nobody seemed to care if it got me into trouble. That was 'cause there was nobody to care. When we sang, I decided that I was Glodean James—the lead singer—and Anica and Marlena was the backups. Neither one could hold a tune good 'nough to lead the song, but we did the best we could.

It was hard for me to sing like Glenn, 'cause his voice was real high, but I learned some of his songs too. The best one on the record, the same one the whole album was named after, was called, "I Love You More and More." I r'member hearing it on the radio for the first time! I could feel my head and heart racing to get to the finish line. It was hard to believe it was Glenn. The words was easy to learn, so I caught on fast; in no time a'tall I was singin' "Honey I love you more and more," over and over.

I ran down the street tellin' everybody that I knowed this man, that he was my daddy. Folks didn't believe me at first 'cause we didn't have the same last names, and I didn't know how to figure that one out. But eventually my friends came round to just looking at the record cover and seeing for themselves how much we had the same forehead and nose, 'cept mine was smaller. Plus I had that signed record. Marlena told me, "You can't blame us for not believing you when we've never even seen the man in person."

"You just wait," I told her. "He'll be back one day, and I'll in-na'duce him to you."

I learned to sing the song from the radio 'cause I just knowed Glenn was talking to Ruby when he wrote it; you could tell by the way he sang the words, all slow and sad. And if he was singing to her, then he must've been also talking 'bout me. 'Cause I was the proof they'd been together. I figured that his other girls was too young to really understand his words, and with him knowing I'd be listening, he decided to write a song just for me. Anyway, I was here way b'fore his other kids was. I was even here way b'fore Nadine. She herself told me when the two of them met, and I sat down, added all the numbers up, and seen that I was born five years b'fore he ever set eyes on her. And if what I was thinking wasn't so, it didn't matter any ole way 'cause I'd already told anybody who'd listen that the song was for my mama and me. It didn't even matter when folks asked me where she was and why wasn't she married to him in-stead of Nadine. I fixed that real good. I told all my friends that Nadine come round to our house one day, when we all lived to-gether in Texas, and she seen my daddy and stole him right out from under our feet. I told them that she put some kind of spell on him and he left us and never looked back until my mama hunted him down and made him take me. My friends thought Ruby was cool and that Nadine was wicked.

I think that way, way deep down inside me, in the place where I kept secrets, I was feelin' a li'l bit of what Miss Odetta said she felt for Glenn—I didn't know, but maybe I was a li'l bit proud, 'cause it sho' did make me wanna talk 'bout Glenn with a smile, even if it was only 'bout his music.

The first chance I got, I called my mama in North Carolina

and told her 'bout Glenn's song on the radio. I'd asked Nadine if I could call Ruby, but she told me that they was on something called a "budget" and long-distance calling wasn't covered. She told me that I should let Ruby call me instead. Well Lordy be, if I waited round for that, I'd never talk to my mama. I hadn't talked to her in I don't know how long, and Nadine wasn't gonna stop me! Plus, my mama didn't have all the money that Glenn and her is s'posed to've had; maybe that's why she didn't call me. So I did what I wanted—I called Ruby anyway. Not wanting Nadine to know, I snuck into the back of the kitchen and brought my voice to a whisper and talked on that phone to my mama.

"Hi, Ruby, this Regina, you r'member me?"

"Gina, you so silly, girl, of course I do. You my chile, ain't you?" It was funny how Ruby was all nice when I wasn't with her. But I tried not to pay too much mind to it.

"Why you whispering?"

"'Cause Nadine say I cain't call you. Why come you ain't called me?"

"Oh 'cause of the time difference. You always 'sleep when I'm woke. . . . Benny tells me to say hi."

I knowed she was stone outta her mind. But that was okay; she didn't know no betta'. I let her words go by me.

"Hey, Glenn wrote a song for you. It's called 'I Love You More and More.' You should listen for it on the radio."

"How'd you know he made it for me?"

"I just know!" I could just feel Ruby smiling on the other end.

One day, things took a turn for the worse at Glenn and Nadine's. A woman called and claimed that Glenn had left her

220

with a baby boy that was only a few months older than they oldest child Candace. I could hear Nadine crying on the phone:

"Glenn, I can't believe this! Who is this woman, and what is she talking about?"

I overheard Nadine tell Glenn that she wasn't gonna keep taking care of me when he was out gallivanting through the city without her knowing. She also yelled at Glenn for lying to her 'bout me staying through the school year.

"Glenn, I can't believe that you had me enroll Regina in school, when she was only to be here for a month. Why did you trick me into this, Glenn? I can barely care for my own children."

Nadine was crying loud now. What trick was she talking 'bout? And what was this month business? I didn't believe that my own mama had been in on some kinda plot to get me to stay with folks who really didn't want me. I wanted to call Ruby again, even if it meant that she would be mad at me, but I waited. But I did plan on asking her 'bout this trick.

"I need you here with me, Glenn. And the girls need their dad."

I knowed she wasn't talking 'bout me, 'cause I didn't need nobody's "dad." Nadine'd said all she needed to say.

Marlena and me decided it was time to learn to smoke. I figured if Huckleberry could go and run off with Jim the slave and the carpetbaggers and make his own way, then so could I. And another thing, Huck had learned to smoke the corncob pipe while he and Jim was traveling down the river hiding from his pap. I told Marlena and a group of our friends that I learned how to smoke from my mama.

"Ooh, you did?" they all ask me at the same time.

"Yes indeed, I did," I told 'em. They all loved my talking ways. They said I reminded 'em of the Beverly Hillbillies, 'cepting I was black.

We all went to the Kmart, and I showed 'em how to put a pack of cigarettes down they pants and walk out the store. Marlena wanted to pick the cigarette flavor, so I let her. I figured that there was nobody who was gonna get mad at me if I got caught anyway, so I dared myself—and stole them cigarettes in a blink of an eye.

"I want Kool Longs 'cause that's what my boyfriend smokes," Marlena said. We all agreed without pitchin' fits. Once we was safely outside, and seeing that we got away with it, we took the pack of Kool Longs and divvied each one to a member of our gang. On account there was five of us, we was sure to get two cigarettes apiece to start with. Since I had to go and open my big mouth, telling 'em 'bout how I knew how to smoke, they told me to go first.

"Why don't you go first, Marlena, since your boyfriend does it?" I tried.

"I said he was the one who smoked, not me! Anyway, you said your mama showed you how, remember? Now don't tell me you're a scary-cat-chicken?"

I knowed one thing I wasn't, and that was a chicken. Them was fightin' words. I took one of Marlena's cigarettes and lit it. I r'membered back on how I seen Ruby do it, and I did what I thought I saw. I inhaled the smoke fast, and as I did, my head took off on its own and started spinning. Not only that, but I started choking and wanted to throw up all at the same time. That didn't stop me, though—no siree. I looked at smoking like a game I had to win, and I didn't stop till I won. And I don't mind saying, I was sicker than a junkyard dog with rabies.

After getting away with borrowin' the tobacco sticks, we decided to move up to taking tennis shoes. Lord, I loved Converse tennis shoes. All the kids who had money wore 'em. And since Nadine didn't have money to buy me stuff with, I went and got stuff for myself. If I didn't borrow it from the store directly, I'd borrow money from the tennis ball cans that Glenn kept in the kitchen cupboard. I found 'em one day when the ice cream truck man came round and I watched Nadine go and get money to pay for the ice cream. I figured that since he was my daddy, then whatever he had for her, he had for me. Plus, how could anybody keep track of all them nickels, quarters, and silver dollars when they wasn't round anyway?

I didn't mind the stealing part even though Donna Janine'd told me 'bout not being punished till I turned twelve and now I was. I called it borrowing, not stealing. Sometimes, at night, just before I fell off to sleep, I would ask the good Lord to forgive me for my borrowing. I also promised that if Glenn ever sold some of his records, that he would pay everybody back. And if Glenn didn't, then I would one day.

"Glenn, if you don't get home as soon as possible, I am leaving," I could hear Nadine telling him for the hundredth time, over the phone. I watched as she cried like a baby but quiet-like, with her hand over her eyes. "Your kids don't even know you, and you've only seen Regina once in the four months she's been here. And I can't control her anymore. All she does is stay out with that Marlena girl, leaving the house and playing like she goes to school. Last month she missed more days than she attended. And when she's not with her cronies, there's the issue of the phone bill. She's been calling Ruby without asking. And she's violent; she's busted out the windows of my car. She is a problem! When are you coming, Glenn?" Man did Nadine seem sore. I kinda liked how she got all tough with Glenn. It made me like her a li'l betta' 'cause she reminded me of the folks I come from. Maybe if she was more like that all the time I could get on with her betta'—but I knowed that would never happen.

It was true. I did bust the windows out Nadine's car and rob her house. I did it 'cause my friends dared me to, and I'd decided that if somebody dared me to do anything I'd do it just to show I wasn't no sissy. Marlena told me that I should get Nadine back for what she did to my mama, so I did. Anyway, I didn't feel so bad for Nadine. From where I stood, she wasn't thinking 'bout my Ruby one li'l ole bit and not much 'bout me neither.

After a while Nadine was sounding like a rat caught in a trap right b'fore it got the cheese, and I sho' didn't see her "Glenny-poo" running home. If it was me, I would've left his sorry ass a long time ago. One thing I learned from Ruby, she didn't stay too long with no man who didn't wanna put up with her. Nobody would've had to tell Ruby or me twice that we wasn't wanted. Plus, Nadine should've knowed 'bout this other boy he s'posedly had. She should have seen'd it coming—I sho' did! Far as I was concerned, she got everything that was coming to her and more. After all, didn't she know that Glenn belonged to my mama first?

When I wasn't sneaking off and sleeping either in Marlena's or Anica's room, I would go to Glenn and Nadine's house and make my bed in they living room. The only real reason I came back to they house was so that I could use the phone. Almost every day I'd sneak and call Ruby to see if she'd come and get me. I don't know what Nadine was complaining to me for; she called Los Angeles every day, and I knowed that was long-distance too. I called Ruby 'cause I wanted her to know that the so-called daddy she sent me to be with was nowhere to be found most of the time.

"Now, Gina, you got to give yo' daddy a try. Folks do have to work, ya know," she'd say to me. I got to hate that word *daddy*. I tried to ask Ruby 'bout the trick Glenn played on Nadine 'bout me living with her for just a month, and she said for me to get my ass outta grown folks' way. And that whatever happened, it was none of my business. "If you'd just let the adults run your life, I bet you'd just shrivel up and die with nothing to do." I stopped calling Ruby so much, and I tried saving the calls up for a while, till I thought I couldn't hold the beggin' in me no more; then I'd call and beg longer. Ruby always said the same thing. "Girl, ya gotta give yo' daddy a chance." After a while I stopped asking her to come and get me. But I just kept on callin'.

Nadine was madder than a rattlesnake who'd been stepped on when she found out 'bout how bad my callin' had got. She stomped into the room I was in and threw the phone bill papers on the table.

"What is the meaning of this?"

"What is the meaning of this?" I yelled back at her as my eyes rolled in the back of my head. I knowed by now that Nadine wouldn't hit me, so I let myself get mean to her.

"I can't stand this anymore! And another thing, I will not allow my husband's ill-mannered child to talk back to me, so you had better watch yourself, young lady!"

"And if I don't watch myself, what you gonna do, white lady?"

"I'll show you what!" Nadine came towards me real quick like she was gonna hit me. Without even knowing it I was kicking her trying to get her off me.

Nadine grabbed her stomach and tried to scream, but nothin' came out her mouth. She backed away from me. I watched as Nadine's face turned all shades of red and her mouth started trembling. "Oooh!" She left the room with her arms wrapped round herself. I was real sorry. I didn't mean to hit her. I was just scared she was gonna hit me.

"Your dad will deal with you when he gets here," was all she had the nerve to say to me.

"Fine then," I said to her. That's if he ever gets here, I thought to myself. I heard Nadine cryin' in her bedroom, and since I didn't wanna know that I prob'ly was the cause of it, I ran off and stayed with Marlena a few days.

One morning, when I was back sleeping at Nadine and Glenn's, I heard the front door open real slow-like.

"Hello, Regina," the voice called out to me. "Shouldn't you be up and getting ready for school?"

I narrowed my eyes to focus on who was talking. It didn't take me long to see that it was Glenn.

A mumbled "Hi" was 'bout all I got out. B'fore another word could be said, two screaming children came running for the tall man with the big forehead. Nadine went towards the kitchen, playing like she never saw him. I watched as Glenn hugged the two girls.

"Candace, Delia."

"Daddy!" they both screamed, sounding like li'l sissy girls on one of them TV shows. I mocked they faces under my breath without saying they words. In all my natural-born days I ain't never wanted to call nobody Daddy other than Daddy Lent, and since he was always home, I never had to worry 'bout running up to him and saying nothing.

I guess I just didn't have them feelings that was s'posed to be down there, deep inside of you. The stuff that made you wanna holler out a name of the one you love, like "Daddy" or "Mama," and make you run and drop inside they arms. Nah, I didn't have that. I would've wanted to die first than to call Ruby or Glenn by Mama or Daddy. I guess I didn't like them like that. Nobody was gonna make me use them names—nobody.

I watched as them girls climbed in his arms, and he scooped 'em up like they was his favorite sherbert ice cream that he couldn't wait to lick. They didn't seem to wanna let Glenn go. And I hoped they wouldn't. The longer they kept him busy, the less time I had to be with him b'fore I'd be leavin' for school. I didn't bother to look at Glenn when he said hi to me and placed his hand on my shoulder. I don't know why he had to touch me. I went to the bathroom and wiped my shoulder off with my washcloth.

Usually I'd leave right after Nadine walked her girls to school, to keep her from seeing me while I was on my way to Marlena's. That way she wouldn't know where Marlena lived. But this morning, Mr. Glenn wanted to drive me to school. I was hell-bent on finding my own way. Not only did I not wanna be seen with him, but I sho' didn't wanna be caught dead in that car he drove. All my other friends' families had station wagons or trucks, just like the ones I used to ride in out at south Austin. But Glenn, he had to go and buy a big, green, wide car that could sit 'bout twelve people. It was named after the bus—

Continental—and I could see why! Glenn came round to my side of the car and opened the door for me. Careful not to let none of his body touch me, I scooted up against the car and slid into the front seat. Glenn pushed in the button to lock the door, then shut it. I was happy I didn't get none of his cooties on me.

I rode with Glenn to the school that day in quiet. I didn't wanna talk to him a'tall. I had nothing to say. Far as I could see, he was as much a stranger to me as the ones Big Mama and Ruby told me not to talk to. What difference did it make that he was s'posed to be my daddy? A stranger is a stranger.

Folks had already claimed that I was gonna be like Ruby, fast and quick with the mens. I wondered that he might've been thinkin' the same and mistake me for her. For all I knowed he could be just like Mr. Benny, and wanna touch my titties. And for all I knowed he might wanna do it with li'l girls. Any fool with a mind could see that he had kids by so many folks it seemed to me it didn't make no difference to him who he laid down with. So from the second we got in his car I didn't let his hands outta my sight. And to make sure he couldn't touch me, I kept stuffin' my body deep, deep inside the crack between the door and the car seat. Lord knows I would've rather been dead than to let any part of him touch me.

All the way to my school I could only wonder on why Ruby wanted to have me with this man. I wanted to know what Ruby thought was so good-looking 'bout him. I looked hard at Glenn, and I tried to find what she seen. I couldn't. I really wanted to like this man that my mama was so stupid for at one time, and for the life of me I was having one hell of a time bringing myself to it.

When I was on that plane flyin' to see "my daddy" I thought it would be the same for me as it was for her with Glenn. I figured that Glenn would hurry to see me every day from his job. And that we would go for walks and laugh at anything that suited our fancies. Or maybe he'd give me piggyback rides or a flower. I thought that's how it'd be for me. But it wasn't. I hardly knowed how to spell his last name that didn't even have nothing to do with me. If he was really wanting to claim me, Glenn would've had my name changed right off, just so that he could do right by me and my mama. But then again, Ruby and her boys, and Glenn, Nadine, and them li'l sausages, all had the same last names too. Maybe he really wasn't my real daddy after all—maybe my being kin to him was a rumor, just like everything else was.

While he drove, Glenn just kept his hands on the steering wheel and stared off into the yonder. I thought for sho' that he would try and say something since he hadn't seen me for so long, but no, he was quiet as darkness. We drove in quiet. By the time we pulled up to my school, I was more than ready to get out the car. And that's when my so-called daddy decides he wanna talk to my back when I turn to leave.

"Regina, Nadine said that you have been calling Ruby, even after she has asked you not to. I'm telling you now: do not call your mother for at least the next month. You need to give yourself a chance to adjust. Do you understand me?"

I placed my hand on the handle of the car door and pushed it open. I could feel my blood turn. "Yeah. I heard you," I mumbled under my breath. Mad as hell that he thought he could tell me what to do after only ten minutes of being with me in months, I slammed his ugly car door shut and turned to walk away. I heard him again.

"Make sure you come right home after school."

I didn't say a word as I walked off.

I could see it in the way he held his head. I ain't sure what it was, but I knowed it was coming. Maybe it was the way he never looked at me straight on. Or the way I never called him by his first name, or any other name for that matter. When I wanted anything from him, I'd just call out *"Hey."* And he would tell me hay was for horses, and I'd think he was stupider than anybody. When he didn't come after I called him, I would throw things at him, and he'd play like I wasn't there. Or he'd turn round and throw 'em back at me: pink sponge rollers, rolled socks, house shoes. It took a long while b'fore he did that.

I knowed without a doubt that it was coming after I kicked and hit Nadine. I knowed again when I didn't come back home after school one day. Two days. Three days, deciding that it would only be a matter of time b'fore he was gonna get rid of me, so I might as well stop being round him and his family. After all, I was gonna be leavin' 'em anyway. When he'd asked me where I'd been, I told him that I was sleepin' in a Laundromat next to a dryer. And when I got hungry, I ate li'l donut holes from the garbage cans in the back of the donut store. He didn't say one word.

I thought for certain it was comin' the time I got sent home from school for taking on the Garcia twins. One of the boys tried to cut me in line in the cafeteria, and I tripped him. When he got up and hit me, I snatched somebody's tray out they hand

and smashed what was left on the plate in his face. I didn't know the boy had a twin, who told me that blood was thicker than water right b'fore he punched me in the nose and they both dragged me up and down that cafeteria. I got sent home for a day. But that still didn't do it. It still didn't make Glenn pay me no mind.

That Christmas I could see that my so-called daddy had nothing for me. He gave me a jar of "tightly packed in vinegar" pickled pigs' feet that had been wrapped in a too-small elf's stocking. He didn't even bother to wrap the jar first. There was no tree. No decorations like all the folks on TV and my friends Anica's and Marlena's families had. Nothin' but them pigs' feet. Glenn didn't even have the nerve to come and give me the gift hisself; instead, he shacked up in his room and sent Nadine out to do his dirty work. That was it! I called Ruby.

"Hi, Ruby." I couldn't get the words out my mouth b'fore I was crying like a baby. "I don't wanna be here no more."

"What happened now, Regina? What did ya do?"

"Glenn gave me pickled pigs' feet for Christmas." Ruby told me that I was being silly and to stop telling stories. I hung up the phone on her, and she didn't call me back. Bigmouth Nadine must've heard me and ran and told Glenn. Next thing I knowed, he had his belt.

"Lie down 'cross the chair, Regina."

I couldn't believe what I was hearin'.

"Don't make me ask you twice. Now lie down!" I didn't move. I just looked Glenn right in his eyes and dared him to hit me. He did. Each blow he took left me hating him that much more. And by the time he was through, I had nothing left for Glenn or his family.

"You cut my skin." I pointed to the mark that Glenn had left on me. "You cut my skin!" I screamed at him again, this time spitting fire in his face as I waited for him to say something, anything. But he didn't. Glenn walked away from me and tossed the belt in a corner. I hated him, and I knowed that I would feel that way for the rest of my days.

I didn't cry not one single tear. I tried at first, but nothing would come out. Deep inside, something still wanted him to like me and want me more than anything in the world. I needed him to look in my eyes and know that I was his special girl, his first child. I wanted him to see that I was Ruby's girl. The li'l baby that they'd made when they really liked each other—b'fore Nadine. I needed him to show me how to call him "daddy" and let me feel what that felt like. But he was no betta' than any of those folks who wasn't even kin to me. I'd wanted to like him, to make myself believe that I came from a daddy. I wanted to have the same time with him everybody else had with they daddies. I wanted all that. But I didn't have none of it, and it was clear I never would. I left Glenn and Nadine's house and walked to the all-night Laundromat, where I spent the night sitting in one of them baskets next to my favorite dryer.

"Regina, I have to talk with you." I'd come back to Glenn and Nadine's to get a change of clothes, and Glenn cut me off at the door. "Nadine and I feel as if we are not able to reach you. We feel that all of our efforts have failed and you aren't happy with us anymore. This leads me to my only option. You have to leave. I've looked into a couple of places for you to stay—a possible boarding school. Or, if you like, you can try and go back to Ruby. I'm waiting to hear from her about this. What do you think of what I've just said?"

I didn't think shit 'bout what he just said. I'd knowed right 'way that he was gonna be saying something like this, so I already had a plan. I had tried begging Ruby to let me go on back with her, but I could see that she was just too busy to be bothered with me. So I tried to see if I could stay with Marlena's family. I told my friend the whole story of what was going on, and never once did she offer to have her family adopt me; so I figured they didn't have a way to make that happen. The only person left was Anica Bushfield. I knowed her mama was all tied up in the church, and knowing how church folks loved helping kids, I asked Anica to ask her mama if I could come stay with them, and she said she would.

CHAPTER TEN

NO ROOM IN THE END

WHEN ANICA'S MAMA said yes, I could come and live with 'em, I was so surprised I didn't say a thing. Anica jumped up and down and screamed 'nough for the both of us. I was glad I wouldn't have to see Nadine and her precious, perfect, light-bright children anymore and that she didn't have to feel like I was just dumped off on her—even if I really was. Glenn let me move in with ole Miss Bushfield, the Bible-toting Jesus freak, without blinkin' twice.

"Bible-toting Jesus freak" was what most anybody called ole Miss Bushfield. Everybody knowed that Anica's mama was strange. Not just b'cause she walked round preaching to folks who didn't wanna hear her "Gospel" as she called it, even after they told her to be on her way. It was the way she looked that made most folks wanna think on her as different. Her eyes was set real far apart, which made her look like she could see round the corner and watch whatever you was up to. And if that wasn't 'nough, her upper lip was turned up like it got burned, making her look like she was a growling fish with lips. And to top it all off, when she talked, it sounded and felt like she was spittin' S's at you. Secretly, I knew she couldn't help the part 'bout her lip, so I never made fun of her. Plus, Big Mama always said not to poke fun at people and they defects. The grown folks believed that if you mocked such folks, you could take on they ways. Lord knows I didn't wanna have none of that. I liked the way I look just fine.

So I tried to stay quiet when everybody made fun of ole Miss Bushfield. But when I tried to tell Anica why people said things 'bout her mama, she reminded me that at least she had a mama, and she knew where she was at all times. I let Anica slide on this, on account they was nice 'nough to let me stay with 'em, even if my way was being paid for this niceness. Glenn had promised ole Miss Bushfield that he would send her money for taking me in for as long as he was away, and since he didn't know when he was coming back for me from Los Angeles, she stood to make a whole bunch a money. Now, she was no Widow Douglas, and she seemed all right, to the naked eye, but as the grown folks would say, "Ya sho' cain't judge no book by its cover."

Everything got off to a smooth start. Glenn paid Miss Bushfield for the first two months and promised her that there'd be plenty more where that came from. He gave her a number she could reach him at if she needed to and left. I don't r'member any fancy good-byes with Glenn, and by now that was fine with me. I secretly hoped that I never had to see him again.

It was pretty easy settin' myself up in Anica's room. I didn't have a lot of things to take with me from Glenn and Nadine's, and what I did have fit right into a plastic Glad garbage bag. It was kinda good sharing a room with Anica. She had more space than any child I'd ever met. The room looked like it used to be a attic or something spooky where ole dead folks kept things that nobody wanted. I reckon it was the way the roof went up and down and how the li'l cobwebs hung on the corners that made it come off scary. Anica had tried to make it look as girly as possible with the pink walls and posters of singers, but it still needed a lot more as far as I was concerned. The best part 'bout the room was the bathroom was attached, and that meant we didn't have to run downstairs every time we needed to go. I was happy 'bout the bathroom part, 'cause lately my belly didn't seem able to hold on to nothing for any 'mount of time.

I thought I'd like being with Anica and her mama based on how nice they'd both been to me. But things started looking different after I moved in.

It wasn't longer than a minute b'fore mama and daughter was out shopping at the 5-7-9 store for clothes that neither one had no business wearin'. Lord knowed that Anica's rear end was 'bout as wide as two jumbo watermelons put together. Anybody in they right mind could see that she couldn't fit nothing that was a size 5 through a 9, unless she was to buy two of everything and sew 'em together. And her mama was no betta' off. When I asked the two of 'em how come they didn't wait for me to come back from visiting Marlena b'fore they went shopping, ole Miss Bushfield had a few words for me.

"I don't remember having to check in with you about nothing I do, missy. In my house I'm the boss, and I say how things is done. Now if you need somebody to take you shopping and buy you some things, then maybe you should call yer daddy. It's his job to care for you, not mine. I'm doing the good Lord a favor, not yer daddy!"

"But I thought Glenn gave you money to take care of me

too? I need some new shoes." It was true; I hadn't had new shoes since I stole the pair from the Kmart store. I had never noticed the fishing pole that was sitting in the corner next to the 'frigerator, but I had cause to notice it now. Miss Bushfield was sure quick with the hands, 'cause in the bat of an eye she was whoopin' on me with that pole like I was her own child! I let her get a few licks in; then I grabbed the small end of the pole that was doing all the hitting and broke it in half. The tears that wanted to fall so bad down my face waited at the edge of my eyes for me to blink. But instead of crying, I stared that ole dog down to her soul wit'out looking away or saying a word, I dared her to hit me again.

"Listen here, you li'l rogue! I'll kill you like your backwoods no-'count mama should've, if you think one time 'bout hitting me back. You li'l heifah, ain't you about as ungrateful as they come? See here, Anica; see what ya drug into our house. I know you was only trying to help out a friend, baby, but always remember, the very dog you rescue from the street is the one that'll turn around and bite the hand that feeds it."

I looked over to Anica, who I thought would help me out by maybe sayin' a word or two to her mama, but she never said a cotton-picking thing. She just looked away from me and turned her eyes towards her stanky mama—then took a plate of banana puddin' and sat down at the TV to watch *The Wizard of Oz*. I didn't care 'bout neither one of them anymore.

After a month and a half, I tried calling the number that Glenn had left for ole Miss Bushfield to use if something came up, and it didn't work. I tried turning the numbers round as many times as I could, thinking that maybe ole fish lips had got the number wrong. I even called the Hollywood operator and

tried to find Barry White or Glodean James, hoping they'd get
me to Glenn, but they numbers wasn't listed. But no matter
how many ways I dialed them numbers, Glenn was nowhere to
be found. It was right then that I saw that Glenn and Nadine
and maybe even Ruby was in on the trick to lose me. It was just
like when us kids played hide-and-seek back home and you
tried to find the best hiding place so you could never be found.
Or when you wanted to dodge the kid with the cooties who
wanted to hang out wit' you and your gang. Instead of telling
'em where your clubhouse really was, you'd send 'em off in the
wrong direction 'cause you didn't wanna be bothered.

Then, that Monday, soon as I came home from school, ole
Miss Bushfield told me, "You need to find someplace else to
live. There ain't no more room in my house."

"Why I have to leave; didn't Glenn pay you already?"

"That ain't none of your danged business what goes on between me and yer daddy."

Something inside of me just closed shut. When I was in
south Austin, I used to play with doodlebugs. I remember I'd
take a straw from a broom and try and tickle 'em and they'd curl
up into a tight ball. Right then, I felt just like one of them bugs.
Seein' how I couldn't stay no more, later on that night, I snuck
out the house and went to Marlena's. I told her 'bout how
Anica's mama'd told me to get out, and Marlena let me stay the
night with her.

The next day I thought I'd go back to the Bushfields to get
the rest of my things. I'd already learned how to look for truant
officers from Marlena. She told me that they watched the
streets for kids who didn't go to school and if they caught you
they'd take you to jail. Marlena said that I should be on the

watch for a white, brown, or beige-colored car that would have two mens riding in it as they stared out into the streets and bushes for kids. I kept my eyes open and stuck to the backstreets as best as I could. It was morning, and I figured Miss Bushfield to be off to work, so I walked straight to her house.

Once I got to the house, I walked to the backyard and tried to open the back door, but it was locked. Since I was the only one who didn't have a key, and was usually wit' Anica, the back door was left open in case we was to be separated—but not today. I tried jimmying the door, but it wouldn't open; so I started looking to see if there was any other way to get inside the house.

I seen that a window was cracked open, leading to the kitchen, and I pulled it open farther, dragged a garbage can over to it, then crawled into the house. Something inside me didn't feel so right 'bout this, but I kept on going anyway. As I was on my way up the stairs I thought I heard something behind me, but I knowed it couldn't be true 'cause everybody should've been at school or work. After stopping to listen closer, I decided to turn round to see what the noise was. Ole Miss Bushfield caught me round the collar from the back. She punched me so hard in the forehead with a balled-up hand I didn't know my tail from a hole in the ground.

"Whoa Nelly, what the hell are you doing up in my house when ain't nobody supposed to be here?" There she went, upside my head again. "How'd you get inside? I'm calling the police and let them know you breaking an' entering. Now get on up them stairs before I come after you. And stay till I come get you!" She pushed me up the stairs. After catching my balance, I took two stairs at a time; then I slammed myself in the room. I could hear her slowly coming after me, shoutin' that my daddy didn't pay her 'nough to be harboring burglars and that I was for sho' not going to be slamming a damned thing up in her house. "As a matter of fact," she said, talking out loud to nobody, "your daddy ain't paying me nothing at all. As a matter of fact, he's nowhere to be found. You gots to go, child; there's no more room in the inn," she screamed, laughing at the same time.

"Yes, Lordy. No room in the end." She laughed in a scary kinda way.

"Now I don't mind looking after my brother's flock! Thank you, Jesus! But I sho' ain't no danged shepherd. These days the shepherds gots to get paid! Hallelujah! In Jesus' name! That's right! Get paid. In the name of Jesus."

I knowed now that this woman had gone plumb fool. And that my daddy wasn't any kin to me a'tall! Nobody in they right mind would do this to a child of they own.

I started changing my clothes as fast as I could. Putting on the best things I had, and somehow knowing I wasn't 'bout to see my stuff no time soon, I picked my favorite red Converse sneakers and a pair of blue corduroy pants and shirt with a glittered rose on the front. I also took the plastic baggie that was holdin' my special things, like my mood ring, and put it in my back pocket. While I packed, I locked the flimsy door behind me, just in case the ole woman tried to bust in on me. I picked up Anica's phone. Calling the police was all I could think to do. It was clear to me by now that all Miss Bushfield was gonna do was hit me. Specially now since Glenn wasn't sending no money. I'd been thinkin' on how I hated him b'fore—this time it was for real! I didn't know the police's phone number, but I knew that all I had to do is dial the operator, and if I told her it was a emergency, she would put me through to the proper authorities. I had seen people on TV do this.

"Operator? Can you connect me to the police?"

"Is this an emergency?"

"Yeah."

"What's the nature of your problem?"

"I've been beat up real bad."

"By who? Is the person still there?"

"No." Just in case the police would wanna speak with ole Miss Bushfield and have her talk me outta wanting to leave, I decided to lie.

"Please hold."

"Hello, is this the Richmond Police Station?"

"Yes. How can I help you?" the man on the other side of the line asked.

"Hi. I was wonderin', if I didn't have no place to go, could I come down to where y'all at?"

"Yes, you can, young lady. Are you all right? Do you need help?"

"Nah, I'll come to you. What's yo' address?"

I wrote the number he gave me down on my mind.

"Hey, wait!" I told the man with the deep voice. "If I come down there, are y'all gonna lock me up in one of them rooms with the metal doors where you keep real bad people?"

"No, we don't do those sorts of things to kids."

"All right then, I'm on my way," I told him, hoping he would wait for me.

I knew I couldn't get out the house through the front door without being caught by the two-faced Jesus freak. So I went to the window that was facing the front of the house, opened it, and jumped the two stories, landing mostly on my feet but scraping up my knees along the way. My knees burned a li'l when I tried to move, so I sat crouched down to let 'em get used to the stinging. Then I was off. I walked into the church 'cross the street from where I was to see if I could find some of that holy water Marlena had told me 'bout. She said if you took the water and placed it right b'tween your eyes, then God would bless you with no harm and protect you for all your days. I figured I give it a try 'cause maybe her Italian God was doing a betta' job than the one who looked after the black folks.

While I was sneaking round trying to find the sink-shaped thing that held on to the water, I saw that a door was open to a office. I didn't see nobody inside, but there was a purse sitting right there in broad daylight, so I opened the purse real fast and took the first thing I saw: a ten-dollar bill. Closing everything back like it was, I tiptoed out the crack of the door I had come in through. I was 'bout to forget the holy water holder and just leave when I seen that it was right in front of me all the while. I took my first and second finger like Marlena had said her preacher did and dipped 'em in the water. Pulling my fingers out, I made a circle in the place right b'tween my eyes and played like I was drawing a cross, just like Marlena had told me. Then I left. But not before asking God to not be mad at me 'bout the money. I figured that God, of all folks, would know why I had to do it. Lord have mercy, did I feel bad, though. I walked out the building and stared at the house ole Miss Bushfield lived in. After sticking my tongue out at her and giving her the middle finger, I started down Rector Street telling myself that I was never gonna come back here again.

By the time I walked up the steps that led inside the Richmond Police Station and stood at the front door, my insides was doing something I had long forgot all 'bout. Ever since I came to Glenn's, I hadn't paid much mind to what my insides told me. From borrowing from Kmart to borrowing from the Lord, I did what I seen fit. But this time something spoke up to tell me what to do, and I listened. I listened good too. It was clear to me that outta all my li'l gang, I was the only one that didn't have a place to go to at night where folks really wanted them to be round. I was tired of it. And I was also tired of knowin' that no matter where I was, anybody could just say that they didn't want the likes of me and send me off. My mama had done it. Then Big Mama. Then my mama again. And now, my so-called daddy was doing it!

But I wasn't gonna give up on wanting to see if there was somebody out there for me. Deep inside me I heard a voice saying to me that there was somebody and that I just hadn't come up on 'em yet. I told myself to believe what I heard, until the Lord hisself was to tell me different, and somehow I knowed that if he was to tell me, I'd know. And like Huckleberry or Nancy Drew, it was time to take the matter of "me" into my own hands. Just like Huck, I knew when it was time to leave, and like Nancy, I knew when it was time to call the police. I figured that they could do a much better job than any of my peoples had so far. I also decided that no matter what, or how, I was never gonna let another grown folk get close to my heart—and that included my mama. Not even if she really begged for a long, long time.

The police building was made outta red bricks, and it sat in the middle of a green lawn. I didn't notice any trees or flowers, just grass trying to grow. As I entered through the big double doors, I stood and looked for somebody who could help me. I saw a man sitting at a li'l stand, talking to folks as they come in. I watched him for a spell, wantin' to see if I could see his mouth moving b'fore I walked over, thinking he was telling people what to do.

"Hi. I just called down here and talked with somebody 'bout turning myself in."

"What seems to be the problem, miss?" the man with red hair crawling all over his face asked me. He also had red freckles that matched his hair. When he talked, the hair that was laying 'cross his lip moved at the sides.

"I ain't got no place else to go," I told him, with my eyes stinging. For the life of me, I wasn't gonna let Glenn and his stupid-ass wife make me cry, or the crazy old Bible-toting Jesus freak neither. I put my hand to the li'l patch on the side of my head and started twistin' again. I could see Big Mama, in my mind's eye, talkin' to me 'bout going bald for messin' with that patch of hair, but I made her go away fast. I knew if I let myself think on her, I'd be sho' to break right there on the spot.

The redhead came from behind his li'l desk and showed me to the main lobby. He told me to wait right there and that somebody would help me shortly. I watched as people came and went. Mostly the ones that came was wearin' handcuffs, and looked like they hadn't seen the betta' part of day. There was always a policeman pushing 'em forward to make sure they wasn't gonna try and get away. I watched and waited, all the while thinking on how I should just run out this place. Not only was folks screaming to be let out them rooms wit' the metal bars on 'em, but all I saw was mens—nowhere in there did I see any girls turning theyselves over to policemen.

Even though I wanted to run from that ugly redbrick building somethin' awful and never stop, I just couldn't let myself go. It was like I was under a spell that was turning everything in my body to lead. So I let the thought of runnin' pass right through me and I plain ole sat there. Plus I knowed the police to be all right—on TV they always helped folks out—so I sat and watched the goings-on.

A short time later a man come up to me and asked if I was waiting for somebody. I told him I had just spoke to somebody on the phone and that I wanted to turn myself in. He asked if I had done anything wrong that I wanted to tell him 'bout, and I said no. I figured more wrong had been done to me than me to others, so it really wasn't a lie. He pulled out a piece of paper hooked on a board with a metal clip. The board had a pen on a string hanging alongside it. He asked me my name and a hundred million other dumb questions. I told him my name and where I had come from. I was tired of messing with grown folks who was no good, so I decided to make up whatever I wanted, just like they did. I told the man that all my folks had moved and left me for dead. I explained how I came home from school and all that was left was my tennis shoes, which had been sat on the side of the curb. I didn't even bother mentioning Miss Bushfield and her low-down dirty self. I sure as hell didn't wanna go back to her ugly ole house.

When he finished asking me questions, I asked him if they was gonna lock me up in one of them rooms with the gates on 'em. He said no and promised that those rooms was not for kids, but for me to settle down and everything would work out fine. I told him I wasn't too good with somebody putting me in a room and closing the door, that it was hard for me to breathe when that happened. He told me to just hang on and let him ask the questions and again, that everything was gonna be fine.

Fine! Everything was not fine! I should've knowed that nobody could keep they word for all the gold in the world. For as sure as I was gonna stay a girl and die, them no-good, low-down, lying-like-a-dog police people locked me right on up! That's right! They went and got this woman, dressed just like the men, and had her put her hand on my back and lead me dead smack in the middle of that iron metal cell with the metal bed and cement floor. They called it the holding tank, and said I'd be where I could see what was going on round me. And that since I was a minor, it was the only way I could be safe from harm's way. I guessed I should've run while I still had the chance.

CHAPTER ELEVEN

WHAT CHILD IS THIS?

THE NEXT MORNING, I woke up in the same holding tank I'd gone to sleep in the night b'fore. I couldn't believe that these folks had lied to me 'bout not locking kids up behind bars. These was the police—they wasn't s'posed to lie. It was like I did something wrong in trying to do right. All I r'membered from the night b'fore is having a long slow cry that just pushed me off into sleep. Now that I was awake, my body and eyes was empty, and my head hurt so bad I could've hollered some more just so I didn't have to feel it. But I didn't. I sat and waited and hoped for somebody to come and get me.

I wondered if God was still paying attention to me or if he was too busy with all the other people in the world. I 'magined him to be sitting up in his big chair watching over all of us and thinking to himself how dumb I was for coming to stay with a daddy that didn't want a thing to do with me. And for wanting a mama who seemed to be telling me she didn't want me. Or even for turning myself in to police folks who lied right through they dingy teeth. I sho' hoped God wasn't pointing at me and laughing.

Sitting on the edge of the hard, gray metal cot, I waited in the quiet of the morning. Inside this place, there was no birds singing or blue skies. No trees bending as the wind hollered through 'em. No, in this place there was just white bars and gray beds. There was also hallways that had sounds that repeated themselves while you walked down 'em. I heard the keys coming before I saw anybody and prayed that they was coming for me. When the man showed his face, I didn't bother to look at him where he could see me; instead, I barely cut him a look out the side of one eye. I wanted him to know I was mad.

"Come on; it's morning. Let's get you out of here." He acted like he was telling me something special. I'd already spent the night on his lie, and now he wanted to try and do right by me. I hated his fat ass. The more I tried to believe the things that grown folks told me, the more I felt like a window closing tight against a storm. I wasn't never gonna listen to or believe nobody again!

Waitin', waitin', and more waitin'. I waited while the sergeant-man said he was getting my paperwork together. I watched as they all seemed to not know what was going on. After a spell, a policeman who was helping the one who helped me said it wouldn't be much longer; I was already in they system, and a record was already started for me. I looked at that man like he was stone crazy.

"What's that mean, I'm already in yo' system?" I asked, my insides going tighter by the minute.

"Your name was logged into the system about two months ago. Have you ever been in any trouble before?" the officer said to me, and closed his one eye at me real fast. He had a sly grin trying to run 'cross his face at the same time.

"Nah, I ain't done nothing to nobody. Never!" So this is why they kept me overnight! I almost peed on myself. I couldn't for the life in me figure on what he was talking 'bout. Could it've been the folks at the church knowed who I was and called the police and told 'em? No! That was just the other day. They couldn't've got word that fast. I went round and round with myself, trying to know who called on me. Nothing I could think of made sense to me, 'cause if somebody had told on me that long ago, why didn't I get in trouble for it then?

"We tried to reach one Glenn Hathaway, but we can't locate him," the officer explained. "We got his number from our data, and after reaching his wife, Mrs. Nadine Hathaway, we have learned that Mr. Hathaway is out of the area and unavailable at this time. And Mrs. Hathaway is unable to supply care at this time. Therefore, we will be transporting you to Martinez, to the Edgar Children's Shelter. It is a place where children can be safe."

I couldn't hardly get from one breath of air to the next, with what was happening to me. It was like the world was gone and I was the only one left. There was nobody to call and tell what ole Miss Bushfield, Glenn, and all the others had done. And there was nobody to come and pick me up. All I could see was mouths movin' in circles, then flattenin' out to smiles with no meaning behind 'em. Just words falling on themselves.

There was one person I could call to let know where I was, and where I was going.

"Can I call my friend Marlena please, Mr. Policeman?" With everybody actin' so crazy, I just wanted to talk to somebody I knowed. I let the phone ring a coupla times, but figurin' Marlena had already gone to school, I hung up and followed the officers to their car.

I got into the backseat of the police car. When I asked the woman and man why I had to sit in the back like a robber or somebody in trouble, they both said it was to protect me. I knew they was lying, but I didn't fight 'em. I sat back and fixed my eyes on the station that I had spent the night in and told myself I would never wind up in a place like that again.

We drove mostly in quiet. The only talking that did happen was b'tween the two police people. I didn't pay them much mind, though; I was busy wonderin' where they was taking me for real. For all I knowed they could've been taking me out to kill me and then dump my body someplace. And if they did, who would care? I tried to think on betta' things. Would the Martinez shelter be someplace like where Oliver Twist lived? Would I have food to eat? Or maybe I was gonna be like the li'l happy white girl Annie who after all the troubles she had, ended up with some nice folks who wanted her for real.

As we drove down the road, I could see the sun struggling to break free from the clouds that was bullying her, tryin' to keep her from shinin'. Everywhere I looked there was large and small humps and bumps, looking like mountains, covered with grass. We rode through places called Hercules and Rodeo to get to Martinez. I imagined that Rodeo was a town where cowboys lived and learned to rope bulls and cows. As we drove through, I tried looking for barns and farms. I saw a few farm animals spread out here and there, but no corrals or barns. I later learned that Rodeo was a town like any other, with a name that wasn't even said the way it looked. I never understood how the one word *rodeo* could also be a town where folks lived called "Row-day-o." I guessed that it was sort of like the words *kernel* and *colonel*. Me and my sixth-grade teacher had a knock-down, drag-out fight when I flat-out refused to believe that a colonel in the army wasn't the same as a kernel of corn. Or that cents wasn't the same as sense. And what really made me mad was when I couldn't switch the words round so that a kernel in the army could also be a colonel of corn. I never worked that one right in my mind; I just learned to see that sometimes that's just the way things went, confusing with no hope of ever making sense. The situation I was in now sure didn't make sense, but I tried not to let them tears in my eyes spill out as the car pulled to a stop.

The sign read 100 GLACIER DRIVE, and underneath the numbers there was the words THE EDGAR CHILDREN'S SHELTER. The road we was on split off in two directions. The one on the left took you to somethin' called the Juvenile Detention Services; the one to the right led us to the shelter. We parked the car in a place that was marked for visitors, making me think that I wasn't gonna be stayin' here, only visiting these people. We walked into the gray building with white trimming, and I was told to sit down on a chair in front of a desk that had a li'l white card saying INTAKE.

On the other side of the desk was a man who was bald right down the middle of his head, leavin' what looked like two bushes on each side of his ears. After handing the bald-headed man a big ole gold envelope, the police people told me good-bye, and that they hoped everything worked out for me. It was real strange to me to be watching the police folks leave. I didn't know 'em at all, but somethin' inside me kinda wanted them to stay with me a li'l longer—at least till I knowed for certain what was going on. They'd lied before, but they was still police after all.

When the police people left, Mr. Porter, the man behind the desk, opened the envelope, pulled out what was inside, and read what it said. I watched as he thumbed through the few pages, and caught him as he looked me over. Finally, his face caught my eyes and stared right at me.

"It says right here that you have an enlarged protrusion on your forehead." He looked up over a pair of glasses I hadn't seen a few minutes ago.

What the hell was he talkin' 'bout? I didn't know what no pro-true-zhun was.

"See here." He showed me as he pointed to a piece of paper that had what looked like a body with no insides to it. The arms, legs, head was all there, and two li'l beady eyes poked out from the face. That's where I seen the X he was pointin' to. It was right on top of the left eyebrow.

I didn't remember saying nothing to nobody 'bout no pro-tru-zhun. I didn't even know I had one. I put my hand to my forehead and there it was, sho' as day, a knot the size of a big marble, stuck right there under my skin. I must have been so busy make-believing that I plumb didn't even feel the thing growing on my head. For a second I couldn't recall how a marble came to be there. Then outta nowhere, I r'membered that ole Miss Bushfield and how she'd punched me upside my head with her balled fist, with a ring on it. That must've been how I got the knot. I decided not to tell what really happened, 'cause I didn't want him to think I was some kinda sissy, so I said, "Yeah, I bumped into the corner of the 'frigerator and knocked myself." I hadn't even told the police 'bout how the Bible-quotin' Jesus freak had punched me in the face. From here on out my mouth was gonna be zipped, and the key was where nobody could find it.

He looked at me over them glasses, like I just stole something, and kept right on readin' the papers he was holdin'.

"I see here that you have a birthday in a couple of days. You'll be thirteen, is that right?"

I was quiet. It was like half of me knew he was tellin' the truth and the other half was fightin' to have him shut up.

"I guess so," was all I said, hunchin' my shoulders. I didn't even r'member tellin' the police people 'bout all that. Maybe that was 'cause of the information they had on me b'fore. It didn't matter to me, though; I never did take to birthdays. And I'd never had a party that I wanted to recall. 'Cept maybe the one time that Ruby showed up to Big Mama's outta nowhere for my birthday party—I cain't r'member the year. I can see it as if it was happening right now.

I'd told a few of the kids from my Sunday school class and some more from my regular school 'bout my party and that they was invited. I don't know how Ruby found out, but she did and she came. I had prayed and wished for her to come, and for once she did. When I seen her pull up, I went running to her car, and the first thing I wanted to know was how long she was gonna be stayin' so I could leave with her. "How long you stayin', can I go with you when you leave?" I asked in one breath. She said, "Hush up, chile, and give yo' mama some sugar." I took that to mean yes, and after I kissed her, I went and packed a brown paper bag. That whole day I forgot 'bout my party and the people who came to it. I hid behind trees, spyin' on Ruby, keepin' my eye on her in case she tried to leave wit'out me. At one point, after she sat down to play cards with the other grown folks, I jumped into the small boxin' ring my "cousins" made, and put on gloves and started punchin' the air. Since the card table Ruby was sittin' at was right next to the ring, I figured she'd watch me, and if she seen how good I was, she'd wanna take me home with her. At one point I believe I saw her look up and laugh at me. The rest of the time during my party, I didn't do nothing else but keep my eye on my mama. As the day got shorter, and the dark was roundin' the bend, I went and put my bag in her car. I tried to stay 'wake as long as I could so I could keep a eye on Ruby, but somewhere in it all, I fell off to sleep.

Well, the grown folks say some peoples wasn't good with good-byes, and my mama must've been one of those people, 'cause she sho' did leave without me, bag and all. I guess I should've got used to gettin' left, but I never did. I always believed my mama was meaning to do right.

Mr. Porter pushed a button and talked into the phone. He told whoever was on the other end that he was a-bringin' one down. I followed him as he got up and motioned me to come along. We walked down a hall that was all done up with windows, from the top of the ceiling to the floor. I counted: for every four windows was a door like the ones we had seen in gym classes. They had big metal handles that pushed open from the insides.

Once we came through the long hall, Mr. Porter pointed back in the direction we had come and told me that was where the boys lived, to the left, and that the girls was to the right, closed off by two big ole orange doors. On the one side of the windows was the parking lot and driveway I had just come in, and on the other side was the biggest backyard I had ever seen in my life. I could hardly believe my eyes. I seen kids of a lot of different sizes and colors outside. They was swingin' off monkey bars and playin' tetherball. I even saw a table with a black girl and white boy sittin' real close to one another. The girl had her arm restin' on the boy's shoulder, and she was talkin' to his ear.

And there was grown folks of all colors, who must've been watchin' the kids. Mr. Porter showed me through a door and asked me to sit down while he went to get a staff member. He must've gone outside, 'cause I heard kids yellin' and laughin' and callin' his name.

I sat down and again thought back to that birthday party many years ago that Ruby had came to, and I put my mind on the li'l white boy who was there. He was from my school class and was the first one to show up. He came, holdin' a small present, making me think he really liked me. His name was David, and I'd invited him to my party 'cause I wanted to ask him to be my boyfriend. As soon as he got to my house, with his gift in tow, I grabbed David's hand and took him out back to the old silver Airstream trailer that Big Mama had at the back of her property, where she kept visitors right along with her government food supply. Once we was inside and I closed the door, I asked David if he would be mine, like the li'l sayin' on the heart-shaped valentine candy.

For a minute David was starin' at me like he just been playin' with the Ouija board game and seen a ghost. Then he cocked his head to the side and said, "Girls ain't supposed to ask boys to be their boyfriends." After that he threw the wrapped jacks and ball he'd bought straight at me and run out the trailer.

That Monday in school, our teacher pulled me behind the flip-over chalkboard and said that it wasn't right for li'l black girls to ask nice white boys to go out with them. The teacher smiled and told me that David's mama wanted her to separate us so that he wouldn't be disturbed by me.

Seeing that he was ugly any ole way, I just dropped it. After all, I was tryin' to be nice and help him get a girlfriend.

* * *

I looked up and saw a lady standing in front of me. She was light brown with dark hair. Her small eyes turned up at the corners, and they was shaped almost like they was closed when she smiled at me.

"Hi. Regina, is it?" she asked. "Welcome to the shelter."

I smiled back a li'l bit and said hi. I watched closely as she moved 'bout the room, closin' and openin' doors and drawers with keys that was holdin' on to the belt loops on the pants she was wearin'. As I watched her, kids came running through the hallway, calling out, "Miss Rubie! Miss Rubie!" At first I thought my mind was playin' tricks on me. I wanted to know how could it be so, that somebody here had the same name as my mama? Was that possible? Other people started coming in, and there was screaming and hollering going on all over the place. I heard Miss Rubie's name called out again and again. And I watched to see who was gonna answer.

"You guys need to mellow out! Can't you see that I'm with a new intake!"

There she was right before me. Miss Rubie. Somebody here, all the way in California, have the same name as my mama. I let myself believe that since Ruby couldn't be with me, the Lord must've sent someone with my mama's name to look after me. I thought that was kinda nice, even though I didn't like Ruby so much anymore. But maybe this is where I was meant to be after all.

"I know somebody named Ruby too," I told the woman while she shut the door to the room we was sittin' in. "That's my mama's name." She answered that her first name was Jocelyn and her last name was Rubie. I asked her how come she had two first names. She just smiled and told me it was the name her parents gave her. I liked her. She talked to me nice, like I was important or something. I learned that she was from a place called the "Fill-a-peens," had never been married, and that her last name, Rubie, had been with her family for as long as they was all born. Listenin' to her just made me think on my own name and wonder why come it had to be so different for me.

Through the glass windows that went round the room I saw eyes starin' at me. The real small kids had to hold on to the windowsills and peek in. From the looks of how they eyes was all stretched into they foreheads, I figured they had to be standin' on tippy-toes. Miss Rubie shooed 'em away from the window and started asking me a bunch of questions like did I have anybody to call, a place to go on weekends. My eyes must've had 'nough, b'cause all on they own they just broke down. Miss Rubie had to give me a piece of toilet paper to wipe my face dry.

"Come on, Regina. I'll show you to your room. I think you've probably had enough for today."

I got up slow and followed Miss Rubie to a room where all I saw was beds. There was 'bout ten in the room, but only five was made, and now mine was gonna make six. I had a small cot, not too different from the one that was at the jailhouse. But, unlike the jailhouse, here there was other kids with me. At the foot of my bed was a pile of sheets and blankets.

Miss Rubie helped me make my bed and didn't go on asking me a whole bunch of questions. She seemed to tell that I wasn't able to talk no more. After we was through, Miss Rubie showed me where to turn the light off and left the room. Right before she was gone, she turned round and told me, "If you need anything, sweetie, just let me know."

I smiled, and pulled my belly tight as I nodded real fast. Please don't let me cry again, Lord. I wanted her to just go b'fore everything inside me fell out onto the floor.

I sat on the edge of the bed and felt the air squeeze out the plastic mattress pad. If I didn't know better, I would've thought I was sleeping on a bed for kids that went wet on themselves at night. I scooted back onto the middle of the bed. Then, using my big toes on both feet, I peeled my Converse shoes off, one at a time, and listened to 'em hit the floor. I didn't even take my clothes off; I just leant back until my eyes got heavy. All these kids round made me r'member Big Mama's. For a minute I thought 'bout what all them was doing. But I couldn't stay thinkin' on 'em too long 'cause my eyes wanted to close. The last thing I thought on was how Big Mama'd left me on that bus all by myself and how I ain't never heard from her since. Then I stopped thinking, and fell off to sleep.

CHAPTER TWELVE

THE RULES

"GOOD MORNING, pumpkin. Rise and shine." A voice spoke to me as someone pulled the cord that belonged to the blinds, raising them high into the window frame and making the room and everything in it come to life. B'fore I could rub the night from the corners of my eyes, I could see the brightness of day through my closed lids.

I sat up in the small bed as my naked toes landed on the floor. My socks must have come off in bed during the night. Pulling my hands from my eyes, where they was rubbing away the sleep, I tucked 'em under my legs and stared as this big-hipped stranger swayed round the room, waking up each girl as she opened another blind. In all my days, nobody had ever woke me up by coming into the room all happy and carrying on. The most I can remember is somebody, usually Big Mama or Lula Mae, telling me the first time round, "Get yo' rump up now and don't make me tell you twice!" as they slammed things all through the house and stomped holes in the floor on they way to the kitchen. And if I needed to be reminded, the covers that was keeping me all warm and sleepy would be ripped off b'fore I had time to take my next breath. Yeah, this place was strange, with its happy people. As I woke up more, I seen that there was other girls in the same room with me, and they was of all different kinds and ages. And all the covers was match-ing, so nobody got more than the next. I was still havin' a time r'membering the day b'fore. I just sat there and let my mind chase itself through the fields of my mem'ry. I watched as those hips led "Miss Pumpkin" through the room.

"My name is Regina," I said, letting the words roll out my mouth like a dare. There was so much other fussin' going on from the other girls being woked up I didn't think she heard me. I started to repeat myself, but was cut off by the sound of her voice.

"Why of course I know that, sunshine," the white lady called back over her shoulder at me as she gently grabbed a girl's big toe and shook it from side to side real fast. The girl wanted to sleep more, so she dragged the dingy light blue blanket that was covering her body over her head, trying to block out the sun and "Miss Happy Trails." I watched her grab somebody else's foot and shake it softly. As I listened closer, she was calling each girl "pumpkin" as she passed their way. Secretly, I was a li'l sad that she wasn't saying them silly names just for me.

"What's your name?" I asked her, seeing that she knew more about me than I knew of her, and we ain't never met till now.

"My name is Ms. Claire Kennedy," she told me as she made her way over to me and crouched down to look dead into my eyes. Hers was light brown, with specks of gold. She placed her hands on my kneecaps to steady herself, and the heat that came from her touch turned into ice as my whole body froze on the spot. "Welcome to the shelter," she said. Her smile was the widest I had seen yet. And she was so close that I could not only feel her breath touch my face every few times, but I could smell the food she must have just ate before coming to our room. It smelled like a bowl of Cream of Wheat with brown sugar and Pet evaporated milk. I loved Cream of Wheat.

Ms. Claire Kennedy kept standing right in front of my face, and I felt everything in my body go hard and stiff. No stranger had ever been that close to me without wanting something from me. But this time I wasn't afraid like the other times. I felt like I knew her niceness b'fore, a long time ago, b'fore I was ever scared. I reminded myself that it didn't matter how nice this Miss Claire Kennedy was. They all started out that way just to trick me into thinking they really liked me. But in the end, they all disappeared or sent me away.

I turned my face and stared at the ceiling. I could feel the wetness welling up behind my eyes. Ms. Claire Kennedy moved away from me and walked outta the room, her backside switch-ing and twitching as she quickly disappeared. Shake it, but don't break it, took yo' mama nine months to make it, I thought as I turned to watch the other girls get up and start dressing. There was six of us sleeping in the same room, and I didn't wanna know nary a one of 'em.

Suddenly Miss Claire Kennedy came trottin' back. "I need you to come with me, please," she said, pointin' at me. "Don't worry about changing your clothes. What you are wearing will do just fine." I looked down and seen that I had slept in my jeans and shirt. I stood up and left the room behind Miss Claire, lettin' the thin-carpeted floor scratch the bottoms of my feet. She led me into the same room I'd been in the day b'fore, only

261

this time there was another woman who looked like she was waitin' on us.

"Hello, I'm Sandy Mason," the lady said to me, and took a chair right next to Claire Kennedy. "Welcome to the shelter."

Man oh man! Was I tired of hearin' these folks say "Welcome to the stupid shelter!" It was like they had to keep sayin' it so I would think I was welcome for something. Miss Sandy explained to me all the rules, as she called 'em. I learned that the kids was on some kind of system called a behavior chart. All we had to do is every day clean our rooms, go to school for the whole day without problems, and get along with everybody we come in contact with. Miss Kennedy butted in and said that for everything good I did, I would get a gold star. And that five gold stars a week meant that I could, at the end of that week, go to the prize closet, where there was a lot of toys and games, and pick whatever I liked. But if I got a red mark—which was bad— I'd have a chance to redeem myself by doin' a extra cleanin' job or something like that. And if I got two red marks, I'd have to get a special okay from a counselor. However, if I got three red marks, Miss Mason said, there'd be no redemption possible, and I would be makin' my life real hard and unpleasant-like.

I listened as best I could, but they was talking pure hogwash. Who in they right mind had ever heard of such a way to talk to kids? All they needed to say was *Look!* If you don't give me no reason to whoop yo' ass, there won't be no ass whoopin's going on. Period. I would've understood that. But red marks and re-demption? I didn't know what they was going on 'bout. They also said that my stay at the shelter was only for a short time, and since I wouldn't be there that long, for me to make the best of it. How did they know that? I wondered, but I kept quiet. After making sure that I understood, Miss Mason left me and

Miss Kennedy alone and went out to take care of the loud and noisy group that was forming outside the room.

"Do you understand all that we've discussed with you, Regina? I know we're giving you a lot of information at once, so I just want to check in with you and make certain you get it."

I lifted my eyes to look at the woman sitting in front of me, and nodded my head that I understood.

As part of the rules of the shelter, they made me give up all my personal stuff. I didn't have much. Just a plastic baggie I'd slipped in my back pocket right b'fore leaving the Bible-toting Jesus freak. I gave over the mood ring I had put on. I'd found it on my way from school one day. I also handed over a half of a smoked cigarette that I was holding on to for a "friend." Miss Kennedy made me throw that away fast-like. She said it was illegal for me to have it on my person since I was underage. She smiled and went on 'bout collecting my things. There was one thing left inside my li'l plastic bag that had been in my pocket. It was a ball of tissue that I'd been saving for a long while. The nice lady wanted to know what was rolled into the paper that I was holding on to so tight. I looked down, waitin' for the tears to fall from my eyes onto my hands, fingers, and legs, but nothing happened. I was dry as dirt. I decided to ask if I could keep the toilet tissue with me.

"No, it will be safer in our care," she said. "Especially if it means that much to you." I gave it to her without a fight, and Miss Kennedy promised that it would be there when I needed it. She also told me that I could come and look at whatever it was at any time.

I r'membered on the day I had thought to save it. I hadn't taken a bath for so long that Nadine told me I was gonna run folks away 'cause I smelled so bad. I then ran me a tub and got in it. I didn't wanna get wet 'cause I didn't wanna wash the place on my face where my mama last kissed me. I didn't bother to tell Miss Kennedy that the toilet paper was holding the last kiss that my mama had gave me.

"Here you are, sweetheart," the hip-swishin' woman said to me, and handed me a pair of tan corduroy shorts and a striped T-shirt. "I'll need you to change into these, and hand over the clothes you are wearing to me."

Both pieces was folded nicely, and I could see a little pair of red feet on the shirt and short pockets. Oooh-weee! I just knew I wasn't gonna be able to take much of her! Now I know I was s'posed to treat all grown folks with a certain 'mount of respect by not talking back and doing what was asked of me. But these folks was asking too much. Whoever heard of people taking all your stuff from you, then tellin' you to make yourself at home? What kind of place was this? "Hey, why come I cain't wear my own stuff?" I asked.

"Because those are the rules," Miss Happy Trails explained as she walked on 'bout her business. Later on, one of the girls told me why they took our things. One reason was that they had to protect against lice, and another was if we didn't have our own things, we'd think twice about running away. Well, it seemed like they had it all figured out, but who would try and run away? Seemed to me, if anybody had paid attention when they came in, they would've seen that they'd be runnin' a long time before they got anywhere.

While I was changing my clothes, I heard a voice call out,

"It's breakfast time," and I sat and watched as the other kids ran out the room. I had no notion where they was going to eat, but I got off my bed and followed behind 'em, snapping the button on my shorts and wigglin' into my shoes at the same time. I didn't see 'em all last night, but there seemed to be a whole lot more kids than just the ones when I first came. There had to be at least thirty-five in all. We made our way to the eating room. It was a long room with real high plastic windows all round just like the halls I had come through with Mr. Porter. I could see outside to the play yard. It looked real big. I could also see that there was a big brown fence wrapping itself the whole way round the yard. It was the tallest fence I'd seen, and anybody thinking of jumping it would need to be good at fence jumping. I decided to let that kinda wondering alone. I took in a deep breath and sat down with the other kids.

Being at the shelter for the most part wasn't too bad. Us kids went to a school that was in the same buildings as where we lived, so we didn't get to go round too many other folks on the "outside," and that was a li'l hard for me. I missed being free with my friend Marlena and even Anica—well, not so much Anica. Even if it was less free, there were still good parts 'bout the shelter. One of the best parts of the shelter was I learned how to swim. Miss Mason and Miss Claire Kennedy took me and the other shelter kids to the city and county swimmin' pool. At first I didn't even wanna get in that water, on account I didn't wanna have to be swallowin' other folks' pee. My play cousins back in Texas told me that city and county pools was for folks who didn't have commodes at home. And most likely, if I swallowed water, it was gonna be full of pee and you know what else. I told this to Miss Mason, and she said that wasn't so, that there was too much of something called chlorine in the water for me to be worried. I believed her and jumped in.

Miss Kennedy was beginning to make my heart tingle whenever I got round her, specially while I was swimming, or at night when she'd come in the room where I slept and teach me how butterflies kissed. I cain't rightly say when parts of her started staying with me even when she was gone. I started to 'magine things again, like how it might feel if I was to get a new mama. All I wanted was to be round her.

Whenever we'd go swimming, Claire—that was what I called her in my mind—would hold her arms out wide and tell me to jump in the water. "Come on, pumpkin, don't be afraid. You can do it!"

When she said it that way, I believed her. In fact, I believed I could do anything. I'd stand on the edge of the concrete—toes gripping hold of the hard ground. Bending over from the waist with my hands above my head, I'd fall in the water, and Claire would always be there to make sho' I was all right.

"Hey there, champ. How does it feel to be so brave?"

I could feel my heart leave my chest and take a sit beside hers.

"Keep that up and you'll be ready for the Olympics."

I didn't know what that meant, but it sounded good anyway. After just a few lessons of learning to kick my feet, catch my breath, and turn my head, I was for certain that I could swim.

I plunged my body out in the water. "I can swim!" I screamed. "I can swim." All the while I was choking on the water that had got caught b'tween my throat and my nose, burning me till my eyes rolled to the back of my head.

"Not quite so fast," Claire told me as she put the flat of her hand under my belly and learned me how to float. I couldn't do it without her, so she never left my side. B'fore long, I could dive in the water and swim b'tween Miss Claire's and Miss Sandy's legs. They would stand in the water, spread they legs open wide to make a bridge, and I'd go under and swim through without kicking 'em or anything! Shortly after that I learned to jump offa diving boards. By the end of a coupla weeks, I was able to fight the water clear 'cross one side of the pool to the next. Both Miss Sandy and Miss Claire said they was proud of me. I felt like somebody's favorite ice cream cone that they couldn't live without.

Seemed like most of the counselors at the shelter was real good at something. They was specially good with working with they hands. I learned how to make crochet stuff from watching Miss Faustino, and from Miss Kennedy too. Outta all the stuff I watched them counselors do, this thing called macramé was my favorite. Once I learned it, I was able to make pot holders and wall coverin's. I even made a lampshade cover and sold it for a lot of money to a lady I met—only thing was she never gave me the money after I gave her the lampshade. The staff at the shelter told me it was a lesson to be learned 'bout trustin' people to things before they actually paid for 'em. I was never gonna do that again.

Being at the shelter was betta' than being anywhere I'd ever lived. I never had to worry 'bout being in the dark with no lights, like we sometimes was out at Big Mama's, or havin' to wait for the grown folks to eat and then gettin' whatever was left over, or watchin' Glenn's real children. No, I was in a good place. Maybe the Lord knowed what he was doin' after all, by callin' my bluff and havin' me leave south Austin. Even though I was likin' being at the shelter, I was scared to like it too much, in case I'd have to go back and live wit' my own peoples. I promised myself not to let nobody know how much I liked being where I was so no one would take it away.

I met Miss Coral Matthews the second month I was in Martinez. All kids who lived at the shelter, by law, had to meet with a social worker within a certain 'mount of time—and my time had arrived. Miss Matthews was a real ole white woman with hair the color of a Big Hunk candy bar without the peanuts. Even though she looked like she'd been round awhile, it didn't stop her in no way a'tall from seeming alive. That woman talked quicker than ole Cousin Eli talked slow. I learned to keep up with her just 'nough to hear what I needed to know. According to Miss Matthews, the county—that's what she called it—had tried on several attempts to get ahold of Glenn so that they could reunite us, and when that didn't work out so well, they'd asked him if he could refer them to my mama, and he did. They'd tried working on Ruby, and asked her if she could come and get me. She told 'em, "Let me see when I can get some money together, and I'll come and get her." But she still hadn't showed up. Miss Matthews never mentioned nothin' 'bout Big Mama, and neither did I. I asked Miss Matthews why I had to live with Glenn or Ruby, since it was clear they didn't want me. Miss Matthews said that my well-being was b'tween my daddy and mama; they was the ones that I belonged to. But I knowed better; what was b'tween them was what got me into this mess in the first place.

"They don't want me." I looked at Miss Matthews and let the words roll into her ears, giving her time b'fore I continued myself. "Anybody with any mind of they own can tell that none of my peoples wants me. I been here almost two months, and ain't none of 'em called. Didn't you tell 'em where I was and give 'em my number?"

Miss Matthews looked like the cat had stole her tongue right out from under her. We sat 'cross from each other in quiet. Miss Matthews was sittin' at a desk, resting the elbow that was holdin' up her arm, while her hand covered her mouth. Her eyes was looking at mine. My heart felt like somebody was sitting right there, in my chest, beating the daylights outta me wit' they fists. When the talking did start, ole Miss Matthews went first.

"From the looks of these records, you've been through this before, yes?"

"Nah. I ain't never been through this b'fore." Why does everybody keep telling me I have? My mind went back to the policeman, who'd told me the same thing.

"Well, according to our information, you were scheduled to come into the system four months ago! All your paperwork was drawn, and your father signed the papers. Did you know anything about this?"

Now ain't that some shit! My mind was spinning fast. This must've been what Glenn was talking 'bout when he said, "I've looked into a couple of places." It was all coming clear to me that Glenn must've knowed that Nadine or Ruby couldn't take care of me, so he had called these folks up and tried to pawn me off on them.

"How are you doing with all this information, Regina? How do you feel?"

I looked up at that lady and thought she was plumb outta her mind. What was she talking 'bout, how did I feel? How was I s'posed to feel?

"I feel fine," I told her as I slumped down into my chair. I wasn't gonna go into how mad I really was on account, it really didn't matter anyway. It wasn't like anybody was gonna do shit 'bout how I was feeling. I turned my eyes on the ole woman who was staring at me. "What?" I asked her as she kept staring. I wanted to know what else she wanted from me and decided to turn her question back to her.

"How'd you feel?" I asked her, thinking maybe I could borrow some feelings from her, since I didn't have any to give.

"I'm not the one who's important here. I'm more concerned for you. As you know," Miss Matthews went on to say, "the shelter is only meant to be temporary, which means a limited amount of time. It isn't our idea to have you stay for any long periods. We will be setting up foster-home visits for you as soon as possible, hopefully finding suitable placement for you until your dependency status can be determined or your parents show up."

"Can you tell me something?" I asked her.

"What is it?"

"What would make somebody want to throw out they own flesh and blood and not even think two times 'bout it? Why do folks go round having babies they don't even have a mind to keep in the first place? What did I do to make this be?" I watched as my words crawled into her ears, playing hide-and-seek wit' the answers she was wanting to give me but couldn't ketch 'em fast 'nough to say.

"I don't know what makes people do the things they do, Regina. And I'm sorry that I don't know."

What was it inside me that made me think anybody was

gonna give me an answer? So far nobody had nothing to give me but bad news. No God would ever want a child to go through all this stuff. Maybe there wasn't gonna be nobody for me after all. I let the talking go off by itself. To a place where mouths was moving in slow motion; words didn't mean nothing, and you didn't have to believe anything. For the first time in my life I wondered what being dead would feel like.

"Regina, Regina, are you listening to me? I will be presenting your case to the judge and recommending that your parents come to a hearing so that we can determine your legal status . . ." She talked on and on, but I plumb stopped hearing her. Finally she seemed ready to close her mouth.

B'fore she got up to leave, Miss Matthews said she had one more question for me.

"Regina dear, I was wondering if perhaps there is someone or another that you might like for me to call, so that we can get you out of here on the weekends?"

At first I couldn't think of anyone, but then I thought that maybe somehow Marlena could find a way for me to visit her. At first I was 'fraid to tell Miss Matthews. I didn't wanna know the truth if Marlena's peoples said no, and that I couldn't come. I finally decided to try her.

"I have a friend, but I don't know if they'll come all the way out here just to see me. But you can go 'head and ask 'em if you wanna."

Miss Matthews said that it would be good for me to give her the names of any friends and that she would see what she could do at least to get me out on some weekends. I gave her Marlena's name and number. I hoped she would come, but deep down, somethin' wouldn't let me count on it. I didn't know how to count on anything.

CHAPTER THIRTEEN

DO YOU LIKE ME?

GOOD AS LIVIN' in the shelter was, the city it was in, Martinez, was hotter than hell. Not only was it dry and boiling, but the ground that our shelter building stood on had more crack lines in it than a road map. It was just what I 'magined hell must feel and look like. Only difference being, you couldn't see the flames of fire shooting through the ground and burning names on the pews that was put on hold for sinners. I'd thought a lot 'bout hell ever since ole Miss Bushfield described it to me. She told me that there was a pew with mine and my daddy's name burned right into it, just waiting for us to arrive. Accordin' to her the Lord had showed everything to her in a dream and let her tell it—God never misled her. I tried not to let what that crazy woman said make a minute of difference to me. Whenever I'd r'member that crazy talk 'bout hellfire and stuff, I'd just try and think on what I learned from the white lady at the Church of the Nazarene with Big Mama—that Jesus loved all the li'l children. Thinking on that put my mind at ease.

Folks said the real reason it was so hot was that we was in the middle of somethin' called a drought and that's why everything looked dead and fried: the flowers that was s'posed to be lining the yard never even had their day. All that was left was yellow stubs where butterflies barely wanted to land. And any grass that had a mind for being green never made it past gold. It didn't seem like a place anything would wanna grow in. Sometimes, if I walked outside barefoot, I scorched the bottoms of my feet. So I learned fast to wear my jellies wherever I went. I was mindful not to stay in one place too long in case they decided to melt on my feet and stick me to the ground like the Wicked Witch of the West.

I'd been living in the shelter for a while, and there was still no word from nobody. I'd been to court four times, and no one came to check on me. Seem like not even the judge could make 'em wanna come. I was wanting more and more to forget that Ruby or any of 'em ever was born. After a while I seemed to forget what they looked, sounded, or acted like. I even stopped talkin' 'bout 'em altogether. When folks asked me if I had any brothers or sisters, I'd just say, "No, I don't." Lord knows I wasn't lying. And the worst part 'bout it was I hardly if ever wanted to be with my sister. I think that somehow, I must've buried her deep down inside with all my so-called kin. From where I stood, not even one of them scoundrels tried to call me and see where I was or how I was doin'. Far as I was concerned, I came from nobody, had nobody, and most of all didn't need nobody—'cept maybe Miss Kennedy.

And I'd already been on two foster-home visits that turned out to be no good. The first one lasted 'bout seventeen minutes flat. It all happened like this: Miss Coral Matthews picked me up so that I could go visit the Rowhen family. Since I was only going for the weekend, all I took in the paper bag was a change of clothes and my toothbrush. Me and Miss Matthews must've drove what seemed like forever in a small, ugly, white county car with a gold sticker on the side. I was so 'shamed of being with her in that car. Anyway we wound up in some place called Pittsburg, California—which was even hotter than Martinez. Once I got inside the house, I met Mrs. and Mr. Rowhen. They was darker'n I was, an' twice as ugly. The woman did all the talking, while her husband sat next to her and said, "That's right, that's right," to everything she said.

"We'd very much like it if you'd come and stay with us for a while."

"That's right. That's right."

"How does that sound to you?"

It sounded like I was gonna be dropped off somewhere I didn't have no business being. Hell would b'come a Sno-Kone b'fore I stayed in some house wit' a man I didn't know.

"The lady's talking to you, Regina. Can you speak to her?" Miss Matthews was nudging my leg and talking at the same time.

"Uh, yeah, that sounds fine."

I followed Miss Matthews out to her county car and took my bag from her. She waved and took off, but not b'fore she told me to be on my best behavior and that the Rowhens was good people. I watched Miss Matthews leave; then I took my bag and went inside the house with Mrs. Rowhen.

"Here's your room. You can put yourself down in it, and when you finish come on down and talk with me and Mr. Rowhen. And by the way, I heard that you can be a handful; so I wanta let you know that Mr. Rowhen, he's got a bad heart, and I don't want no mess."

"Yeah, I hear."

The woman left the room and shut the door behind herself. I wasn't gonna let nobody say whatever they pleased to me and think they could just get away wit' it 'cause I didn't have anyone to take up for me. What did she mean by *handful*? I was outta there.

I was used to climbing out windows, but this time I walked straight out the front door. And all along thought to myself that she could kiss me where the sun didn't shine.

"Where do you think you're going?" Mrs. Rowhen called out to me as I walked down her front path and hightailed it out the driveway. I could hear the Jheri-Curled Rowhen lady saying out loud, "Well I'll be goddamned!"

When me and my social worker was driving up to the Rowhens, I watched the roads she took and the exits she used. I also counted the number of stops she made once we got off the highway. I figured I could make my way back to where I wanted to be. I walked the sixteen or so miles back to the shelter.

They wasn't none too pleased to see me when I got there. "You know there's an AWOL report that has been filed on you, Regina."

"So what?" I told my counselor, not caring one bit 'bout what she had to say to me.

"Well, you probably should've stayed there, 'cause now you've lost all of your privileges for the weekend. Do you realize that, Regina?"

"I don't see why come it matters where I'm at, as long as I wanna be there," I told Miss Faustino as she stood in front of me with her eyes raised and her forehead scrunched up.

"Don't you want to find a nice home to live in?"

"Not really," I answered her with a lie. I thought it might

matter if she was gonna talk with my social worker; that way they would know I didn't wanna leave the shelter. It didn't matter—they kept right on working at tryin' to place me.

The next foster home was a li'l farther outta town. Again, I packed my brown paper bag with a weekend's worth of changing clothes. Miss Matthews said I'd think twice b'fore running from this home—on account we had to drive for 'bout three hours to get there. It was close to Bakersfield. Again we drove up to the house. This time Miss Matthews asked me to promise her I'd give it at least the weekend. I gave her my word; I'd do my best to do what she asked. I meant it too.

I met Miss Deanna Walton. She lived on her own with 'bout four other foster kids and her own natural daughter. Miss Walton had a li'l white girl that she was looking after, and all the rest was black. I wondered to myself, Why'd someone leave a li'l white girl here? I figured she must've been really bad to be put with the rest of us. This time, I let Miss Matthews go b'fore I started counting. I didn't stop till I got to one thousand—then I left. At least one time on my way back to the shelter, I stopped to think 'bout how I gave Miss Matthews my word, but I told myself too bad for her; nobody told her to believe me in the first place. I decided to do what the white girls did whenever they run away. Even though I'd never seen 'em do what they called "hitching," I'd heard 'em talking 'bout it. I got on the side of the road I wanted to be traveling on, stuck my thumb out, and waited till somebody pulled over. It wasn't long till this nice lady stopped, and I got in her car. She dropped me off five blocks from the shelter.

All the foster-home folks seemed to have agreed on the fact that I took way more than any one human being had to give.

How anybody could see all that after one visit was news to me. But if that was the way it was, then that was the way it would be. I didn't give a damn no more. It had been three months since any of my folks had tried to lift a finger and call me to see how I was doing.

My social worker, Miss Matthews, left—she didn't wanna work with kids no more. She said it was too hard for her and she'd had 'bout all she could take. I couldn't help but wonder if I had something to do with her leaving. I knowed I'd kinda been bad to her. Once when she tried to take me to another home, I asked her what color the folks was. When she told me black, I told her I wasn't going, and she said she'd have me locked up in Juvenile Hall for being "in-cur-ridge-abul." She took me to the folks' house anyway, and I locked myself in the car with her keys and threatened to drive off and run over anybody who tried to get in my way. Miss Matthews screamed at me that she was going inside to call the police, and I finally surrendered. The foster-home lady told Miss Matthews that she already had her hands full and a child like me wouldn't be good for her health.

The incident with Miss Matthews made me get so many red marks that I was off the charts for trying to redeem myself. One counselor said, "There isn't that much redemption in the world," whatever that meant. And 'cause I had so many incident reports in such a short time they wanted to send me to a doctor for my head, to see if I'd had some kinda breakdown. I didn't have no mind to know what these crazy folks was talking 'bout. Whoever heard of going to some doctor so your head could act right? And who cared 'bout marks, redemption, and fool stuff like that? As the grown folks would say back home in south Austin, "That ain't nothing but white folks getting big on theyselves."

One day I asked Miss Claire why I had to go and see somebody for my head. She told me that sometimes when people had things that was too much for them to handle on they own, it could make them b'come overwhelmed and anxious. She told me that when this kinda stuff happened, it was sometimes a good idea to have somebody to talk with, and that's what Dr. Barnett was—somebody to talk to. Claire could make me wanna go and talk to a rock the way she put things. I figured if she trusted the doctor lady, then I could too, so I went and met with Dr. Barnett. But she was no different from all the rest of them fool folks I knowed. All she wanted to know was, "What do you feel?" By the millionth time she asked me that stupid question, I almost told her that "I feel" like jumping 'cross that big ole desk of yours and knocking the mess outta you. But I thought a minute b'fore saying that and was dead set against it in no time. I didn't wanna have to go back to that jail.

I ended up getting a new social worker—her name was Miss Forde. After a couple meetings, Miss Forde told me that they'd made contact with Glenn, and that it might be a good idea to call him and talk with him, and if things went well, that I could maybe go on a home visit with him. I didn't bother to let her know she was wasting good thinking time on Glenn. Anybody could've told her he wasn't interested in being my daddy. But I called Glenn and tried to talk to him anyway. It was real hard to not say mean things to Glenn. Just hearing his voice made my flesh wanna crawl right off my bones.

"Hello, Regina."

"Why you leave me like you did?" I couldn't wait for him to say a word b'fore I came at him again. "I hate your guts and anything that you touch or think 'bout." Glenn was so sorry that all he did was sit there on the other end of the line, letting me talk any kinda way to him. The whole while I was talking to him, I kept wanting to say, "*Na na-na na-na na*, I can say whatever I want, and you cain't get me." The call didn't last for long. "Glenn, why come it seem like you never liked me too much?" I wasn't scared of him. I just wanted to know why he acted like he did. Why couldn't he be different and fight for me like Robin Hood fought to feed the folks in the Sherwood Forest— a story I'd just learned at my new school.

"Regina, it's not that I don't like you. That is incorrect thinking. It's that I don't love you. I've never loved you—I simply don't know how."

I let his stupid words sink into the back of my mind and secretly wished that somethin' bad would just happen to Glenn and he would just go away forever.

"Anyway, it is God's job to love you, not mine. His love is pure and incapable of running out. Therefore, my dear, he can never ever leave you. Believe me when I say that he's the only one who could possibly give you what you need. And I fear that you need a lot. And not only do I not love you, but your mother doesn't as well. She can't love you or anyone else for that matter, due to her selfishness and jealousy. Ruby simply can't look you in the face and not feel contempt for you. Looking at you only confirms her own sense of self-hate; therefore, she'd rather not. Can't you see that? It is as clear as water. Furthermore, not only do we not love you, Regina, but it is high time that you grow up and learn that no one can or will ever be able to love you like Jesus. It is time that you learn to love yourself with the help of the Lord. He's the only one who can help you. After all, you are the one who's decided to stay with the enemy. And believe you me, if you continue to choose to consort with the enemy, you shall suffer greatly."

When Glenn finished talking, my body felt like the devil hisself had crawled down my back and snatched my breath. It took all the words I could find to try and say somethin' to him. "The enemy?"

"Yes, the system that you are now a part of is going to fail you. All they want is to say that you are just another li'l nigger girl who isn't wanted by anyone—*so what!* Just remember, you are not the only one suffering, and nobody really wants to hear it anyway."

By then, I was like a mad baby that wants to say something out loud for the first time but cain't find the words to say it. All the words I was trying to grab hold of got caught in the breath I couldn't take. I hung up the phone on him and his words and asked myself what kinda man would be so mean to say something to me like that. But on the other hand I kinda thought that maybe he was right. Maybe that's why God was making things so hard for me—he was figuring that I was being selfish in wantin' a mama and daddy when there was kids round the world who didn't even have nothing to eat. I hated me for being so stupid and selfish just like my mama. I hated Glenn for showing me how stupid I was. I wanted to go away to a place where nobody could find me. Not even God if he strained his big ole eyes. I wanted to go where you close your eyes and don't come back from it and everybody would be sad and cry. I wanted to be gone. Just plain gone.

The next day I told Miss Forde what was said b'tween me and Glenn. She told me he didn't mean it and for me not to believe a word he said. She was wrong. I knowed that he meant what he said, and any fool with half a sense left to hisself would've knowed too. She said Glenn had somethin' called a semantics problem and twisted words round so that he could come out looking good. She told me that I shouldn't take too much of what he said to heart. I didn't know what all that was meaning and didn't rightly care. But I sho' was getting mad at her for wanting me to keep on fooling wit' that man.

Miss Forde fixed it so me and Glenn could see each other. Ever since he told me the truth, it seemed like he wanted to come round more than ever. The first time I seen him, he came round to the shelter. Lord have mercy, the man had gone from bad to worse. His hair was all growed up high on his head, and he'd grown lip hair to match it. Not only that, but he'd let the hair in his nose grow till it touched the lip hair. I didn't know how he could breathe. If that wasn't bad 'nough, he'd somehow got one of his front teeth to be longer than the other, making him look like a snag-a-tooth fool. I sho' did hope none of the other kids seen him, 'cause I didn't want nobody to think I knowed him, let alone was related to him.

During our meeting time, we sat in a li'l visitin' room that was connected to the main office at the shelter. Glenn could've taken me out for a while if he'd really wanted to, like to McDonald's or the park, but I don't think he wanted to be with me by hisself, so we stayed at the shelter. We never talked 'bout much other than him tellin' me how I was joinin' with the enemy if I was thinkin' I was gonna find love in the world. And that I was in cahoots with the devil for the way I acted towards him. He talked about Jesus and some man named Roy Masters for what seemed like hours. And if that wasn't 'nough he told me I was gonna burn in hell for being a rotten child. The nerve of him! I just got right up and walked out the room on his sorry ass.

Anytime I had anything to do with Glenn—whether it was a call or one of his li'l raggedy visits, it seemed like I got worse and worse at the shelter. I knowed it, but I just couldn't help myself. I would do stuff that was plain ole mean. Like this one time when I peed on the floor in my room and took a girl's Raggedy Ann doll and smeared her face all in the piss. I even ran away one time, but was brought back fifteen minutes later—I didn't know that a police station was right next door to the shelter whose main job was to keep watch for runaways. I'd never listen to what the counselors said, which meant that I never made it to the prize closet. They all said I was failing—all except Claire. She'd tell me that I was in a situation that was very challenging for a child to manage, but that I should continue to want to do better than I was doing.

I started just 'bout every mornin' with a red mark. And by the evening, I was "ir-redeemable," which meant that I would have to try again the next day. Only the next day never came. Seem like every time I had a chance to do a li'l better, I'd just get mad and think, Forget it! Since I wasn't nothing, that meant that whatever I did cain't hurt nobody, so I did just what I pleased. I even went as far as to do the worst thing that I could do at the shelter—I started smoking again. I learned to wrap tobacco butts that I stole from the counselors' ashtrays, or picked up from sidewalks, in the paper that covered tampons. I didn't even know what tampons was, but I'd convince the counselors that I needed 'em, and they'd give them to me. I learned these things from the older girls who came from north Richmond. This was also the start of me taking pills. The shelter was full of kids who could get they hands on anything you wanted, since most of 'em came from families who messed in drugs.

I took pills that made me feel like I'd been dumped in Big Mama's sometimes running washing machine or the dryer in the Laundromat I used to go to. I didn't like them pills too much, 'cause I was good for nothing after they wore off; so I decided to never, ever take 'em again. Somehow I knowed that I would never come back if I got too far out on them drugs.

Glenn came to the shelter to see me one more time. He brought me a bag full of candy with Pop Rocks, and a Coca-Cola along with that. I thought it was kinda nice until I heard from one of the other kids that if I mixed the two, I would die. I told the social-work lady I didn't wanna see him no more, which came as no surprise to her, 'cause he had told her the same thing.

After that, Glenn called me once more. He brought bad news: he told me that Ruby had called and said somebody named Aint Bobbie had died of the cancer. I asked him if Ruby asked 'bout me. He said nothin'. I didn't cry one tear—I had no feelings left for her. What came to my mind instead was the way I'd watch Aint Bobbie feed her babies. She'd take whatever food she was eatin'—be it chicken, greens, or corn bread—chew it up good, and put her mouth to her child's and spit the food right in. The baby, knowing no difference, would gum it some more and swallow, all the while looking in its mama's eyes. That's how I r'membered Aint Bobbie.

Aint Bobbie's dying wasn't so hard for me, but I couldn't believe nobody from south Austin called to tell me themselves. I never cried. I mean I tried to push a tear out my eye, but it wouldn't come. Finally I figured that I wasn't s'posed to care 'bout her dying, and instead I should just see that maybe God took her away 'cause of the time she'd beat me till my knee swoll. Hearing 'bout Aint Bobbie made me wanna know how that ole stank-dog Lula Mae was feelin'—was she sick too for bein' so evil? I kinda wanted for her to have died instead of Aint Bobbie, but I told myself that since I didn't have to see her any ole way that maybe it shouldn't bother me. I figured that all of south Austin was gonna be dead to me, so I should just get used to not hearin' from them and not caring.

CHAPTER FOURTEEN

BUTTERFLIES KISSING

I CAIN'T SAY I rightly r'member when Miss Claire Kennedy started wanting to do more for me than she did for anybody else. But I do know I must've planted myself right inside her heart by the way she seemed to smile whenever I'd come round. Maybe it was when I first came to the shelter and she called me pumpkin. Or when her and ole Miss Sandy would take me and learn me how to swim. I don't know when it was; I'm just glad it happened. And even though I tried not to let on, I couldn't help but let myself fall all out for her. Whenever she'd leave the shelter to go home, I wouldn't want to let her go. I'd always try and find a way to make her stay longer. Sometimes I might play like I had a stomachache, just so she'd take the extra time to call up the nurse—and wanting to know what the matter was, she'd stay on a li'l longer. Or maybe my arms would hold on to her neck and not wanna let go when she'd give me a hug good night—even if I told 'em to. No matter what, something in me couldn't get 'nough of her. I even went as far as to 'magine that maybe one day she might b'come my new mama. After all, the last home I went to visit had a li'l white girl in it and the woman was black, so maybe Miss Forde could let Claire take me.

If anybody was to ask me, I'd tell 'em I liked how Miss Claire told me how to speak better than I did. If I said, "I cain't help myself," she'd say, "You mean, 'I can't help myself.'" At first I thought her to be picking fun at the way I saw things, but she was so tolerating and smiley I knowed it couldn't be true. "There's no such word as *cain't*," she'd tell me. "And if you don't believe me, look it up in a dictionary." I went and looked it up in a dictionary like she showed me, and sure 'nough, there was no such word. Everything seemed to sound better when Claire said it. I even got to loving to hear her call me them sweet names she liked to use.

When I asked Claire why she called me names like "sunshine" and "pumpkin," she said that whenever she looked in my face, my smile was so bright, it reminded her of the sun. And the reason she called me "pumpkin" was 'cause she was fond of me. Whatever that meant. I asked her why she called other kids "sunshine" too—she told me she had to call everyone that so that they didn't notice if she only said it to me. "But don't worry," she'd say, "you're my very special pumpkin."

Whenever I tried to use Miss Claire's words, some of the other kids poked fun and said that I was acting all white, and that wasn't too cool. They also told me that black people wasn't s'posed to wanna be like white folks. So I stopped using her words out loud. Most times I'd think on the way Miss Claire said things in my own head, and then I'd tell myself to save as many of her words as I could, just in case I'd need 'em one day.

Secretly, I learned to tuck her way of talking away in a li'l pocket of my mem'ry.

Miss Kennedy was what I was told to call her. Us kids couldn't call on the grown-ups at the shelter by they first names on account it wasn't seen as respectful. I didn't mind that—it made me r'member being in the South and having to put "Miss" in front of all the names. Even if us kids couldn't say grown-ups' names out loud, I loved to listen to the other counselors call each other by they first names. That way I got to hear Claire's name as much as I wanted. Many times when I was just sitting by myself and thinking, I'd whisper the name "Claire" over and over underneath my breath in the hopes that somehow it would help me change into her li'l girl.

I was one of the few, if not the only, children left behind in the shelter on weekends. But I didn't mind too much 'cause this is when I could have Miss Kennedy all to myself, if I was lucky. If Claire wasn't s'posed to work, I'd hang out with whatever counselor was left to tend to me. But when it was her turn, things was special. She loved to go for rides and show me all the nice sections of Martinez, Concord, and my favorite—Walnut Creek, which is where she lived. The only hard part of the rides was that we had to travel round in a white county van, which I hated 'cause it made us stand out for everybody to see. Sometimes it seemed like people was pointing at us and saying things like we was retarded. When I asked Miss Claire 'bout why we had to ride in a big ole white "retarded" van, she told me 'cause we was special. I told her the only folks I'd seen ride in "special" vans wore helmets on they heads and slobbered on the windows. In our school back home, "special" was the ones to always get to school first, and everybody could see 'em get outta those yellow vans and make fun of 'em or try and get away from 'em in case they carried retarded germ cooties. Claire just looked at me and said not to worry myself 'bout that kinda stuff. Secretly though, I always felt sorry for the kids who rode them buses, and I promised God I'd never poke fun at 'em. I sure hoped that if folks seen me riding in a van, they wouldn't laugh at me.

There was this one time that I went to Claire's house and we didn't use the van. I r'member she had to get special permission from the higher-ups to use her own car 'cause there was no county van that weekend. Her car was blue, and it was big, and I got to sit in the front seat with her just like I did with Big Mama. While we was riding down the road on this particular time, Claire handed me a present—just like that.

"Here, sweetie, I have a little something for you. I wanted to wait to give it to you because you know I can't do it in front of the other kids."

Yes, I knowed that. Miss Kennedy had gave me lots of nice things by then, and I knowed not to rub it in nobody's face. We had worked out a understanding that whatever I got as a gift would have to stay in the big yellow envelope with my personal belongin's till I got into a permanent placement. Right then, I could see that Miss Claire was wanting to love me—just like I'd seen other kids loved when they had mamas, and like Nadine was with her girls. I'd also seen it and felt it while watching folks on the TV, but I never thought I'd ever have it for myself in real life. Maybe God was no longer sittin' down and laughing at me and pointing at how stupid I was. Maybe now he was trying to do good by me.

"You got this for me? What is it?" I asked her, barely able to hold on to myself.

"Yes, it's for you. Go on and open it."

I hardly knowed what to do with myself. I took my time opening the package. Instead of tearing through it as fast as I could, I held it in my hands for a small while. I wanted to hold on to the feeling of someone caring 'bout me.

"Go ahead, silly, open it. It won't bite you, I promise."

I took my eyes offa Miss Claire's face and turned back to my present. Next, I took each corner as slow as I could, peeling the tape back inch by inch. I was wanting to save the blue bow that sat in the middle of the gift, so I took it off and put it in my pocket. Finally, I pulled the paper back and looked at what was inside. I wasn't quite certain what it was, so I held it out from me a ways and studied it for a minute.

"Know what that is?" Claire finally asked me.

"Nope, I sure don't," I answered her with wonder sitting deep b'tween my eyebrows. "What is it?"

"It's a handheld tape recorder with earphones. I guessed that since you enjoy singing and talking, maybe you could use this to record with."

I'd had a tape recorder at school that we was allowed to make music with, but I'd never seen one quite like this. I was so surprised I didn't know what to say. "Oh, that's so nice. I love it a whole lot, and I ain't gonna let nobody else touch it! Plus, I'll make you a tape from KFRC radio station the first chance I get, or I'll sing you something." And I meant it too. I loved my new gift, and I wasn't gonna never lose it from moving so much, like I'd done with most of the things I'd ever gotten in my life. This would be different. It was a gift from somebody who loved me.

"Well, sweetheart, I'm glad you love it. Because I want you to have something special; you deserve it." Praise the Lord! We rode the rest of the way with li'l smiles splattered on both our faces.

From the first time I ever went to Miss Claire's house I was able to tell her how to get there. She told me I had a mem'ry like a elephant and that she was gonna have to watch what she said and did round me. She winked her eye at me while talking. Times when Miss Claire wasn't working, I would run off from the shelter to look for her. I didn't like it when she wasn't close by. It was like I stopped breathing or something. And the only way I could start would be if she would smile at me and call me sweet names. Just to be near her made me wanna do betta' at everything.

One night I just couldn't take it. I decided to see if Miss Kennedy wanted me as much as I wanted her. I told myself that if I went to her house and she let me stay, then that'd mean she wanted me for herself and that I could prob'ly become her daughter. I decided to leave right after dinnertime.

The coast was clear. I got down on my knees and crawled past the staff office. Since the top part of the office was glass, making it so you could easily see who came and went, crawling was the only way out. Slowly I made my way without nobody taking notice. I snuck out a side gate that was knowed for not making any noise. I'd watched the older girls go out that door to smoke so nobody'd hear them leave. Out the corner of my eye I could see inside the office, and I seen Miss Kennedy signing her name out in the big red book that all the staff had to use—she was on her way home.

I made my way to the edge of the yard. After climbing to the top and jumping the big Cyclone fence that went clear round the shelter, I made my way all the way to Miss Claire's house. I crossed highways and hid in bushes along the interstate whenever I seen a police car, and sure enough I arrived at her house in what seemed like no time a'tall.

I knocked on her door a few times, but nobody answered. "Miss Kennedy, you in there, Miss Kennedy!" I tried to keep my voice down 'cause I didn't wanna get her next-door neighbors going. After a while, I decided to sit on the steps and wait for her to get home.

"Oh my God! You startled me. What on earth are you doing here, Regina?" Her white face in the dark looked like it was glowing.

"I wanted to be with you."

"Sweetheart, you know that it doesn't work like this, don't you?" She stared down at me as she asked me that question.

"Yeah, I know, but I still wanna be here with you. I hate being at that shelter. They don't understand me like you do. Nobody understands me like you do. Why can't I just be here with you like normal kids do?"

"I know, sweetheart, but that's where you live for now and where I work. And if we both want it to continue to be that way, we have to put up with the rules. I didn't make them, but we have to live by them."

"I hate them stupid rules. Whoever made 'em must not have or like kids. Anybody knows that if you like somebody and they like you, it ain't easy to stay away from 'em."

Claire moved towards me as I was sitting on her stoop. She put her hand under my chin and lightly shook it. "What am I going to do with you?"

I pushed my shoulders up and down. For a minute I didn't know what to say to her question. I wasn't for sure if she was asking or just talking out loud. But whatever her reason was, I decided to just say what I'd wanted to say, if she was really meaning to ask me. "Keep me, I hope." I sat and studied Miss Claire to see how she was gonna act hearing my bold talk.

All she said was, "Come on inside; you must be cold."

I wasn't cold, but I followed her anyway.

"You know I have to call Mr. Porter at the shelter and let him know where you are, don't you?"

I nodded.

Claire stood for a minute with the receiver in her hand and then said, "I'll take you back in the morning; you'll have to spend the night here, okay?"

"*Okay!*" I listened as she told the shelter folks that she was too run-down to drive me back that night and that she'd have me there early the next day. That night I got to sleep in a beautiful white nightgown with lace round the bottom. I counted five tiny li'l buttons that ran up into the collar and stood up at attention round my neck. I looked like one of them queens in a ole movie. After slowly, slowly, brushing my teeth with Claire's toothbrush, I got in bed. She said she had some work to do, so she stayed up. I waited for her, crossin' everything I could on my body—toes, fingers, legs, and feet—and prayin' that she could be mine.

"All right now, Mr. God, if you can hear and see anything that I'm saying or doing right now, then you know how bad I need a mama. If you ain't too busy and too tired from helping those other folks, please hear my prayer. Amen." Just shortly b'fore my eyes clamped shut from being plumb tired, I could feel Claire slide underneath the covers. Her big toe accident'ly scraped my leg as it was finding its way to the foot of the bed. I pulled my leg up and held on to it all night to seal her touch into me.

She kissed me on my forehead and said, "Sweet dreams, pumpkin."

Not only did Miss Claire take me places and do nice things for me, but she also told me 'bout a man who was kinda like God—his name was Meher Baba. She wore his picture in a beaded necklace round her neck. When I asked 'bout it she told me he was something called a guru. At first, I was a li'l scared 'cause Big Mama had told me that white folks was knowed for being devil worshipers. But after she explained that he was just like Jesus, but from a different place, I felt all right 'bout it again and decided to like her even more. I was figuring that after all, maybe she was God's friend and this was his way of wanting to help out. I was beginning to think that somehow Miss Claire was sent to help me out, 'cause Lord knowed, she sure did have a way with me.

Miss Claire also learned me 'bout reading other kinds of books, like *The Prophet* by a man named Kahlil Gibran and *The Little Prince*. I loved reading whatever she gave me 'cause them books made me feel like I could go to the places she'd been to b'fore. Aside from reading fun books, Claire told me it was time I started understanding that I should take care of my body. She brought me a book called *Our Bodies, Ourselves*. Who could've ever thought to write such a thing? I was too embarrassed to look at some of them pictures and have to read 'bout what happens inside your body. I fanned through the pages, but I thought it was too stupid to really take the time to read it. Plus, the letters was too small for me to read, so I wasn't interested in it.

Outta all the things I got from Claire, the best thing that I liked was how she said that the freckles on my face—spots I one time wanted to scrub off with a S.O.S. pad—was called "angels' kisses," and that God had put 'em there just for me. I'd never heard such a thing b'fore. I wanted to love my li'l spots from here on out. And at night, sometimes before she went home, Miss Claire would come into my room and show me how butterflies kissed. She would take her own eyelashes and lean her eye to my cheek. Then she'd bat her eye back and forth 'cross my skin real fast, and I'd feel the wings of the butterfly kiss my face.

To keep her there with me longer, I asked her how butterflies was made, even though I already knowed the story 'bout the cocoon and the caterpillar. I loved it when she told me how a caterpillar believed it could be more than just a worm and after sleeping for a small while, grew wings and became a butterfly. "You remind me of a butterfly, sweetheart, and if you put your mind to it you can become anything in the world. You have so much potential that you aren't even aware of. I can see that you're really trying, and I'll let Miss Forde in on that. Always remember, you can be anything that you put your mind to."

With Miss Claire I felt like I was wanted for the first time in my life. I even thought that if I wanted to real hard, I could grow wings and fly us both off from the shelter. The way I seen it was, if a caterpillar could turn into something else like a butterfly, then so could I. Maybe I could turn myself into Claire's baby. That way she'd have something for her very own and would wanna take care of it like all mamas was s'posed to do for their children. I let myself believe what she said.

It soon became clear to all that I did a whole lot betta' when Miss Claire was round. At least when she was at work, the staff knowed that I was somewhere close, and it kept them from having to write up a AWOL report or call the police. The other thing that could keep me in line was always knowing that if I didn't do right I wouldn't be able to go anywhere with Claire again.

After some time, my social worker reviewed my situation and had a meeting with the folks at the shelter. After the meeting I was told that I could go on home visits with Claire, seeing how good she was with me. The staff felt it would be good for me to get outta the shelter with someone who wanted to be with me. Miss Forde wasn't so certain, but she gave me a chance against her better judgment—whatever that meant. She just told me to be sure when I was with Miss Claire and was gonna spend the night, that I should have a separate place to sleep.

On one of our first official outin's Miss Claire took me to see the San Francisco Ballet's *Nutcracker Suite*. And I learned that folks who stand on they tippy-toes in li'l pointed, pink satin shoes was called ballet dancers. They was the most beautiful folks in the world to me. I loved how the shoe ribbons danced round the ankles of the ladies and how pretty the outfits was— like the Easter dresses I wore when I was small. I couldn't believe that the big toes could be that strong to hold a body up like that. I wanted to be a ballet dancer more than anything. I 'magined having my very own music made just for me to dance to. I wanted to dance and make folks feel good, just like I was feeling. Maybe then I could be free from people not wanting me and I'd make a way for myself.

One time, Miss Claire got me to dress up real fancy. She made me a light blue corduroy dress with a round collar—she somehow knowed that blue was my favorite color. The dress had rainbows and hearts that she hand-sewed on it, all by herself, and she got the fit just perfect without even measuring me first. We had dinner at the Spenger's Fresh Fish Grotto in Berkeley—a real fancy restaurant—and then drove to see the

San Francisco Opera. Claire told me that the opera was called *La Tra-vee-ah-ta*, and that it was a love story of some kind 'bout love going wrong. Or maybe going right, whatever way; I can't 'xactly r'member. I didn't understand a word of what she was saying, but it didn't matter none. I watched the women in they big skirts and hair and loved it all. I thought it was funny how the men's hair was just as big as the women's. I sat back and watched and listened. I wanted to sing songs at the top of my lungs so that every night people could come and watch me too. Folks would come from far away to watch and listen to me sing in different words and dresses, my hair all big and fancy. Maybe I would be famous. Not like Glenn my so-called daddy famous, where I'd lose my mind to Jesus and abandon my child for strangers to take care of her. But famous where folks would hear that I was good and took care of children and sang 'em songs 'bout love going right.

Going to big fancy shows wasn't the only things me and Claire did. Though I was filled with my ole country ways, like eating and talking at the same time and putting my elbows so deep on the table there'd be no room left for my plate and stuff, Claire learned me how to use my fork, knife, and spoon the right way. She told me to always pick my fork up from the out-side of a place settin'. And if I needed to cut my meat or some-thing, then I should place the knife in my right hand, fork in left, and switch back after I was ready to eat. She said doing this showed that I had manners. I figured these was the secrets that white folks kept from everybody else. I wondered if that's why black folks wasn't let to eat with whites a long time ago. I have to say, where I come from folks never bothered with this sort of stuff—good manners and all. I also learned to put a napkin on my lap and chew with my lips together without smacking. But that wasn't all she taught me—she even told me how to act b'fore getting the food.

"Sweetheart, it's really important that you never go to anyone's house empty-handed. You should always bring a small token of appreciation. And when the dinner is over and you go back home, you must always send a thank-you note." Man, was she smart, even if it did seem like a lot of work.

"Why come we have to do all that just to get something to eat?" I wanted to know.

"So that you can always be invited back. And it shows that you have really good manners." Well, if good manners was what Miss Claire wanted, then good manners was what she was gonna get. Even though secretly I sometimes wanted to do things my own way.

When I was with Claire, my heart didn't hurt. It felt smooth and light, like one of them balloons that floated free up in the sky. But when she was gone, I had a uneasy feeling, like somebody was chasing me, trying to get me. My heart was jumpy, and my belly was full and excited. All I wanted to do was try and keep my mind busy so I didn't have to think 'bout her not being there. Sometimes if she worked three days in a row, I'd go crazy tryin' to stay up, so that I didn't miss the minute she arrived and every other minute she was there. I felt the same way for her that I did for Ruby, b'fore I moved to North Carolina. Nowadays, I didn't think 'bout Ruby too much, if a'tall. I finally saw that it was no good to want things that wasn't ever going to be.

CHAPTER FIFTEEN

SMILE

IT ALWAYS CAME outta nowhere, like something sneaking up on you in the dark when you ain't expecting it and snatching all the wind outta you. No matter how many times I heard them words, I never got used to 'em: "Regina, you're going to be leaving the shelter."

This time, my social worker, Miss Forde, called the counselors on Monday and told 'em to have me ready to leave by Tuesday, midday at the latest. Each time I'd moved, I had no say in the matter. By the time the news reached me I barely had a minute to ketch my breath, let alone make do with the notion that I'd be leaving Miss Claire.

"But I don't wanna go yet," I'd told Miss Claire as she sat me down and let me know what was happening. Since the call came on her shift, the other counselors decided it might be best for her to break the news to me. And since it was her last night before I left, she wanted us to spend a bit of time together.

"I know, sweetheart, but like I've said before, everyone must

move on at some point. The shelter is only a temporary placement. Miss Forde is just trying to find a good stable home for
you." She smiled and offered to help me get packed. "I'll go and
get the request for your personals, and you can start by emptying the drawers.

"Regina," she called out to me before walking outta the
room, "it's going to be all right, honey. I know you're going to
do well."

I waited till she sashayed out the door before I let the air I
was holding out. I tried to cry, scream, or holler, but nothing
would come out. It reminded me of a time when I fell from the
roof onto cement and I had to run round the yard shaking my
hands before my next breath found its way back to me.

Once I got ahold of my breath, I took the pillow off my bed
and slammed my fists into it like I'd seen some of the other girls
do when they got mad. "I hate Miss Forde," I kept saying to myself. "*I hate you.* I hate you." Over and over I screamed inside
my own head and beat that pillow till the middle thinned.

It took me all night to pack one drawer of clothes. I dragged
my time out by folding and refolding my stuff, then slowly placing each item inside the green Glad garbage bag. I wanted to
have Miss Claire as long as I could. When we finally finished
and all my things was squared away, I took the recording machine Miss Claire'd gave me and offered it back to her.

"Here, I want you to hold this till I see you again. I don't
want nobody to take it from me where I'm going; for all I know
they a bunch of thieves." I pushed the small black-and-silver
box at her, but she refused to take it from me.

"No, it's for you, Regina. You keep it. Anyway, I have an
idea. Why don't you make me tapes like you promised, and send

them to me. You know, some where you're singing, and others where you talk and tell me all about your new placement; that way I'll get to hear your voice firsthand. And by the way, pumpkin, Sacramento is only an hour's drive, so I'm sure we can see one another as soon as you settle in and Miss Forde gives the okay." Miss Claire folded the fingers from both her hands round my outstretched one and pushed the present she'd gave me back towards my lap. "You keep it, Regina; it was meant for you to have as your very own."

I held on to my present and didn't pack it with the rest of my stuff. Instead, I placed it on the chair with the clothes I'd laid out to travel in so I could be sure to keep it with me the whole time, away from anyone's pokin' hands.

Miss Claire said good-bye to me later that night. I'd hung out with her while she did her rounds and made certain that all the kids was in they rooms getting ready for bed. My body, now frozen like a life-size ice cube, slowly moved with her from place to place, not caring that some of the other kids was asking why come I got to be up when they had to be in their rooms. After reminding everybody that tonight was my last, Miss Claire and me kept on doing our rounds. Finally it came time to gather my things up and set 'em in the office—which is what everyone had to do the night before they left, to keep folks from wanting to steal your personals. As we set my bag on the office floor, I wanted to grab Miss Claire and beg her to take me with her. But I remained frozen, inside and out.

"Hey you, are you hanging in there?"

I moved my head up and down slightly.

"Come here." Miss Claire pulled me to her and hugged me long and good.

All I wanted was to stay right there forever. Why wouldn't God let me stay right there?

"This is going to be a new beginning, Regina. And you are in charge of how it all turns out." She smiled a closed, thin smile, then kissed me right in the middle of my forehead.

Again the more I chased after my words, the farther they ran from me. I just stood silently—no speech was gonna come my way, no matter how much I wanted to tell her.

"Okay, let's get you to your room so that I can do the shift change with Miss George." Miss George was the new overnight woman. Miss Claire walked me to my room and watched me get into bed. She stood at the doorway with her hand on the light plate and said, "Don't make a big deal out of going, Regina. That way you can show Miss Forde that you are willing to co-operate, show her that you're a big girl." I just listened. I still couldn't feel her words. She switched off the light and walked away.

I laid in bed for a while and watched my thoughts do somersaults 'cross my mind. Over and over I 'magined myself running and holding on to Miss Claire's leg and not letting her go. I even seen myself getting into the backseat of her car and sneaking home with her and then begging her to run off with me. Finally, I heard the handle on the office door open and Miss Claire say good night to Miss George. All a sudden my body started pumping blood like crazy. For the first time since I heard I'd be leaving, I could feel—but it didn't feel good. My breathing got real short and stuck in the top part of my chest. I tried to concentrate on somethin' else to keep me from exploding. Where was Miss Claire now? The *click-clack* sounds of her heels on the tiled floor let me know she was in the kitchen, then the dining room. The noise faded as she made her way

down the hall that would lead her to the double-front doors—
then to her car.

I jumped outta bed and snuck out the quiet door on the
right side of the building. In my bare feet I ran back out to the
fence that circled the yard. I needed to see her one more time.
In a hurry, I climbed to the top and leaned my upper body half
'cross the pieces of metal where the ends of the fence twisted
together then split like baby wishbones. I waited. In minutes I
could see the headlights of Miss Claire's car come slowly down
Glacier Drive. My heart thumping all heavy-like, I wondered
if I should just throw my body on top of her car as she passed.
I don't know what kept me back, but I didn't jump. Miss Claire
stopped at the sign. I didn't want her to see me, so I scooted
back a bit till the fence spikes dug into the skin below my
bosom. I didn't care. I watched Miss Claire make a left onto
Muir Road. As she passed me, I seen that her face was plain but
looked sad. "Please don't go." I whispered the words into the
night air. I watched her drive right past on her way to her
house, to sleep in her bed—without me.

After waiting till I seen the tail end of her car make the last
left that would take her to the freeway, I finally jumped down
from the fence and snuck back to my room. As I hurry and laid
down, I grabbed my recorder and pushed the rewind button and
listened to the voice. It was a earlier recording that I'd tricked
Miss Claire into doing. I'd had her say some nice words to me
and promised myself to never erase 'em. When the tape came
to the end of rewind, I pushed the play button and slid the
player under my pillow. As her voice asked, "Hi, pumpkin, how
are you doing?" finally I could hold them tears no longer. They
started a-flowing. I kept pushing the rewind button till I fell off
to sleep.

We arrived in what Miss Marrion called the San Joaquin Valley close to an hour after we'd left Martinez. At the last minute I got word that Miss Forde had been called outta town on a emergency and wasn't gonna be able to take me to Sacramento. So Miss Marrion, her coworker, filled in. We pulled into a parking lot that sat in front of a great big ole red-and-white-painted house. From the outdoors, the house looked like it had a million rooms for folks to sleep and run round in. I tried to take it all in as fast as I could. 'Cross the yard from where we stood was a park that had green for as far as the eye could see, with tall oak trees like the ones on Big Mama's property. They branches stretched high into the air, as if they wanted to pull themselves up into the sky. This place reminded me more on south Austin than the shelter. Maybe that was a good sign?

"Would you like some help with your things?" Miss Marrion asked in a gentle kinda way as she popped the trunk of her white county-issued car with the gold sticker on the side door and the E that was held by a five-sided circle. I hated them cars.

"Nah, I got 'em," I said to her, pulling my one bag outta the trunk. The plastic sack dropped to the ground with a soft thud. For a minute, I just stood where I was and stared off into the park at a big ole oak tree and wondered if any of my peoples ever thought on me.

"Come on; let's get inside. It's pretty hot out here." Miss Marrion motioned with her arm for me to follow in front of her. With my bag slung over my left shoulder I made my way to the front door.

In the California Wayward Children's Home, I shared a room with 'bout six other girls off and on, depending on who came and who left. There was also a boys' section that was separated on the other side of the building. I met Mary, who was in charge of the girls' section, and Bruce, who was head counselor for the boys. Bruce looked like the jolly green giant without the green Tarzan outfit. And Mary seemed like somebody nobody should wanna play with. When she talked at you, there was no smiling, and she let it be knowed that if trouble was gonna be had, she was the one to set things straight. Mary and Bruce was in charge of leading me and two new boys round the property, so we could know where everything was at. From what I could see, whoever went through the trouble to make such a nice place for kids was all right by me. But even still, if anybody should've asked, I would have gone back to the ugly ole shelter in a minute if it meant I could get back with Miss Claire.

The best part 'bout the new place was the swimming pool. We was allowed to use it if we acted like model citizens and followed the rules. That meant no lying, stealing, hitting, or name-calling. I thought to myself that I could be a model if I really wanted to. And just maybe it would help me get to see Miss Claire sooner.

I also loved the yard that was pushed up behind the house. It was fine, with its tetherball poles, a baseball field, and kickball yard. The tour seemed to be going good till I seen the li'l room that sat right next to the counselors' office at the foot of the big staircase. The room was called a confinement area. It was as big as a small closet and was all white—inside and out. The handle for the door was only on the outside, which mean that once you was inside, the only way to get out was if somebody let you out. The room was used for "children who got themselves way out of hand."

"What does 'way out of hand' mean?" I asked Mary.

She told me, "Hopefully nothing you'd ever have to concern yourself with, right, Regina?"

That closet gave me a bad feelin'. I was gonna have to do my best not to get myself concerned with it.

The first three weeks at the California Wayward Children's Home was working out all right for me. I'd met up with ole Miss Forde, and she said that the director lady had told her I was being good and if I kept it up for a while longer I could maybe have Miss Claire come up for a short visit. When I asked why I had to wait longer she told me it was 'cause of some policy that the home had with all they new cases. If you could get through the first thirty days without incident, then you could earn privileges like phone calls and receiving and sending mail. Lord knowed I barely earned anything at the shelter, but I was willing to keep up the model-citizen thing so I could get what I wanted here at Sacramento. And in the meantime I was gonna keep earning money to buy tapes so that when the time came, I'd be able to mail 'em off to Miss Claire. An' I could have done it, too, if I hadn't've seen that picture.

It was the most beautiful picture I'd seen. The lady's eyes was dark and lifted up at the corners when she smiled, reminding me on Ruby. And she had a smile that made you just wanna dive in and stay for a while—like Miss Claire's. Then there was her hair. Long and dark brown—again, reminding me on Miss Claire's—it laid on her shoulders in soft curls that kicked at the ends like the rounded check marks my teachers would put on my papers when I'd done a good job. Ever since that Elena showed me the picture of her mommy, I wanted to see it all the time. 'Cause even though the woman in the picture was Mes'can, I 'magined her to be Miss Claire and Ruby rolled into one—a mama for me.

Elena kept that picture in a little box under her bed. She didn't know I knew where it was, but I think I loved that picture more'n she did, so even though she hid it away, I watched her carefully and found her special hidin' place.

I looked at that picture every chance I got, always careful to put it back before Elena could discover it was missin'. This time, though, I was a li'l bit bold. I closed Elena's empty box and hid it back where it belonged. I planned on using the picture just for a while and would put it back before bedtime when Elena always took it out to look at it and talk to her mommy. Careful not to hurt the picture in any way, I slipped it into the elastic of my panties, then pulled my shirt down to make certain you couldn't see it. I wasn't s'posed to be in my room at recess, so I snuck back downstairs and went to the tetherball yard.

"Look, y'all wanna see what my mama look like?" I held the picture up so that the girls from my homeroom could see. I was so happy to finally have somethin' to show folks. I was tired of always being the one who had no proof that I belonged to anybody. "Don't we look alike?" I asked, hoping that somebody would say yeah. Nobody said nothing. "Well! Don't we?" I asked again.

"I guess a little bit," Debbie, a girl from the day program, answered as she scrunched up one of her eyes and the left side of her mouth.

"Why is she so light and you ain't?" asked Michelle, who had just come to the children's home but lived in the part for much older girls.

"'Cause she half Mes'can, stupid, can't you tell? Anyway ain't you never seen any real light black folks b'fore? We come in all different colors."

Nobody knowed what to say. They must've figured I was telling the truth on account that there was a couple of other black kids that went to the day-program school and we wasn't all the same colors.

"Well, you do got real white teeth and some freckles. And your skin is lighter than the man my mama used to go out with, so I guess you and your mom do look alike," Michelle added.

For the rest of the day, I showed my picture to all the girls in my classroom and anybody who asked to see it. By the end of the day it seemed like folks was nicer to me than they'd been before. I'd even look at the picture and start telling folks that my mama had been in court for the last coupla weeks trying to take me back from my daddy, who really didn't want me in the first place. Some of the Mes'can kids started actin' friendlier towards me when they found out that my mama was made outta half of them. The more I looked at that picture, the more I loved my Ruby-and-Miss-Claire mama all rolled into one. She looked so pretty, and she loved me so much . . . I couldn't believe it—I finally had a mama of my own.

"*Where's my picture!* Oh God, oh God, my mama. Somebody took my mommy! Give her back; give her back." Elena's screams could've been heard a mile away. "*I want my maaama.*" Now she was in a full-blown holler.

As the cryin' got harder, it pulled me right outta my sleep along with the other girls in the room. Since Elena had been there longer, she had a later bedtime than the rest of us. All at once everybody's heads started pulling up from the covers. I could feel my body shaking as it tried to figure out what was going on. And in a sudden, I realized it was the picture. I had forgot to put Elena's picture back! By now she was drooling all over herself, and her face looked like it was caught in slow motion. Next thing I knowed she was running through the room tearing stuff off the walls: the fire extinguisher, the emergency exit sign, and even the li'l pictures they let us draw then tape to the walls. I didn't know what to do.

"*Goddamngoddamngoddamn!*" She kept repeating the Lord's name in vain all over the place, at the same time running over to each bed and screaming "goddamn" over and over in folks' ears. By the time she got to me I could hear the staff running up the stairs.

"What's going on in here?" Mary the head counselor said as she got to the top of the staircase. "It's bedtime, ladies; I wanna go home. What's all the racket about?" By then everybody was up and wandering the hallway trying to figure out what was going on.

"Somebody stole Elena's mama's picture; she's tripping out."

"Move out of the way! Let me in!" Mary yelled as she pushed past the crowd of kids. "Can I get some backup up here?" she shouted over her shoulders, and in no time, there was three other grown folks trying to get kids to go back to their rooms. Elena was tearing up her own sheets by then.

"Okay, girls, someone should start talking."

"Somebody took my mommy's picture. I swear it was right here." She pointed to her cigar box. "I put it right here where I always keep it, and now it's gone." Elena kept right on crying.

By now I was sittin' up in the bed wondering how I was

gonna get that picture back in that box, under the bed or wherever it was now. I couldn't believe how stupid I was. My head
started spinning as I tried to think of what to do.

"Are you sure you had it in your box?" Mary asked Elena.

"Yes, every night I put it back in my box right after I pray.
Then I put the box back under my bed so that my mommy can
be with me all the time."

"Who'd you show the box to last?" Mary wanted to know.
My hand slid underneath my pillowcase. My fingers found the
black-and-white picture with the pretty Mes'can woman on it.
I didn't mean to keep it—I just wanted to hold it for a li'l while
longer, and I must've fell asleep.

"I don't know. I just say my prayers, put my box back, and go
to sleep. I didn't show it to nobody else."

"Okay, ladies, everybody up and out. We're going to do a
strip search." Mary's voice moved through the room like a echo.
My insides started jumping.

"Let's move it, ladies."

As I went to get out my bed, I started to pull the picture out
from under my pillow and slip it up the sleeve of my pajama top.
Mary must've heard the sound of the paper scrape against my
skin as I bent it so it'd slide easier.

"What's that in your hand, Regina?"

"What? Nothin'," I answered back while my heart tried to
beat itself right on outta my chest.

"Let me see what is in your left hand now!" Her face was
glowing red.

"I said nothing; why you trippin'?" I yelled back at Mary.

B'fore I could get another word out she had called for backup
again. "That's it, young lady. This is not how we do it here!"
She moved to grab me, and I jumped on another girl's bed,

holding the picture behind my back. "We will not tolerate stealing and lying!" The backup folks came runnin' in, and Mary shouted at 'em to hold me down.

I yanked the picture from behind my back and told 'em if they touched me I'd tear it to pieces.

"Nooo!" Elena screamed and started hollerin' up a storm and scratching herself. I decided right then to tear the picture in half so that we could both have a mama. I wanted to take that part of the face that smiled and made me know my mama loved me. As the other counselors held on to Elena, I tore the picture and tossed Elena the part of her mama she could look at when she prayed—the half with the eyes. I turned and ran smack into Bruce, whose jolly green giant body was blockin' the door. He grabbed me by my arm. I balled the smiling part of the picture into my free hand as I tried to hit him as hard as I could. He yanked my arm behind my back and locked my neck behind his elbow.

"Let me go, you fat mother—"

I never got to finish my words. His one hand twisted my arm up higher while the other one slammed 'cross my mouth. "Let's go," he said as he pushed me towards the stairs.

All the way down I tussled and turned. By the time we got to the first landing, I could see somebody standing at the foot of the stairs: they was holding the li'l white room door open. I shook my head from side to side 'cause Bruce's hand was round my mouth. I was screaming, *Please no! No, please not the white room. I get too scared. Please no.* Nobody heard me. As I landed on my hands and knees, the door slammed behind me in a way where it sounded like flesh landing on flesh.

"You are not comin' out till you can behave!" Bruce called out, and walked away breathing hard.

"I can be good. I can be good. It's all right. You gonna be all right." I kept saying this to myself over and over while I waited in the white room.

At first I screamed bloody murder as I slammed and kicked and scratched at the walls and door. I called for Miss Claire and Ruby and Big Mama and God. And everybody ignored me. "I'm sorry, Elena. I didn't mean to steal your picture. I'm sorry," I cried over and over again. I sobbed myself to a quietness. Then somebody came over.

"When you can give us more of this, we'll let you out."

I couldn't tell whose voice it was but I answered 'em back. "All right. Okay. I can do it." I sat down on the floor. The only sound that could be heard was my hiccups as I tried to quiet myself down more. After a while, when I stopped only hearing myself and the sounds of kids running up the stairs getting ready for bed, I tried to open the hand that was holding the picture inside it. At first it seemed like it was stuck and my fingers didn't wanna give. But slow-like, each finger gave way to the next, and b'fore long I could see what was left over from the picture being tore. It wasn't near the same—in addition to the tear it had kinda melted in my hand. I tried stretching the picture out so I could see her mouth smiling at me, but it was too squished up. I had ruined it.

Shortly after I was let out the closet I was kicked out the California Wayward Children's Home in Sacramento. I never told another soul 'bout my half Mes'can mama, but her face troubled me for a long, long time.

CHAPTER SIXTEEN

GONE

BACK AT THE SHELTER everything seemed to fall right into place. Miss Forde had sat me down and told me how disappointed she was with me 'bout how I acted in Sacramento. And even though she was upset, she seemed a li'l softer than usual. But I didn't let myself trust that. I knowed in no time a'tall she'd be back to her regular self. After she talked with me, Miss Forde met with Miss Claire, and they came up with a plan of action—as they put it—to make certain that I started following the rules and could have some success. Miss Claire, she never asked me 'bout why my placement failed in Sacramento, and I didn't mention it a'tall.

I was told that if I did everything right, like respect other folks' property, stay outta trouble with the counselors, and not run away, then in a while, I might be able to go and spend time with Miss Claire Kennedy in the right way. I promised to do my best to be good and follow all the rules. Miss Claire closed her eye at me real fast and told me welcome back. I was happier than I had ever been in my life. And even though I promised not to run off to Miss Claire's house, every night when she left I wanted to go. I just never wanted neither one of us to leave the shelter again.

"Pumpkin, I will be going on vacation for ten days to Hawaii."

The words just lay there. I felt like a balloon that was let go after being full of air, flyin' round a room with no place to land. Seemed like I hadn't been back two days b'fore things was changing again. "How long you gonna be gone?" I asked her.

"Ten days, like I said; then I'll be back. I'm going to visit my father. He lives there."

"If I lived there, would you take off work and come and see me?"

"If you lived there, I would be there with you, and you would go to the University of Hawaii, because you're smart enough. And I wouldn't have to visit you: I'd always be there with you."

On the night b'fore Claire left, she sat me down on the couch and plaited my hair like I'd taught her to do. She'd gotten so good at it that I didn't mind letting her when she offered. I could feel her fingers touch my scalp as she lay each piece of hair over the next, pulling on it gently, mindful not to hurt me. "Here is a calendar that will show you when I'm coming home, sweetheart," she said, handing me a Holly Hobbie calendar with a big circle round the fifth of August to the fifteenth. Ten whole days. I didn't know if I could hold out that long. I took the calendar from her and ran to post it over my bed. Then I ran to the bathroom. I didn't want the other kids to know I was cryin' over some white woman, and I didn't want Miss Claire to know I was scared for her to get on the plane. I hid out in the bathroom for a while. Then I took some powder that we had

313

underneath a sink and rubbed it all on my face, playin' like I was disappearin', like Casper. If Claire wasn't gonna be round, I didn't wanna be there either. And at least that way I could keep my word with ole Miss Forde. When I walked back out to where Miss Kennedy and some other kids was sittin', they asked how come I had wet marks on my face. I told 'em that the powder burned my eyes and made 'em water.

I cried for the whole ten days she was gone. One of the older girls in my room told me that Claire's plane prob'ly went down, since I hadn't heard from her. I stopped eatin'—I wanted to starve myself just in case Claire's plane was down and she didn't have no food. If she didn't have none, I didn't wanna have none either.

The day she left I was so mad I couldn't take hold of myself and got the worst incident report I could from the shelter. Right when it was time for the shift changes, I ran outside to the back gate and waited for the cars to make the left down the street that leads to Muir Road—the street that takes you toward the highway. I sat down and forced myself to take a dump right smack dab in the middle of my hand. When the first car left the yard, I threw the smelly stuff, aiming at the back of anybody's window. The first time, I missed. The second time I hit a probation officer's car that was coming from the Juvenile Hall place next door. B'fore I knowed what was going on next, the car stopped, and the man got out and chased me all the way back towards the shelter. I tried to run inside and hide, but he got me as I was rounding the building on the side with the quiet door. He filed a complaint and incident report against me and threatened to have me booked into Juvenile Hall if it ever happened again. I even had to clean the windows of his car—including the ones that didn't have nothing on 'em. I was told that Miss Forde would be notified. I spent the rest of my time in my room counting the days of Miss Kennedy's return.

I hardly dared to believe it, but Miss Claire was back from Hawaii ten days after she left—just like she'd said. I figured out that that was the second time somebody did what they said they was gonna do. The first being when Odetta came and got me from the Perezes'. Not only did she keep her word 'bout coming back, but she brought me something called a lei as well. It was a perfect circle of purple and white flowers sprinkled with tiny drops of water and packed in a plastic see-through box. When I asked Miss Claire why she gave the present to me, she told me a story:

"When I was a young girl and met my father for the first time, he gave me a lei. It didn't look too different from the one that I am giving you. After my father gave me the lei, he also gave me a name, a Hawaiian name. It's Kua-hava-e-atoa. It means 'a lei that is strung wrong—but is still perfect in its own right.' My father told me that the prettiest leis he'd ever set his eyes on were always strung a little wrong, so I should never look for things to be perfect."

Her words was beautiful—no wonder her daddy loved her. All I could say was thank you. My mouth must've been clear 'cross my face by the way I was smiling and all. I couldn't believe that she wanted to tell me such a thing, and that I was the one who got to hear her own daddy's story. Nobody I knowed had ever told me nothing so nice 'bout a daddy b'fore. I wore that lei till the flowers fell off; then I saved the string it was strung on. I put it in the gold envelope with the rest of my personals.

I cleaned up my act a bit after Miss Claire came back. One day Miss Forde told me I would get to go on a home visit with Marlena and her family. I had got so caught up in Claire, I almost forgot 'bout my friend. And to tell the truth, I wasn't so sure I wanted to visit anybody else. But Miss Forde thought it would be good for me to go with my old friends since she'd gone through the trouble to set everything up. Plus, she was starting to have second thoughts 'bout me spending so much time with Claire. So after going by and doing a investigation of the Ballentinos' house, Miss Forde said they was qualified. According to the county, there was real strict rules that folks had to go by in order to have a ward of the court in they midst.

Once the weekend was decided on, I got real happy to see my friend Marlena. It had been a long time since I'd seen her. Marlena was the middle girl of four kids. She had a younger sister, Greta; a older sister, Stella; and a older brother, Sam. Marlena was the wildest one of the whole bunch. Everybody said she was wild 'cause she thought herself to be black. I didn't know nothing 'bout that. But I did know that she could get any boy she wanted. She was sure boy crazy, and her claim to fame was that she'd gone all the way! Marlena could even take boys from the girlfriends they already had. I didn't know what I thought 'bout that, bein' that that's what Nadine did to my mama, but I liked Marlena, so I guessed it was okay.

That first weekend at Marlena's I met a boy. I already kinda knowed him from b'fore I went to the shelter, but back then I didn't really pay him much mind. After all, I sure wasn't 'bout to get caught up wit' no nasty boy and wind up like Ruby. No siree, Irene.

The boy I met again, his name was Will. Marlena kept telling me that whole weekend that Will was "head over his

heels" for me. I couldn't see what in the world for. But I let her
go. She told me that since I was livin' round so many girls, that
it might be a good idea for me to get to know Will—'cause I
should spend some time with boys. "After all," she said, "I've already gone all the way with my boyfriend Michael."

"Ooh-wee, that's nasty!" I told her. Then I wanted to know
everything. What did "all the way" really mean?

Marlena told me that all the way means that you let a boy
kiss you, and then if it feels good, you let him stick his finger in
you to test you out and see if you wet. If you wet down there—
then it meant that a boy could stick his thing in you!

"Oh, hell nah!" I told her. "Ain't no boy ever doin' that to
me and leavin' me with no baby I don't want." I told Marlena I
knew all about that, and that it was fine by me if I never went
all the way, and she could go all the way to hell, just for bringin'
it up to me. There was no way I was gonna end up going all the
way. No way!

My first thought when I seen Will was, he was the biggest
boy I'd ever set eyes on. He had to look down at me when we
talked. He sure was pretty for a boy. He looked better than most
girls I knowed. He was blacker than me, with skin the color of
chili beans, and he had black hair that parted to one side. But
his eyes is what I liked best. They was slanted up at the sides
even when he didn't smile. Maybe he was so beautiful 'cause he
wasn't from round these parts. He was half Guam, and the other
half was from Hawaii.

I didn't wanna be by myself with Will, so when he came by
Marlena's house, we all hung round her front yard, listening to
Marlena's brother, Sam, play Fleetwood Mac from their garage.
My favorite song off that album was "Rhiannon." I could sing
all the words. Later that night, all us kids was hangin' out in

Marlena's den room, listening to records and playin' spin the bottle. We played the records so that her mama couldn't hear our voices. At first, I didn't really wanna play, in case I was being tricked into doing something I didn't want to do. But seeing that they was all gonna call me chickenshit, I gave in. At first it was easy watchin' everybody do things that was silly, like kiss somebody on the lips, or fart on the spot (the boys loved to make each other do that).

The time came for Will to get the bottle, and he spun it. It landed right in front of my crossed feet! I looked up and raised my eyebrows at him.

"What you want me to do?" I asked, fiddling with my pant hem.

"I don't know. What do you want me to ask you to do?"

"Don't be stupid!" Marlena yelled at Will. "Ask her to kiss you."

"Will you kiss me, Gina?"

He had nerve callin' me Gina. I never said he could. But then I kinda liked the way it sounded. It was like my name, "Gina," rolled off his tongue but stayed close to his mouth, making me turn and wonder if he was twirling it on his tongue. Since Will was from a place off Hawaii, he talked different than the rest of us. That must've been why I liked the way he called out my name.

"Let's go outside," I told him. "I don't wanna let everybody watch."

The two of us walked outside in Marlena's backyard where it was dark—we didn't want nobody spying on us.

"Have you ever kissed a boy before?"

"Yeah," I told him, not exactly lying. I'd kissed a boy when I lived with Ruby in North Carolina. But I'd forgot 'bout it until

CHAPTER SEVENTEEN

A CHRISTMAS WANT

I THOUGHT THAT I'd never spend a Christmas with folks who wanted me there just b'cause I was me. And I'd gave up a long time ago on believing that a fat white man with some talking reindeer and a red nose was gonna come down a brick pipe and bring me anything I wanted, especially after the pigs'-feet Christmas with Glenn. Far as I was concerned, the only people that could have something like that happen was the people in the books I read.

Without my knowing, Miss Claire had gone and fixed it with my social worker so I could go and spend four days with her and her peoples for Christmas. I could hardly believe this to be so. I'd wanted so bad to go with her that I just couldn't let my mind think it. Plus, b'cause Marlena and her family went to they "I hate black folks" gran'mama's house, I had nowhere else to go.

Claire told me that at first Miss Forde was a li'l uneasy 'bout letting me go with her. She said that there was rumors that she'd let me sleep with her when I stayed at her apartment and that that gave some folks a bit of concern. I knew this was my fault, since I was the one that had told the other girls when I came back from my visits with her what we did. Now kids was saying things that had everybody up in arms. Some of 'em would flat-out call me names, and say I was funny. Not funny where everybody was laughin' at you, but funny actin'—like in gay!

"You sure do act like she's your boyfriend," they'd say, or, "Is you two funny, or gay or something, 'cause she ain't your mama, so why you sleep in the same bed with her?" They was real stupid kids, and I could see why nobody wanted them. I wouldn't want somebody who could think them sorts of things. Now, deep down, I was feelin' kinda stupid for telling 'em where I was sleepin' when I went to Claire's. On the one hand I didn't understand why folks seemed to have a problem wit' it. After all, me and Sister shared the same bed for as long as I could r'member. And another thing, didn't all kids wanna sleep next to they mamas? Miss Claire took me aside and tried to explain what the matter was.

"Sweetheart, there are a lot of people, who are ordinarily good people, that for one reason or another, have chosen to believe rumors as opposed to the facts. I'm really sorry that you've somehow become involved in this situation, and I plan to get to the bottom of it. In the meantime, I want you to act as if this had never happened; that way you won't give others a reason to want to say anything negative about you. Just remember, sweetheart: it's really important to keep your chin up when it wants to hang down. My only request is, please don't discuss in detail what we do when we're off the shelter grounds. We both have a right to our privacy, and it's no one else's business."

322

I just loved the way that Miss Claire could take something dark and heavy and turn it into light. But the back-talking didn't stop there. And no matter how hard I tried to act as if what other folks said didn't bother me, sometimes it was dog-gone hard.

Sometimes if the kids wanted to be real smart, they'd accuse me of tryin' to be a white girl. They was all getting mad 'cause I was tryin' to say good words instead of the country ones that I'd used all my life. Like I said before, I used *father* instead of *daddy,* and I think somebody might've heard me say "Oh my God" a couple times too many. When they started in, all I would do was turn round and say what I learned as a real li'l girl when folks would call us kids names: "Sticks and stones might break my bones, but words will never hurt me." They could say what they wanted, but I sure wasn't gonna feel sorry for the kids who was making fun of me even if they was jealous, 'cause they didn't cry no tears when I was stuck sittin' in that shelter and they got to go home.

Mrs. Elizabeth Kennedy, Claire's mama, was coming to pick me up at five o'clock, and I was bringing four changes of clothes, like Claire had told me, along with the two presents I had made for her and her mama. I'd promised myself to be as nice as I could, figurin' that if Miss Claire's mama liked me a whole lot, then maybe she'd wanna keep me, since all her kids was grown. I couldn't seem to keep from always looking to get me a mama. It was like something inside me wouldn't stop till it came to pass. I told myself to try and speak some of them words that I had heard Claire use, thinking that she must've got 'em from her own mama. I was prayin' to the Lord that maybe older Miss Kennedy was gonna take me for her own so that I could be part of Claire's whole family.

Early on in the week my social worker had come and taken me out to eat. She called it lunch. I called it nasty. She ordered me a runny li'l potbellied egg that was on top of a piece of bread, but instead of cheese, it had this lumpy yellow sauce that tasted like lemon gravy. Plus it had the nerve to have a tiny piece a ham on it. The eating place was called the Velvet Turtle. If you asked me, I'd say they caught that turtle, boiled it, and tried to pass it off as real food. Anyway, I picked at my "lunch" as Miss Forde told me 'bout this foster home I was gonna have to visit when I came back from Miss Kennedy's. I realized right then that I didn't care so much for ole Miss Forde. As she talked, the big mole that was stuck to the side of her top lip moved up and down. I couldn't stop my eyes from playin' with the mole on account it was so big. And I couldn't stand how she wore funny li'l shoes with points that strapped what I'd 'magined to be her ugly li'l feet right in 'em. Anyway, her lips was dark and big—reminding me a li'l bit of Mr. Benny. As a matter of fact she looked like she could've been kin to him.

"I have a family that's interested in meeting with you, Regina." Sniff, sniff. Miss Forde also had a funny way of sniffin' the air round her. She made me feel like she was smellin' for something she might've lost—like her manners. After a while I started sniffin' too. I just didn't do it out loud.

"Is the people you want me to go see black or white?" I asked.

Her mole came to a stop as she kinda lowered her eyes at me. "What difference does that make, Regina?" By now her hands was taking her napkin from her lap and putting it in her plate. She stopped eatin'. I could see for my own self that maybe something I said wasn't so good. I didn't see why it had to be trouble; after all it was me I was talking 'bout, not her.

"Nothin', forget it!" I answered her. Lunch was done.

"Why does it matter what color the family is, Regina?"

"B'cause I'm scared that black folks don't really want me. They always leave me like I'm a mistake nobody wants to fool with. Plus, they beat me and call me names and holler at me, when all they have to do is just be nice sometimes. Why come everybody black gotta be so mean and act like they can't stand they own kids? You don't see my own mama or daddy or any of my kin breaking they black-ass necks to get over here and take me home, now do you? And another thing, all I ever heard was that nobody paid anybody 'nough to take me in. Somebody was always having something to say 'bout money. It's the white people like Claire who is trying to be good to me and show me I can be anything I want to. And she ain't never asked for one dime. That's the difference it makes."

I watched as Miss Forde's face got hard like a rock. She reminded me of what that ole ugly Lula Mae looked like when she was 'bout to go into one of them "Don't make me have to tell you twice" moods. Anyway, I knew she couldn't hit me, so it didn't bother me that her "panties was all tied in a knot"— like I learned to say at the shelter.

"I think I understand, Regina. You don't know who you are, and you are heading for an identity crisis. Understand this. You are *black!* Always have been, always will be; and nothing you can do will ever change that. This white world that you so want to be a part of does not see you as anything other than that! And it is high time that you start taking responsibility for who you are. Now, I don't want you to believe that what you said is true for all black people. You'd be surprised how many black families there are that are willing to love and support black children."

That might've been true through and through, but from where I stood, I'd never met them kinda folks b'fore. And I didn't get anything she said to me 'bout wantin' to be white. As a matter of fact, she was soundin' pretty crazy to me—I just wanted somebody to be nice to me.

"You need to think about what I've said, Regina. We are running out of options for you, and I think a nice black home would be a good thing."

I half listened and thought that Miss Forde didn't know 'bout the option of Miss Claire's mama. I decided to wait till I met with her again b'fore I brought it up.

The older Miss Kennedy came at five on the dot, and I was ready to go with her. The front office called and told the unit staff that my ride was here. I grabbed my bag and started off. Almost forgettin' my two presents, I turned round and went back and got 'em off my bed. I had made a plant hanger out of jute for Claire and a crocheted patchwork afghan for her mama—I knowed that ole folks liked blankets to keep 'em warm—at least Big Mama did. The older Miss Kennedy was nice, just like Claire, and they sounded the same when they talked.

"Hello there, darling," she called to me, and pulled my body right smack into her bosom. She was warm, and had a big chest. She took my bag and put it in the backseat, which I thought was a nice thing to do. After sliding in the seat, she told me to put my seat belt on, and I did. I liked how she told me what to do. It made me feel like she was thinking 'bout me. Then, we was on our way.

"Is Christmas your favorite holiday, Regina?"

"Yeah!"

"What do you want Santa to bring you this year?"

"I don't know."

"Isn't there anything you would like?" she asked me.

"Um, anything?" I answered back with my eyes as they lifted themselves up to help me out.

"Well, you have to ask for something." Somethin' told me that she was tryin' to get me to ask her for what I wanted. So I did.

"Okay then." I played along. This was the first time in a long time that somebody was asking me what I wanted for Christmas. Sometimes out at Big Mama's somebody might ask me if they r'membered, but if they didn't, you got what you got. And most times Big Mama would say that Ruby wasn't sending no money, like she always did, so not to expect much. One year, though, after a lot of begging and pleadin', I got a Easy-Bake Oven I'd seen on the TV 'bout a hundred times, and all the girls in my school was saying how they mamas was gonna be buying them that oven for Christmas. I think Ruby must've come up with some money and sent it to Big Mama—but I didn't know for certain. I thought I was gonna be cooking some bread or rice pudding up in it, like I'd seen Big Mama do, but the best I made was a nickel cake with red hots stuck in it since the li'l oven was heated by a lightbulb, not real fire.

Claire's mama asked me again. "Well, Regina, tell us. What do you want for Christmas this year?" I thought back on what I'd always wanted for Christmas, more than anything in the world. And figured just maybe I could get it this time.

"I want him to bring me a family."

I looked at her out the corner of my eye and saw her noddin' her head up and down, but she didn't say nothing.

327

Claire came to her mama's house later on that night. I was so happy to see her, I ran right up to her, grabbed her hand, and held on to it tight. She told me the reason why I couldn't've left with her was b'cause some of the kids was really making a fuss 'bout us goin' off together. And that the unit staff was even havin' problems with it, so she saw fit that we should leave in different cars. I just listened and said nothing. In my mind, though, I couldn't for the life of me understand why come some folks didn't just mind they own business.

I came to Claire's mama's house on Christmas Eve. She told me to call her by her name—Elizabeth. *Elizabeth* sounded pretty to me, and I wanted to please her, so I did. Elizabeth told me how her family had Christmas the night before, so that they could spend a longer time together. I thought that made sense. After a while, a bunch of folks started coming over, and they all wrapped they arms round one another and seemed real happy to see each other. I could feel something inside me pull for what they had. Us girls was told to go into the kitchen and start get-ting the food ready to put out. Claire had a sister, and she came and helped us too. As I watched 'em go 'bout they ways, again I felt a quickness go right through me. It made water come to the front of my eyes faster than I could keep up with it. I didn't know where the sadness was coming from, but lately, anytime I got round folks and they families I just couldn't stay myself— even wit' Marlena. It was like I was wantin' so bad to just be mushed in and be like everybody else. I wanted for folks to come up to me and say, "How's ya' mama, girl? Where she at?" And I'd point them over to where my mama was standin', and right before they'd walk away, they'd say, "You sure do look just like her." And there my mama would be, givin' me a look and smilin' 'cause she knowed how much she loved me and was proud that I was hers. And before our eyes would leave each other, she'd wink at me. I'd lower my head from the weight of my own smile.

To keep the water from falling out my eyes, I held on to my breath and started countin' the carrot sticks I was layin' on the plate. One, two, three . . . By the time I got to forty, I could breathe again wit'out cryin'.

I swear b'fore God that I was on *The Lawrence Welk Show.* The only thing missing was Lawrence Welk hisself. Elizabeth could play the piano real good. She busted out with "Deck the Halls," and everybody started singing together. I secretly made fun of people who acted like this. When I would watch them Christmas specials on TV, like John Boy and them, I thought they was silly and corny. But seeing folks act like that in real life wasn't so bad; they was just having some fun. Claire, who was standing 'cross the room, gave me the eye, which was a code that said something without words. I learned to understand that eye thing back home with Big Mama and them, and you didn't want to see it twice. Anyway, I pulled outta my corner in the couch and started singing with the folks. I was doing all right for a while, till Claire had to go and tell everybody, "Hey, everyone, we have a singer in our midst! It's Regina! Just listen; she has a great voice."

"Come on over, Regina, and sing with me!" Elizabeth called out. The North Pole ran through my body right at that minute. I mean it was true that I liked to sing. Specially in the talent shows at the shelter and for the staff and the other kids. But not here in front of a bunch of people I didn't know too good.

"Nah, I mean, no. I cain't. I mean, I can't do it," I said back. Oh, Lord, my words was getting all caught up on my tongue. I know they was seeing me as a country bumpkin who couldn't even talk right, let alone try and sing. So I stopped and thought 'bout what I wanted to say real good.

"You guys go right ahead! I'm just fine being right here," I said, and didn't even stumble over my words. They didn't give in so easy. I ended up singing "O Come All Ye Faithful."

We sang, ate, and drank our fool selves stupid, right on up till midnight. They even had a clock that had a bird come out and say "Cuckoo, cuckoo." We all sat around that tree, with its nice lights and decorations. It wasn't one of those silver trees that you had to take out a box and put up, each year losing another branch somewhere b'tween the box and another year gone by. And it didn't have the li'l four-colored, plug-in wheel that made the silver turn different colors, like the one we had at Big Mama's. No this was a real live tree. I'd seen small trees and skinny ones too, but this was the best one yet.

Since she was the mama, Miss Elizabeth was gonna be handing out the presents. But first we had to start with the stockin's. Oh my lands, I ain't never heard of such a thing in real life. There was a stockin' just for me. And it was made in the likeness of a Converse tennis shoe, connected to a checkered-board sock that was blue and white. The Converse was red, with a blue star caught in a blue circle. It looked just like the real thing. I had seen Claire working on that same Converse stockin' at the shelter. And when I asked her who it was for, she told me a friend's li'l daughter who loved Converse just like me.

"Here, pumpkin, this is for you." Claire had lifted the stockin' from where it rested and handed it to me. "Merry Christmas, sweetheart." As I reached up to take the stockin', she said, "I love you, pumpkin."

My whole body stopped what it was doing. My hands seemed

to be frozen in the air as they grabbed for the Converse tennis shoe that was made just for me. Right then I could've died and not even missed myself. I couldn't think of a time when somebody had ever said such a thing to somebody like me. *I love you, pumpkin.* I knowed right then that she was sayin' what was true. My heart was a merry-go-round, and the words was the li'l horses that you see going up and down and round and round. For a minute I felt like I did the time Miss Francis had me stand up in front of the class to be welcomed—I didn't know what to say then or now. For another minute I sort of hung on to the stockin' and looked at all that she had done for me—and just me alone. I finally looked up at Miss Claire, and I could feel my throat go dry all at once as I let them strange words I couldn't r'member ever speaking b'fore fall out my mouth. "I love you too," I said as I rocked my legs sideways in my chair and didn't know what to do next. I didn't know what I was s'posed to do with the "I love you" part, but I just tried to hold on to them words from both of us.

_____

CHAPTER EIGHTEEN

FOR THE LOVE
OF YOU

WHEN I CAME BACK to the shelter after Christmas, being there didn't feel so good for me. I had failed what was called a group home and a couple of foster homes faster than you could spell *shit*. I failed the group home on account of taking hits off of a marijuana joint. You would've thought I known betta' than to mess with that stuff, 'cause of all the kids in the shelter who was there b'cause they folks was either drug addicts or in jail for some kind of drug problem. Plus, I'd even promised myself and Claire that I was gonna be somebody one day and that I'd never touch the stuff, but being at this group home, it was too hard to keep saying no. The more I resisted, the more I was called a pussy or was threatened to be beat up. I tried to tell my social worker that the girls at that home was pushing dope and selling their tails out to boys left and right. But no, she didn't wanna hear me. Miss Forde swore up and down that I was trying like hell to get back to the shelter and Claire.

"Regina, I am sure that Mrs. Richards, the director of the home, would never allow any of the ladies to involve themselves in potentially criminal activity. I know that you are doing your best to get back to Claire Kennedy, and I won't permit it." I hated her! Once again she had stuffed me in some place where I had no business being. And just like that Sacramento home, she'd just walked in one day and said, "It's time to try another placement."

The home itself wasn't so bad. The owner lady really tried to do right by us girls. I learned how to take pictures with a camera and develop 'em on my own. I even got to go to a place called A.C.T. It was a big theater where you go and get on stage and learn how to act by puttin' your energy—as they called it— into something good. All in all the place was fine as long as the grown-ups was round. But at night when they went home to they own families, some of them girls would start cutting up something terrible.

I got tired of trying to tell Miss Forde 'bout what was going on, and just decided to give in and smoke the grass that had been offered to me a million times.

"Here let me show you. You just hold the lighter at the end of it and inhale like you do a cigarette." Jennifer, one of the girls, and me sat out back of the house one night. We was not in the sight of our housemother, so I took the chance and inhaled a hit of the reefer like I'd been doing it all my life. I already knew how to smoke, so the inhaling part was fine. With my lips circled round the tip of the end paper, I sucked in as much as I could each time. At first, I couldn't see what all the talk was 'bout; it was no different than a ciga . . . rette. But then, slowly, or fast—I didn't know which way it was coming at me—Ohjesusinheaven! I could feel everything in my body beating at one time. And the lights. The lights from the other houses started connecting into one big line of light. I needed to get outta my skin. I jumped up from the back steps and took off down the street, not knowing where I was going or why. There was voices telling me to run. Run far away! By the time they caught up with me, it took three people to tackle me to the ground. Not to mention three fistfights with the girls and the housemother, 'cause I thought they was all out to poison me. Smoking that grass left me senseless in a closet for three days; I was too scared to come out. And it was the only place where I could watch what folks did without having to look over my back. Not only that, but I got to go and visit Miss Claire for a overnight, and when I got back, I was so scared to sleep by myself that I creeped into one of the girls' beds and went off to sleep. The next day the girls asked me why I had to go and sleep with somebody when I had my own room.

"I was scared, that's why."

"If you are so scared, how did you sleep by yourself at your white-lady friend's house?"

"I didn't sleep by myself; I slept with her." Once word got back to the director, Mrs. Richards, I was sent back to the shelter real quick-like.

That wasn't all that was going on in the air at that time. There was some strange something called Proposition Thirteen that was passing, and that sent all the grown folks into a tailspin. I kept hearing folks left and right talking 'bout they didn't know if they was gonna have a job from one minute to the next. They was asking why it always seemed that when cuts was gonna be made in the president's house, old people, children, and the crazies got it first and the hardest. I asked Claire 'bout what all that talk meant. She told me somethin' 'bout some man named Howard Jarvis and how he wanted to help pass some bill that would take money from the poor and the people who was tryin' to help 'em, and give it to the people who made 'em poor in the first place.

Right 'bout then, Miss Forde, my social worker, told me that she had 'bout had it up to here with me and my incident reports from all the failed placements, and that if I didn't get it right, they was gonna change me from a 601 to a 602, meaning I would be seen as a child criminal. She said that with all the cutbacks, nice folks didn't have time for my shenanigans and notions of being put into a white foster home. And I had betta' straighten up and fly right! Under my breath I said, "Yeah right, Miss Forde." It was a new expression I'd learned at the last placement.

My dream of having Claire take me as her own had never been talked 'bout. I didn't bring it up b'cause I wanted my social worker to figure it out for herself—that way it wouldn't be like I was tryin' to be with somebody white. And it could be her own idea, not mine.

I could see that Miss Forde was mad at me b'cause I didn't like the last foster home she'd tried to get me to go to after I came back from the group home that lasted only one month. But I swear b'fore God that I wanted to like them folks. They seemed nice 'nough and all, but they just didn't talk to me like Claire and her mama did.

After Miss Forde had dropped me off at the folks' house, she ran to her car and drove out the people's yard like she had just r'membered she had left something cooking on her stove. She didn't even look back once. I had a high mind to think she was tryin' to pawn me off on these people.

That weekend, with the new family, I got the bloods. The foster-family people had planned to take me campin' in they big motor home. They plans was cut real short. Not only did I soil the woman's white sheets to look like somebody had been killed on 'em, I got the cramps so bad I couldn't stretch my legs out, so I had to stay bent over in a ball the whole weekend and cried. Since the smell of food cooking made me throw up, my condition got to be too much for the foster-family lady, since they loved food and had to cook it in the same room I was layin' in. After I throwed up for what seemed like hours, the lady thought that I might be with a baby, since she ain't never heard of no fourteen-year-old girl carrying on as much as I did with my menstr'ation.

"Do you think you might be pregnant?" she asked me.

"Hell nah!" I told her and rolled to face the wall so I didn't have to look at her face. That was it! They turned the big motor home round and headed back to wherever they was from. The first thing the foster lady did, after parking her tacky trailer on wheels, was go call Miss Forde and tell her to come and get me quick. I heard her. She was tryin' to make it sound like I was more than she bargained for.

"Oh, Miss Forde, now you know we've always been willing to take on the kids and help 'em out, but this one, honey, she's a piece of work."

Miss Forde was there first thing on Monday morning. She told me that the foster-home lady said that I was rude and sassy, and that they had no room for my kinda young ladies. "Regina, I don't know what is going on with you and these foster-home placement failures, but I think I might have an idea. I have a feeling that you think by being shocking with your behavior, that nobody will want you, and you'll be able to stay at the shelter." She didn't even try and believe that my period was real bad! She just went on with another one of her own stories 'bout me.

"Now I can see that you've gone and run a number on all these other people, getting them to think that you are something special, but I'm here to let you know, it won't work with me! You aren't special. And since you have folks believing that you aren't foster-home material, we are considering putting you into a residential treatment facility. Because of the cutbacks, the shelter is on its last leg, and if you keep this mess up you will be heading for Juvenile Hall. You want to act crazy—I'll show you right where you can go!" She told me the place she had in mind was a center for kids who needed a whole lot of structure. I was to be visiting the Guideways Residential Treatment Center in two weeks.

Oh my Lord. This just couldn't be. Why was they gonna do that to me right when I'd found somebody that I really wanted to be with? Couldn't they just see that Claire wanted me? Why come nobody was askin' her to take me in? I wish I knowed how to ask 'em myself, but I didn't want nobody to think I wanted to be with her real bad, 'cause then they might not give her to me. I let my mind sit on the time I'd asked Miss Claire if she'd ever wanted to have kids of her own, and she'd said "ab-so-lute-ly"; and somehow I made that mean she was hoping it could be me.

Finally, I got the nerve and asked Miss Forde if Miss Claire could ever take me home with her for good, and she cut her eyes at me like I had just stole her soul.

"That's the problem with you now, Regina; you don't know who you are. You need to be with your own kind. As far as I and the Department of Social Services are concerned, black kids need to be in black homes. Anyway, a law is in the works to be passed so that they will never be able to adopt our black children."

Who was "they," I wanted to know. And what did that have to do with what I asked her? Right then and there I saw that she was a damned fool. Anybody who was paying attention could see that my own kind sure as hell didn't want me. Why was she so stupid? I couldn't see why folks was wanting me to go back to nothing. How come everybody else like Oliver and Annie got to go to folks who really wanted them? Why did it seem like only the white ones got to get kissed by the prince and live happily and stupid ever after? Was that really the way God meant for it to be? Why was there always more black kids than white ones left in the shelter? Why? Deep down, I hated the color black.

I made plans to be spending the weekend with Marlena. Her mama and daddy was going away, but nobody bothered to tell my social worker or the counselors anything 'bout it. We knowed that if anybody found out, I wouldn't be able to go on a home visit.

Mr. and Mrs. Ballentino left me, Marlena, and her li'l sister Greta in the charge of Stella, Marlena's oldest sister. She was somewhere in her twenties, so she could boss us with no trouble. B'fore they left, Mrs. Ballentino told us not to have any boys hanging round the house and then told Stella to keep a close eye on Marlena. We all knowed she was saying that 'cause Marlena was the one who was so boy crazy. "Okay," we all said together. What her mama and daddy should've knowed but didn't was that Stella had a boy of her own down the road, and she had plans that did not include us three girls.

"What are we going to do?" Marlena asked with a open mouth once the coast was clear.

"Nothing!" her sister Stella told her. "You guys are just going to hang out and do like Mom and Dad said and keep away from boys!" We all three stood and looked at Stella like she was a policeman, giving us orders. "Look, I'm going down a few doors to my friend's house, and you guys had better just hang out and be cool." We agreed and promised Stella that we'd sit round and listen to music or something, all of us suspecting what she was up to anyway. "All right," she said as she cut out, "I'll be down the block if you need anything." Now Stella was gone too. And we had that big ole house to ourselves.

"Come on, Regina; let's go and get Will and Michael. Won't nobody know if we bring them over. Plus, once my sister gets with her friends, she won't even remember who we are."

"Won't your mama get mad at you?" I asked Marlena. "What if we get caught?"

"Girl, you are such a fraidycat. Don't worry; I'll never get caught. I already had Michael in my room once while my parents were home. They didn't even know."

I couldn't believe that girl. As the grown folks would say, she was way too fast for her own good. But I liked Marlena a lot. She treated me just like I was her sister, maybe even better. I figured I owed her for comin' to get me so many times and forcing her daddy to come all the way out to Martinez to pick me up. He never asked for nothing. Not money or even a thank-you. I used to hear Big Mama complain 'bout how my mama never did nothing to help her out with us, and maybe if Ruby had sent a li'l money or something every now and again, she could have treated us better. Marlena and her family treated me nice, for no reason a'tall, so I wanted to be nice back. And since I didn't have no money, doing what she wanted seemed just as good.

"Okay, then, let's go and find 'em." We told Greta not to say nothing, and she crossed her heart as a promise.

We found Michael first, and he found Will. I don't know where it all came from, but the next thing I knowed, we was all at Marlena's house drinking Chateau LaSalle and smoking Kool Longs and huddled up all together like a sports team. I hadn't smoked for a while, but the alcohol made me wanna have a cigarette, so I did.

Oh, was we partying. I was no stranger to drinking. I had learned that at Ruby's. Many a night I had sat up with her and her friend-girls under the carport, playin' spades and rummy, drinking all kinda stuff. One time I even poured myself a glass of Lancer's and waited while my head wobbled and I fell off to sleep.

I watched as Will made his way over to the couch that I was sittin' on. He asked Greta to move so that he could sit by me. Greta caught my eye and rolled hers as she moved over. Will sat down and took the empty glass outta my hand. "Look like you feeling pretty good there." I let him know that I could hold my liquor, and that, yes, I did feel pretty good. Somebody put a record on, and David Gates and Bread was singin' soft love songs. By now I was standin' up and singin' "If" right along with David Gates. Everybody was singin' now. All us girls, that is.

Marlena sidled up to me and whispered in my ear, "You know you gonna give him some!"

"What?" I asked her. "Give him some of what?"

"You know what, and you might as well go on and do it. Me and Michael love doing it."

"Yeah?" I asked with suspicion.

"Yeah. Girl, it's really nothing to be all tied in a knot about. All you do is let him play with you a little bit, get you all hot, and you won't even know when it happens."

I didn't know how to tell my friend that I was scared. I'd never gone all the way before. And I sure couldn't let myself end up wit' no baby. Not now, not never. Even though I'd read books and learned from listening to the girls I lived with 'bout all the different ways they let a boy have 'em, I still wasn't sure how to not end up pregnant.

Hell, I didn't know what I was feeling no more. Seemed like I was never gonna really have what I wanted, and there was plenty of what I didn't want just for the asking. I wondered how come life was like that. Why was it that just 'cause I really wanted something—like to live with Miss Claire—it couldn't happen? But if I told that ole nasty social worker of mine that I couldn't wait to fall into the arms of a wonderful black family—she'd move faster than Superman. And not only that, but it was clear to me that Miss Forde was gonna have her way—and that I might not ever see my friends again, or even Miss Claire. So what did it really matter what I did? Nobody was gonna give a hoot anyway.

Fine, I told myself as my insides started doin' double flips; he could have whatever he wanted. I wondered what harm could it really do, and if I didn't like it, or didn't wanna see Will afterwards, I'd be gone anyway. But more than that, I liked Will. He told me he had waited a whole month to see me and that he couldn't stop thinking 'bout me. I'd thought 'bout him too. Ain't nobody ever waited for me like this before. And from the way things was looking, wasn't nobody gonna be waiting anytime soon.

His lips was on mine. They was big and swallowed up half my face. We found each other's tongues and sucked like if they was tryin' to get away from us. My eyes closed, my heart pumpin', I wrapped my arms round his neck, and he lifted me up in his arms like I was his baby.

"You guys can use my room." Marlena's big mouth made me come up for air.

"Do you wanna go?" I asked Will, not believin' I was asking him that question. I didn't care no more 'bout what was gonna be. I was tired of doing what everybody else wanted me to do, and getting nothing for it. What difference did it make anyway?

"Yeah, let's go." Will carried me into Marlena's room.

He laid me down and then fell on top of me. "Are you sure you want to do this?"

"Yeah. You?" I asked.

"Yeah."

I closed my eyes and felt Will's hand touch my skin. I jumped and got all tingled like if I was cold or something. Then, without my wanting it to, all my mind could see was the hazy figure of a man with me in a car, and I asked Will to stop, figuring I might be doing something wrong. I was also wonderin' if God could see me, and if so, what he was thinking 'bout me. But Will never stopped. He put his mouth back on mine, and I was quiet. It was like I forgot he was there at all until I could feel the wetness sliding out my eyes, down my face. My voice was nowhere to be found. It had left me here in this place with no words to say how I was.

The next thing I knowed, I was hitting, pushin', and telling him to get offa me. I didn't even remember who it was that was on top of me. There wasn't a face, just a body—a big heavy body. My mind flashed back to how I'd seen and smelled that smell my mama had in that room when Mr. Benny was taking her prettiness away. Is that what was happenin' to me? Did what I was doing with Will make me a ho'? Right then, I knowed what shame smelled like.

"Please, get offa me." But he didn't. He kept right on pushing himself on me. I could see Big Mama's boys coming into my room and calling me names like prick-tease and cocky—was that what I was being? I felt my body go cold and hard like when I was tryin' to fight Big Mama's gran'son Lenny offa me. Then at the same time, I just let my body go and stared off into the darkness. For a minute, part of me wanted to know if he'd only taken what I'd agreed to give, and the other part needed to know just what it was I'd gave him.

There was a quietness in the room that me and Will was in. I could feel that I was laying on top of something wet, but I didn't know where it'd come from. I didn't hear or feel Will slide offa me or pull on his clothes and zip, fasten, and go. I just wanted to know if he'd taken some of my pretty with him.

Will was too big—in every way.

"Marlena, come on in here!" I screamed at her, mad as hell that I had lost my mind for a few minutes of pain.

"I got blood everywhere! Why is blood all over me?" I moaned. Marlena told everybody to get out the house. She said that I had a nosebleed and that I wasn't doing too good. My girly parts was on fire, all right. I felt like I had fell on the bar of a bicycle, going full speed while standing up as the chain fell off.

"Oh, man. You're bleeding a lot. What the hell you guys do in here?"

After all that, that was all she could say. I didn't wanna let nobody know what'd just gone on—even though they knowed that we was kissing and stuff. By now most of the other folks was gone, and if they wasn't, I was just gonna say I had a bloody nose like Marlena had told me. I didn't wanna give nobody nothin' to talk 'bout. Will had left, but I didn't see him go. I think I r'membered somebody asking me if I wanted anything, and I just said no and went to the bathroom to check if I was still bleeding. After wiping myself up, I went back to Marlena's room and sat down on her sister's bed as she changed the sheets to the one I'd been in. I pulled my body close to me as I wrapped my arms round my knees. For the life of me I couldn't feel nothin'. My private parts was on fire and felt swollen, but other than that, I couldn't find what it felt like for me. I secretly wished I was a tape recorder and could rewind what'd just happened. Once I had my clothes back on, I turned round to speak with Marlena. Right then and there we made a pact not to tell nobody 'bout this.

For a few days at the shelter I was walking round like something was stuck b'tween my legs, and I was in a daze. I tried holdin' my legs closer together, but the more I did, the more it hurt, and when I went to the toilet it burned. I was pulled into the office, and one of the counselors asked me what was wrong. She said that I hadn't been the same since I came back from the weekend. I didn't say too much. I just told her that I didn't feel good. She kept on asking me if there was anything else I wanted to tell her, and I shook my head no. I stood to go to my room and turned round and told her I had blood in my panties and that it hurt real bad between my legs. The counselor didn't give it two thoughts—we was on our way to the shelter nurse. I told

the nurse that I should go to the doctor because I was in terrible pain, and they drove me to the county hospital.

I had to get four stitches and was told to soak in Epsom salt
till I wasn't tender anymore. I remembered Epsom salt from
south Austin and wondered what Big Mama would've done if
this happened with her. If I knowed 'em the way I thought I did,
they'd all prob'ly say I got what was coming to me.

The doctor asked me what had happened, and I told him I
didn't know. He looked at me and asked me how it was that
I didn't know how I got a half-inch tear in my private parts. I
don't know what came over me, but right there and then in a
breath that was so full of wicked, I got turned round and let my
mind do all the talking. I just sat there and listened to myself
let words fall right out my own mouth, like a witch with no
teeth to hold her poison words inside her mouth. I could only
watch, while they slid out biting everything in they path.
There was nothing to hold my meanness in its rightful place.
Them words came falling out one by one, not caring one bit
'bout what would be.

"I was raped. I was with my friend this weekend, and it happened there, at her place."

Once I started my story, I couldn't stop myself. It was like the
devil hisself was whispering in my ear. *That's right, keep on
lying*, he said, *'cause don't nobody love you anyway. You don't matter to nobody.* For the first time in my life, I was the one sayin'
empty words that had no meanings. It was like paper ghosts on
Halloween was now getting to say what they really felt like. I
wasn't sure what really happened an' whose fault it was, but I
wanted to get that fault away from me for sure. Plus, I thought
that if I told 'em that I was raped, then that meant I wouldn't
have to leave the shelter and Miss Claire. I didn't care 'bout

myself; I just wanted to be with her. I told myself that they would have to do a big investigation and that that would take a long time, months, maybe even years—at least that's how it was done on TV. Didn't matter to me how long it took, I would be with Miss Claire just that much longer—anything was betta' than nothing at all. I just kept sayin' I was raped. I was raped. I was raped. I kept lettin' them words tumble outta my mouth, and I watched the room while everybody in it stopped breathing the same air. We was all in that place where there was no talking, no moving. Nothing. I could almost hear the lying words crash into themselves in midair then fall and hit the ground, only to wait for somebody to come along and claim 'em.

I never knowed that words was so mighty. That they could make everybody stop in they own tracks and change things real fast-like. Seemed like no matter what was said, there was always a ear willing to listen and turn what I was saying into something with meaning. Words could make folks who regularly don't hear, listen. There is also special words that if said with the mind of getting what you wanted in a time of danger, could make you get real strong, like a mama when a car is rolled over on her baby and she can lift that car all by herself. Like a knife, words can come and cut you 'cross the heart and bleed you for everything you worth. Or like a magic stick they can slow down time. Words can make believers outta folks who don't believe. And b'fore you know what was even said, a commotion is started that you can't even see. You can't see it 'cause all you looking at is what you want, specially when it's the thing you wake up every day and breathe for. All I wanted was to use the magic in words, to help me get my way for once. To not let them take what I wanted away from me. I was tired of believing every time somebody said something to me, only to have 'em turn round and deny on what was said without a concern in the world. I was tired of it. I was tired.

"Do you have any idea who may have done this to you?" the doctor asked me in front of the counselor.

"Well, it was night and it was dark, and I was sleeping in my friend Marlena's bed. I was tired, so I went to bed before everybody else. Her and her family was sitting in the living room where I left 'em." The doctor nodded at me to go on. "Well, I was laying on the bed just 'bout to go on to sleep, and somebody came through the window, and before I could yell or anything, they had a hand over my mouth. Then he blindfolded me and tied my hands up. I was tryin' to pull away from him, but he was big and real strong. He laid down on top of me. Then he pulled out his thing and stuck it in me. I couldn't scream."

I watched them lies spill out onto my clothes and cover me with a cool darkness. I didn't care. I couldn't care. I never knew where to stand up and let that care help me stop those demon words of shame. All I pictured was me waiting for folks to come and get me, and nobody was showing up. I seen Glenn running to his kids while they came tumbling down a slide, and his arms was open wide to catch 'em so they wouldn't fall and hurt theyselves. I even seen Ruby driving down the street in a new Cutlass Supreme, her boys ridin' 'longside her. And I see me swinging on a ole rubber tire that was tied to a oak tree back on Big Mama's property. And there was one of Big Mama's gran'kids—standing on the side of the tree. He was wanting to ride the tire swing, and I wouldn't let him 'cause it was still my turn. He turned round and picked up the biggest rock he could find and slammed it into the side of my head, making me fall off the swing. There was nobody to tell—nowhere to run. I knowed right then that I was nobody's child. I belonged to no one. I put my hand over the knot that was coming and swore to God that one day I would be somebody's someone and they would care if I cried.

"Do you know who he was?"

"Yeah. I think so."

"Can you tell us who did this to you?"

I couldn't believe myself. My mouth was gonna do it again. It was gonna open itself and just say whatever came to my mind. It was gonna blow life into something that wasn't real— something imagined. It seemed like I wasn't me no more. I wasn't the part of me that knowed betta'. My mind took over. All I could see was me and the green plastic garbage bags that was gonna hold my belongin's when I had to leave the shelter. And Claire, she prob'ly wouldn't come to work that day 'cause she just wouldn't wanna see me go. I couldn't leave her. I just couldn't. All I could see was that anytime somebody left me, they never cried or tried to get me to stay; they always just let me go. I never put up a fight, either; I just went along with whatever folks wanted me to do. But this time I didn't wanna go. No, I didn't wanna go to no stupid residential treatment fa- cility. I was gonna stay in the shelter. The way I seen it was that if Miss Claire couldn't take me home to be with her and her family, then I wasn't gonna be with nobody else either!

"Naw. I can't. I can't tell you." My counselor answered that the only way they could help me was for me to tell the whole truth. All I could hear was the words I'd just said still hangin' in the air like they was waiting to be caught, dusted off, and put back in they place of darkness. With the twist of my magic stick, I could say the words to undo what I was 'bout to do. They would've said that I was just a stupid girl who didn't know what

I was doing or saying. And I could've got away with being just stupid or ornery. But then I thought if Miss Forde could have just a li'l more time to see how good I was for Claire, she would change her mind.

CHAPTER NINETEEN

AFTERWARDS

BY FRIDAY MORNING, three days after I told my story 'bout the rape, Claire had come back to work, and I was the first thing she tended to when she arrived.

"Tell me now, who did this to you?" Miss Claire was sitting in front of me and asking me 'bout what happened on the weekend. She had found out 'bout the rape incident and was trying to get me to talk to her 'bout it, since I wasn't telling nobody else too much. I couldn't find the air in me to push the words out and call his name. I didn't know who to tell on.

"Sweetheart, if you don't let us know, we can't help you."

I started crying; not 'cause I was hurting or nothin', but 'cause I couldn't stop myself from spreading the lies. Like a pallet laid out for all to sit on, I spread them fibs wider than I myself could see. I lost sight of where it all stopped.

"I don't know who it was. I think it might have been my friend's friend. Or maybe it was Will; you know I told you 'bout him before. Anyway, there was a lotta boys there that night; it

350

coulda been any of 'em." I watched her face draw her eyebrows in together. "Or maybe I don't know who it was." I looked into Miss Claire's eyes; they was trusting me so. Right then I did the worst I could do. I said, "I really do think it was Marlena's father." I didn't even see my mind had left me till it came back round the way and tried to snatch what was said back. But I had said too much—I couldn't grab hold of them words and take 'em back.

Miss Claire's mouth closed tight, and she hung her head down low. That was all I could say 'bout it.

Tuesday came round soon 'nough. Miss Forde had told me she was coming in and that we was gonna go and talk 'bout what was gonna happen to the placement she had set up for me. I was called to the main office when she arrived.

"Hello, Regina, how are you feeling?" I answered, Fine. We went to one of the closed rooms where folks talked 'bout stuff they didn't want the kids to hear.

"So I hear you've been raped."

"Uh-huh." I looked down at my hands and started biting the dry skin around my fingernails.

"Considering all that's at stake here, one might hope that you'll cooperate a little more. In light of this new information about the alleged rape, things are a bit up in the air. I need to find out what's going on and hear your side of the story for myself."

I didn't wanna say nothing.

"Since the ball is already rolling for you to go to this new placement, you're going to have to go to court and have a new dependency hearing. In the meantime, the courts are also going to be sending an investigator out to the Ballentinos' house to find out more about what happened, so that charges can be pressed where they're needed."

Oh hell, I knew I was in for it now. My chest was pounding like somebody was trying to get out. "I don't wanna press no charges against nobody. I wanna drop the whole thing. I don't wanna get nobody in trouble. Just forget it."

"That's just too bad," she came back at me. "You are an un-deraged minor—a ward of the court no less. There is no way the system is going to let someone get away with this. Plus, you don't have to press the charges. We will!" Miss Forde slammed the palm of her hand down on the table and looked at me and kept right on goin'.

"These allegations are really serious, Regina, and if they are as you say, the state will arrest and prosecute Mr. Ballentino, be-cause he was the adult in charge of your well-being. If we find him guilty, his life will not be the same as it was. I want you to think long and hard about what happened that night."

I just wanted somebody to throw a bucket of water on me so I could melt right then and there, like that wicked-ass Witch of the West. I wondered if anybody had made my mama and daddy tell the truth when they would sit back and tell me all those lies just to get what they wanted. I didn't see nobody running to in-vestigate 'em for the wrong they was doing. Ruby still hadn't got no money to come and get me. She'd been telling the same lie for fourteen years, and ain't nobody caught her. And Glenn—what 'bout him? Why they got to get away with it all? No matter how I tried to make my mind right, the lie I told on my friend's father was red-hot and burning a hole right on through me.

The heat of the false words moved through me like a bad batch of Big Mama's homemade chili. I couldn't hold nothing on my stomach for too long. I had to spend long bouts on the commode. My nerves was getting bad right along with my guts. I told Miss Forde that I would need some time b'fore I could talk 'bout it again. In the meantime I went to see my head doctor and sat in quiet the whole time. More so than worryin' 'bout that doctor asking me over and over if I wanted to talk 'bout it, I couldn't help but figure out how I was gonna tell Miss Claire—if I even decided to tell her. I r'membered the pact I'd made with Marlena and realized that I'd already messed the whole thing up and that she was prob'ly not gonna wanna talk to me if word got back to her father. I decided to wait till later on that night, till I could get Miss Claire alone with me, and I'd try and come clean with her like they was always tryin' to get us to do in the shelter—"come clean" so that we could move on from here and start anew. I hoped I could do just that.

"Miss Claire, I gotta talk to you; I gotta tell you something." I could feel the wet running to my eyes like a sprinkler that was hooked up to a knotty hose and the knots was being undone one at a time. "I lied." The tears came pouring out me. "I lied on Mr. Ballentino and I'm sorry." Phew, I'd said it. My body was starting to feel light as a cotton ball. Now that I'd said what was true it didn't matter to me too much that Miss Claire might be mad at me.

"Why did you lie about Mr. Ballentino, Regina?" Claire asked, her face quiet with wonder.

"B'cause I knowed that they was gonna send me away from here and from you, and I couldn't take that. I don't ever wanna leave you." I watched as Miss Claire's eyes filled with water, and she turned her head so that I couldn't see directly in 'em.

"Look sweetheart, I think that you should leave your well-being up to the people who are caring for you. Regina, I believe that everyone has your best interests at heart. Plus, you never know when you could be getting in the way of God's plan. Trust me, sweetheart. It's all going to work out. And another thing: no matter what, you should never try and gain what you want for yourself at someone else's expense. That will only mean that you didn't get it fairly, and therefore it can never be truly enjoyed."

She sat 'cross from me and told me how happy she was for me telling the truth. "Just remember what I've always told you: your life is up to you, honey, and you have done the best thing, by telling the truth and all on your own," Claire told me. She leaned to me and grabbed ahold of me tight. We sat there like that, just for a while.

I'd always heard the grown folks preach that "the truth will set you free." From how I was feeling, them was the truest words I knowed. The darkness that was covering my heart was gone, and I could feel it beat again. I couldn't 'magine how folks could tell stories for years and not fess up to 'em, leaving people to believe whatever they was to tell 'em, and not think one thing 'bout how they lies might destroy a life that was innocent. I wanted to know why most of the folks I knowed didn't know that for themselves, since they was s'posed to be the grown-ups. They was the ones who should've wanted more for me than I wanted for myself. That's how come God gave us to 'em in the first place. I was glad to tell what was so, and watch what wasn't go away. And now I was hoping Miss Forde could see that Claire helped me find the truth, and because of that, she wouldn't make me go away.

CHAPTER TWENTY

SOMEBODY'S SOMEONE

I OFTTIMES WONDERED what made things like the sun and the moon wanna take turns and change off the way they did; giving each a time to shine and be as special as the other. I also figured that the sun and moon was hangin' in the sky by secret strings nobody could see, not even if they looked with all they might. And I made up for myself that God was the one responsible. That he held things up in the sky with his big ole hands. And he used the clouds as his resting posts when his arms would get tired. He did that so that the clouds wouldn't feel left out. I even 'magined the old man in the sky hitched his suspenders on the stars so he could stay steady while workin'. And the stars, in they own way, was able to help him keep things the way they was—pretty and abiding. Above all, I was happy to know that God was there to make certain everything had something to keep it going—even if it was a thing as small as a raindrop sliding down the throat of a blade of grass to keep it alive or a mama whispering "I love you, baby" in her child's ear when it needed it most. No matter what—there'd always be something or someone for everybody. Somehow I made myself believe that God, in his plan, had made sure that nobody would never, ever in a million years be left on their own without being held up or helped out.

Claire, who was all for what was right, made me write a letter to my friend Marlena and her family, to tell 'em how 'shamed I was for what I'd done. Claire said that sometimes apologies could be like a sweetness wrapping round somethin' wrong, making wrongdoings seem that much better. I thought 'bout her words for a while and wondered if it could work for Lula Mae, or my mother or my father or Big Mama for that matter. They knowed they was wrong for the things they'd done, and now I knowed it too. Deep down inside I was wishing that they could maybe make apologies to me.

Accordin' to my social worker, I was to have no more contact with the Ballentino family. They were no longer interested in me having weekend home visits. I listened to Miss Forde go on 'bout it, and when she was finished I thought on calling Marlena and letting her tell me for herself. I really wanted to let my friend know how bad I felt for what I'd done and that I should've never lied on her father like that. Lately after doing anything sinful, something inside me wouldn't let me feel too good 'bout myself. It was like I'd be touched by a heavy darkness as it crawled past my eyes and had a sit on the rest of me. And the harder I tried to keep quiet and tried to get away with whatever the sin was, the more my heart, mind, and belly would start acting up, and the deeper the darkness would rest on me. Only when I made my mind up to set things right did I seem to find rest and feel the shadows pass. I made up my mind to call my friend.

After my social worker left, I snuck into the staff office and punched in Marlena's number. I'd planned that if one of her parents picked up the phone, I'd hang it up.

"Hello, Marlena." It was her. "This is Regina. Is your father real mad at me?"

"No, but girl, you know you should've never said those things."

"I know. I'm really, really sorry."

"Yeah. Just don't let that shit happen again. You know that you can't come visit for a while, right?"

"Yeah, I know."

"Well, just let some time pass, and my parents will come around. Don't worry, girl; you still cool with me."

"Okay, thank you. Bye, Marlena."

"Bye, Regina."

I hung up the staff phone and slipped out the office so nobody could see me. I sat down in the TV room and let all that'd just happened sink in.

I couldn't say why the words sounded different not coming from my social worker, but when Marlena said I couldn't come to her house for a while I wanted to cry. Even though she told me to let time pass, somehow deep down, I knew I prob'ly wouldn't be seeing her again. I thought back to the rest of what Miss Forde had told me when I asked her if my friend's daddy was mad at me. She said, "No, he's not mad at you, but he sure is sorry you had to go and do something like that. And Mrs. Ballentino is really upset." My heart hurt for Mrs. Ballentino. She always welcomed me in her place and made sure that I had a li'l something to bring back with me on my weekend visits from they house. Once she gave me some li'l dumplin'-like things she'd made from potatoes and covered in spaghetti sauce called "no-key." I'd liked 'em very much.

I wanted to ask Marlena 'bout Will—I needed to know if he'd been seen round the neighborhood lately—but I didn't. As I sat on the couch, I lowered my head and thought that maybe he'd gone back to that Hawaii place and thought that it would be a better place to be. I figured that maybe one day I'd go and find him and let him know just how sorry I really was too.

I went to court a few days later. I can r'member sitting in the courtroom on that cold brown bench. My social worker said that my daddy was s'posed to be coming and maybe even my mama would be there. I figured that neither one would show and didn't let myself get too hopeful. Anyway, I wasn't gonna go wit' 'em even if they did come. I was sick of the both of 'em.

It was the first time in a while I'd had to be in a courtroom. I sat in a seat next to Miss Forde while a man came in and put the court in line: "Order in the court." His voice boomed the daylights outta me. I listened as the man sittin' behind the big ole desk ask folks for the business at hand.

Miss Forde stood up and moved in front of a standing microphone. "Your Honor, I am here to present case number 45351—Regina Ollison. It is an emergency review for custody hearing."

Miss Forde went on to say, "Regina's problem continues to be one of having to live somewhere. For all practical purposes, she's been abandoned by both parents. She now resides in the Edgar Children's Shelter in Martinez, California. All attempts to secure possible reunification with family members have failed. As you can see, Mr. Hathaway isn't present, and the minor's mother—a Miss Ruby Carmichael—isn't either. The court should note, on behalf of all the social workers who've been involved with this case, that we've tried numerous attempts to contact both Mr. Hathaway and Miss Carmichael, and of this date neither parent has shown an interest or concern for the minor. Although the minor's father has made appearances at the children's shelter, his visits have been sporadic at best and unpredictable. Staff has requested at this time that visitation rights between minor and father be reevaluated in that minor tends to become volatile and agitated after their visits. Her mother continues to reside in North Carolina, and her father resides in Richmond with his wife and two children. At no point since dependency was obtained has he been involved in planning for his daughter. In addition to the problem of the shelter, Regina is a very immature young woman who requires constant supervision and monitoring of her behavior. Impulse control has improved, but not to the extent that she could function independently." Miss Motormouth went on to tell the judge that I was living at the shelter but that I needed more of a one-on-one placement, so that I could get the individualized treatment that I needed.

While I waited for 'em to finish, I tried to run through all the homes I'd lived in since I was small, and I believe I lost track after thirty. Suddenly, the judge spoke louder than he had before: "Minor will remain at the Edgar Children's Shelter until a permanent solution is sought out. Case number 45351 is concluded, court dismissed." The judge man slammed his li'l hammer down, and the court was over. They even had the nerve to give me my own number, to keep from having to call me by my rightful name. I figured they must've had a shitload of Reginas to have to give me a number instead. I thought about the number that they used to talk 'bout me. I'd already knowed 'bout my number b'cause I read a piece of my file that was hanging outta Miss Forde's brief bag. I tried not to let it bother me that I wasn't called by a name. Instead, I added all the numbers together and got eighteen. I figured it would be my lucky charm number, and that's how old I'd be when I could have my own house, where I'd make a room for Claire, and nobody could tell me what to do. That way I could pay her back for taking care of me.

Miss Forde explained I'd been named "a ward of the court." It meant that I didn't belong to Ruby and Glenn no more. I now belonged to the state of California. I was its property. And as quick as a flash my mind figured that since I belonged to the state and Miss Claire worked for the same folks, that now it would most likely be easier for her to become my mama if she wanted. I couldn't wait to see her to let her know.

We drove to the shelter mostly in quiet, me not quite knowing what all of what I'd just heard meant. When I did talk I went right for what I wanted. I asked Miss Forde that if Ruby and Glenn didn't want me if that meant somebody else could have me. She said techn'ly yes. But that the courts would decide that based on all the evidence they had 'bout me. She told me that if somebody was interested in wanting me that it would take a long time to get what was necessary to take care of me, 'cause I belonged to the state. I asked her if folks got paid for taking care of kids like me. She said they did. Then I asked her how come more people didn't do it if they got paid for it. I asked her how come they didn't let folks of different kinds live to-gether. I asked her what matter was it if they color was a li'l off. But she didn't have no answers. She just kept talkin' 'bout red tape or something.

We pulled up into the driveway of the shelter like we had done so much before. I knew it was Miss Claire's day on, so I ran into the building and slammed through the double doors. Out the corner of my eye I could see Miss Forde signing me back into the shelter.

"Hey, slow down," she shot at me. But I didn't stop; I just changed to a skip wit' the same pace. I was in a hurry. I came to the orange-colored doors that kept the girls' section closed to the rest of the buildin'. Pushing with both my hands, I slammed through while the doors hit the sides of the wall with a big *boof!* That's when I seen her.

Miss Claire was in the corner of the kitchen, balled up in a lump on the floor. I stood real still, not knowing what to do. There was noise all over the place—kids running wild as al-ways—but nobody seemed to be paying her no mind. She looked like a li'l girl tryin' to squeeze her broke-up body into the crack b'tween the wall and the stove. Her feet was pointing at one another, and she had a piece of what looked like toilet paper in her hands, which was hangin b'tween her knees. As I came closer, I looked on while she took the wrinkled-up paper and spread it out wide 'nough to cover her whole nose as she blew a whole ball of snot right into the middle of it. My own hands was landed by my sides. I picked up one of my feet then the other, and I tried to move as close to her as fast as I could.

"Claire," I called out to her, surprised at myself but not giv-ing a damn if anybody heard me call her out by name or not.

She looked up at me with eyes that was swoll and the color

of cherries too ripe for the picking. Trying to put herself back together, she moved a li'l and slung her hair back out her face. There was a small piece of hair layin' by the side of her mouth stuck in the wetness on her cheek. I reached down and moved it away and asked her what the matter was. She dropped her head back in her hands and started hollerin'. I could feel her cries pulling on something way down deep in me. So I sat down next to her. She was shaking like a baby who wanted a bottle that was right in front of it, but it couldn't get it no matter how hard it fought. No sound was coming out.

My heart hurt for her from the front through the back. Like somebody had took a hammer, maybe like the one that judge was holdin' earlier, and hit me clear through my body, then wrapped me in a strange heaviness and left me for dead.

"What?" I asked her. "What you want? Whatever it is, just tell me. I'll get it for you!" My own eyes was startin' to water.

With what sounded like a deaf and dumb person trying to get the words out they mouth and all outta breath at the same time, Claire gave me soft grunt words with no meanings. It was like she was fallin' from something and couldn't catch herself. After a minute, she finally said something.

"I want you to know that I tried, sweetheart. I really tried. I was there for you today; I was there. I want you to know that I did the best I could. I did everything I could do to try and make it happen. I did everything the way they told me to do it. I tried to do it right, just like they'd asked me to do. I even met with your father, to ask him to just give you to me."

I tried to make heads or tails of what she was saying, but it wasn't making no sense to me.

"What are you talkin' 'bout?"

"Oh my God, Regina, I want you to know how much I love

you and what you mean to me." She looked in my eyes, and I saw what she said to me. "I tried to get you for my foster child today. I tried to become your foster mother, but they wouldn't give you to me. I wrote letter after letter and tried to get someone to listen to me, but they wouldn't listen." She was slobbering all over herself by now.

"They said that I wasn't what you needed. They said you needed more than I could offer you. Oh my God, sweetheart, I am so sorry. I know that I'm not black, but what does that have to do with anything? Can you tell me that? I just wanted to give you a better chance at this life."

All sound came to a rest. It was like the first time I dived into the water with Miss Claire, and my ears and everything filled up fast with a stinging feeling. I was floatin' up high. High in the air, where nobody could see me. Then all of a sudden, I started to fall. Fallin' through my whole life fast, and there was nothing to catch me. I kept on goin' and goin'—more and more slowly. From where I was, I looked down at her, and I didn't see nothing. No tears. No sad eyes. Nothin'. I was light. Light as a feather that fell off a bird. No, I was a butterfly—yeah, a butterfly. Claire had told me all 'bout them. I lifted my wings and wrapped 'em round her neck and breathed air out at her as I tried to quiet her heart. I wanted to take those eyes and rub 'em with a salve, so the hurt could go back to where it came from. Or maybe I could take the tip of my wing and brush it against her face, back and forth, so that Claire could again believe in butterfly kisses—and let them make her feel betta', like she'd done for me.

I tried speakin' the words that was runnin' through my mind, breaking their neck to get to her and rest in the creases of her pain, sending that ole nasty sadness back to its grave where it belonged. I was wantin' to tell her that it was all fine. It was all rightly fine. In the whole of my life, nobody had ever did what she'd done for me. I wanted to let her know that for the first time someone had stood up and fought for me, just plain ole me. Not for the money they would get from the county, or whoever—but b'cause they just liked me. But most of all I wanted her to know that no matter what—no matter what—it was more than good 'nough to know that finally, finally somebody had wanted me for their own someone, just like I'd 'magined. I wanted her to know that this was more than anybody had ever wanted for me.

Sometimes when you in a dream, you think it's real, and you believe you said what you was thinking. That's how it was for me. That's how it was.

I packed up all my things in boxes and green Glad garbage bags. After all the moving I'd done up till now, I still didn't have nothing nice to carry my belongings in. The county wasn't allowed to spend funds on stuff like suitcases and so forth. After all, they wasn't in the business of vacations and traveling. That's what Miss Forde told me. I didn't really care too much 'bout what she had to say.

I'd already been to visit the facilities I'd be stayin' at in Redding. Miss Forde had put that together for me real quick-like. I could tell that she really wanted to get rid of me—but I wasn't gonna let her stupid self bother my mind. I was gonna go to Redding and do whatever it was they wanted me to do.

My visit to Redding showed me that there was no black folks anywhere to be found—except for the two other girls and me that lived in the home, which confused me 'cause I thought Miss Forde was real concerned 'bout that. But I didn't care anymore. The new placement I was s'posed to be living in was called Guideways, and it could take a lot of girls at one time. There would be twelve girls to every staff person—that didn't matter to me either. All I could see was that Guideways was 'bout as far away as they could get me from the shelter—and Claire. When I asked why I had to go so far away, Miss Forde told me that it was one of the last stops for me b'fore they'd consider me for a place called Napa State. Wherever that was. She also said that it was as far away from Martinez as she could get me. Deep down I know Martinez wasn't the only reason she wanted me far away. No matter what, though, I wasn't gonna show her that it mattered to me, I just said I wanted to leave Martinez anyway.

That day came soon 'nough. On the day I was leaving, I overheard the staff talking. They said that Claire was gone on a work leave and that the big boss had told her she had crossed the professional line and that she had broke something called ethics. Plus, they said that it was awful how she'd been accused of maybe being gay and un-pro-fession-al with a minor. I didn't even care 'bout that either. My body was empty for caring.

My body was now tired, and I couldn't seem to make it wanna do nothing anymore. The place b'tween my bosom seemed dry. I don't know—maybe I was just finally all dried out. There was no more tears to cry.

The white county car with the ugly gold sticker was waiting outside the door. Everybody was waving bye to me, and I couldn't even tell what they was saying—and deep down it really didn't make no mind to me. Earlier that day, Miss Forde had told me that if I could just be good, then she would try and arrange for Claire to visit me in a few months—after I settled in and all. She finished up by saying some real encouragin' words: "But most important of all, Regina, you have to be good."

I had to be good. I listened to her words, and they made me think on the times that Lula Mae would beat the shit outta me, then say, "You betta' not cry, or I'll give you somethin' to cry for." Even though what she was doing would hurt me so bad, I wasn't s'posed to let on that I didn't like it. That's what Miss Forde's words felt like to me. I held in all that Miss Forde said to me, knowin' well and good that it wasn't her words that made my mind wanna 'magine what good could be like. Right then, I was r'membering the time just b'fore I left to go and visit Redding. I seen Miss Claire as she was leaving her shift, and we said good-bye. Her eyes was small and drawn up like she'd been crying for a long time. Just looking at her made me wanna die right there and become the next bit of air she breathed in. I didn't know how I was gonna be able to go on.

"I'll keep fighting for you, pumpkin," she said to me as she placed her hand under my chin to hold it up. "I'll always be here for you, and I love you more than words could ever convey."

It felt like I died right then—or maybe I did; I don't know. I wanted to know how somebody could get that close to love and have to say good-bye. I just stopped feeling. Miss Claire started to walk outta the big orange doors that led out the shelter, and I just stood right where she left me.

"Hey." She turned and looked at me. "I know I don't have to say this to you, but for me, and more so for yourself, please be good and take care of yourself, sweetheart, and I'll miss you.

And most of all know that God loves you and will never leave you. He's the one that really counts."

I made up my mind. It would be for Miss Claire that I could be good. Not for Miss Forde.

I was imaginin' that no matter what, I could do and be whatever it took to make Miss Claire proud. I wanted to make her prouder than anybody had ever hoped they could be for me. She'd been the one to show me how to have hope when there was none—she'd told me it was all in how you seen things. Deep down inside me I knowed that no matter what happened here on in, I'd forever know what feelin' special really was. It ain't had nothing to do with the color of nobody's skin, but it had all to do with just saying kind things to folks and believing in 'em. That's what love was: when somebody did everything in they power to make someone feel special—and that's what I got. I got to feel just like them li'l white girls I'd seen on TV, and nobody could take it back from me—it was all mine.

Miss Claire also told me that everybody was full of good and that we all had a way to choose to make it come out anytime we wanted—and I believed her. When I thought on what good was, I could still see myself with her—maybe we was in Hawaii or her apartment in Walnut Creek—it didn't make no mind to me. I was always gonna have her with me. Her words was still tucked in the pocket of my mem'ry, and they would be there when I needed 'em. For the life of me, I 'magined that God wasn't done with us. And for that, I told myself, I could be good. For her I would be good.